Microsoft® Office Publisher 2003

Illustrated

INTRODUCTORY

Elizabeth Eisner Reding

THOMSON
COURSE TECHNOLOGY

Australia • Canada • Mexico • Singapore • Spain • United Kingdom • United States

THOMSON
COURSE TECHNOLOGY

Microsoft Office Publisher 2003 – Illustrated Introductory
Elizabeth Eisner Reding

Executive Editor:
Nicole Jones Pinard

Production Editor:
Melissa Panagos

QA Manuscript Reviewer:
Susan Whalen

Product Manager and Development Editor:
M.T. Cozzola

Associate Product Manager:
Emilie Perreault

In-house Product Manager:
Christina Kling Garrett

Editorial Assistant:
Shana Rosenthal

Text Designer:
Joseph Lee, Black Fish Design

Composition House:
GEX Publishing Services

The Illustrated Series Vision

Teaching and writing about computer applications can be extremely rewarding and challenging. How do we engage students and keep their interest? How do we teach them skills that they can easily apply on the job? As we set out to write this book, our goals were to develop a textbook that:

- works for a beginning student

- provides varied, flexible, and meaningful exercises and projects to reinforce the skills

- serves as a reference tool

- makes your job as an educator easier, by providing resources above and beyond the textbook to help you teach your course

Our popular, streamlined format is based on advice from instructional designers and customers. This flexible design presents each lesson on a two-page spread, with step-by-step instructions on the left, and screen illustrations on the right. This signature style, coupled with high-caliber content, provides a comprehensive yet manageable introduction to Microsoft Office Publisher 2003 — it is a teaching package for the instructor and a learning experience for the student.

ACKNOWLEDGMENTS

A book may look like only a few people worked on it, but in reality, it takes scores of dedicated professionals to take it from a table of contents to a printed package. It's just not possible to thank every person involved in this project, but I will take this opportunity to mention a few key members of the team: Nicole Pinard, the Executive Editor who made this team a reality; MT Cozzola, the Development Editor, Product Manager, and constant companion; Christina Kling Garrett, the (Inside) Product Manager and resolver of problems both great and small; Emilie Perreault, the Associate Product Manager who put together the Instructor Resources; Melissa Panagos, the Production Editor and manager of all aspects of the production process; Susan Whalen, the QA tester who was able to debug these lessons with her usual style and class; and Michael Reding, my husband, whose unending patience and support is a constant joy.

Preface

Welcome to *Microsoft Office Publisher 2003–Illustrated Introductory*. Each lesson in the book contains elements pictured to the right.

How is the book organized?

The book is organized into ten units on Publisher, covering creating a publication, formatting text, working with art, enhancing a publication, working with multiple pages and long documents, using advanced features, working more efficiently, and creating Web documents.

What kinds of assignments are included in the book? At what level of difficulty?

The lesson assignments use Image Magic, a small advertising agency, as the case study. The assignments on the light purple pages at the end of each unit increase in difficulty. Data files and case studies, with many international examples, provide a great variety of interesting and relevant business applications for skills. Assignments include:

- **Concepts Reviews** include multiple choice, matching, and screen identification questions.

- **Skills Reviews** provide additional hands-on, step-by-step reinforcement.

- **Independent Challenges** are case projects requiring critical thinking and application of the skills learned in the unit. The Independent Challenges increase in difficulty, with the first Independent Challenge in each unit being the easiest (most step-by-step with detailed instructions). Independent Challenges 2 and 3 become increasingly open-ended, requiring more independent thinking and problem solving.

Each 2-page spread focuses on a single skill.

Concise text that introduces the basic principles in the lesson and integrates the brief case study (indicated by the paintbrush icon).

UNIT C
Publisher 2003

Using Layout Guides

Elements in a well-designed publication achieve a balanced and consistent look. This balance and consistency occurs only with careful planning and design. **Layout guides** and **margin guides**, horizontal and vertical lines visible only on the screen, help you accurately position objects on a page and across pages in a publication. Layout guides are created on the **Master Page**, a background that is the same for pages within a publication that are defined by a specific master page. For example, each initial page in a newsletter might have a similar layout, as might an editorial page and the final page, so you might want these pages to share the same master page. Your assignment is to create a flyer for an upcoming design seminar. You decide to use a publication from the Publication Gallery, then set up the layout guides to help plan for future placement of objects in the publication. You also want to experiment with a different color scheme.

STEPS

1. Start Publisher, click Publications for Print, click Flyers in the New from a design list, click Informational, then click Bars Informational Flyer in the Informational Flyers list
   A new publication based on this template opens, and the Flyer Options task pane opens as well.

2. Click Edit on the menu bar, click Personal Information, click Secondary Business, click the Select a color scheme list arrow, click Floral, then click Update

   QUICK TIP
   Color schemes are listed in alphabetical order.

3. Click the Close button on the Flyer Options task pane, then save the publication to the drive and folder where your Data Files are located as Design Seminar Flyer
   The task pane is not necessary for the remainder of your work on this design.

4. Right-click the graphic placeholder containing the photograph at 4" H / 5" V, then click Delete Object
   A dialog box opens, asking if you want to change to a design that does not include a graphic placeholder.

   QUICK TIP
   In this book, ruler coordinates are given as follows: 4" H / 5" V. This refers to the intersection of 4" on the horizontal ruler and 5" on the vertical ruler, and is where you should click.

5. Click Yes, right-click the remaining text box at 3.10" H / 3.5" V, then click Delete Object
   The image and text box are deleted from the flyer. When selecting an object, you can click anywhere within its borders, but coordinates are provided to make it easy to locate each specific object.

6. Click Arrange on the menu bar, then click Layout Guides
   The Layout Guides dialog box opens. You use the Layout Guides dialog box to change the margin dimensions.

   QUICK TIP
   You can type a value in each margin guide text box, or use the arrows (to the right of each text box) to change the settings.

7. If necessary, click the Margin Guides tab, then verify that the Left, Right, and Top margins are each set at 0.5", and the Bottom margin is set at 0.66", as shown in Figure C-1
   The top and bottom margins are small enough to allow lots of information to be placed on each page. Layout guides create a grid to help you line up design elements, such as images and text boxes, on the page.

8. Click the Grid Guides tab, click the Columns up arrow until 3 appears in the text box, click the Rows up arrow until 3 appears in the text box, click the Add center guide between columns and rows check box as shown in Figure C-2, then click OK
   The pink lines represent the column guides, and the blue lines represent the column guide margins. The guides appear on the screen, as shown in Figure C-3, but do not print on the page.

9. Click the Save button on the Standard toolbar

50 WORKING WITH TEXT

Hints as well as troubleshooting advice, right where you need it–next to the step itself.

Every lesson features large, full-color representations of what the screen should look like as students complete the numbered steps.

• **Advanced Challenge Exercises** are optional steps, included in two Independent Challenges per unit, that encourage problem-solving and creative thinking.

• **E-Quest Independent Challenges** are case projects with a Web focus. E-Quests require the use of the World Wide Web to conduct research to complete the project.

• **Visual Workshops** show a completed file and require that the file be created without any step-by-step guidance, involving problem solving and an independent application of the unit skills.

• **Capstone Projects** are additional lessons at the end of each unit that allow students to practice skills learned in the unit, with special emphasis on reinforcing the design concepts behind the skills.

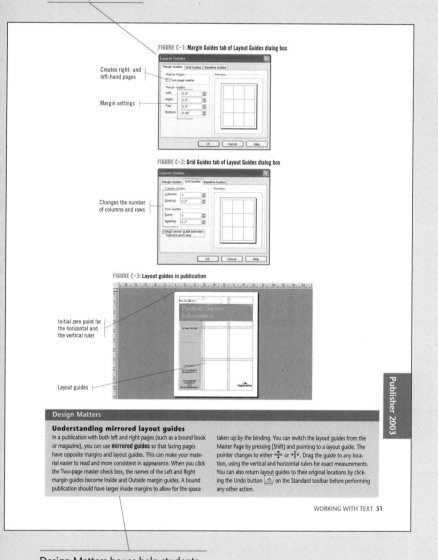

FIGURE C-1: Margin Guides tab of Layout Guides dialog box

Creates right- and left-hand pages

Margin settings

FIGURE C-2: Grid Guides tab of Layout Guides dialog box

Changes the number of columns and rows

FIGURE C-3: Layout guides in publication

Initial zero point for the horizontal and the vertical ruler

Layout guides

Publisher 2003

Design Matters

Understanding mirrored layout guides

In a publication with both left and right pages (such as a bound book or magazine), you can use **mirrored guides** so that facing pages have opposite margins and layout guides. This can make your material easier to read and more consistent in appearance. When you click the Two-page master check box, the names of the Left and Right margin guides become Inside and Outside margin guides. A bound publication should have larger inside margins to allow for the space taken up by the binding. You can switch the layout guides from the Master Page by pressing [Shift] and pointing to a layout guide. The pointer changes to either ≑ or ◂‖▸. Drag the guide to any location, using the vertical and horizontal rulers for exact measurements. You can also return layout guides to their original locations by clicking the Undo button on the Standard toolbar before performing any other action.

Design Matters boxes help students apply smart design principles to their Web sites. Each Design Matters deals exclusively with design considerations, such as using white space, copyfitting text, and studying the use of color.

Instructor Resources

The Instructor Resources CD is Course Technology's way of putting the resources and information needed to teach and learn effectively into your hands. With an integrated array of teaching and learning tools that offers you and your students a broad range of technology-based instructional options, we believe this CD represents the highest quality and most cutting-edge resources available to instructors today. Many of these resources are available at www.course.com.

The resources available with this book are:

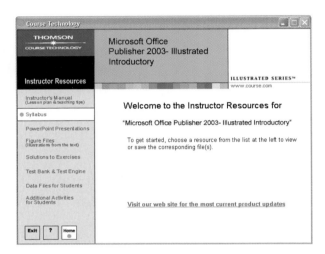

Solutions to Exercises—These contain every file students are asked to create or modify in the lessons and End-of-Unit material. A Help file on the Instructor Resources CD includes information for using the Solution Files. There is also a document outlining the solutions for the End-of-Unit Concepts Review, Skills Review, and Independent Challenges.

PowerPoint Presentations—Each unit has a corresponding PowerPoint presentation that you can use in lecture, distribute to your students, or customize to suit your course.

Instructor's Manual—Available as an electronic file, the Instructor's Manual is quality-assurance tested and includes unit overviews and detailed lecture topics with teaching tips for each unit.

Sample Syllabus—Prepare and customize your course easily using this sample course outline.

Figure Files—The figures in the text are provided on the Instructor Resources CD to help you illustrate key topics or concepts. You can create traditional overhead transparencies by printing the figure files. Or, you can create electronic slide shows by using the figures in a

presentation program such as Microsoft Office PowerPoint.

ExamView—ExamView is a powerful testing software package that allows you to create and administer printed, LAN-based, and Internet-based exams. ExamView includes hundreds of questions that correspond to the topics covered in this text, enabling students to generate detailed study guides that include page references for further review. The computer-based and Internet testing components allow students to take exams at their computers, and also save you time by grading each exam automatically.

Data Files for Students—To complete most of the units in this book, your students will need **Data Files**. Put them on a file server for students to copy. The Data Files are available on the Instructor's Resources CD-ROM and the Review Pack, and can also be downloaded from www.course.com.

Instruct students to use the **Data Files List** located at the back of this book and on the Instructor Resources CD. This list gives instructions on copying and organizing files.

Brief Contents

Contents

UNIT C

Working with Text   49

UNIT D

Working with Graphic Objects   75

UNIT E — Enhancing a Publication   101

UNIT
A
Publisher 2003

Getting Started with Microsoft Office Publisher 2003

OBJECTIVES

Define publication software
Start Publisher 2003
View the Publisher window
Open and save a publication
Enter text in a text box
View and print a publication
Get Help and change Personal Information
Close a publication and exit Publisher
Capstone Project: Study Abroad Flyer

Microsoft Office Publisher 2003 is a popular desktop publishing program that uses the Windows operating system. In this unit, you learn how to start Publisher and work in the Publisher program window. You also learn how to open and save existing files, enter text in a publication, view and print a publication, use the extensive Help system, and change Personal Information. ▰▰▰ You work at Image Magic, a small advertising agency, as an assistant to Mike Mendoza, an account executive. Mike asks you to create a flyer announcing the location of the agency's new office. You decide to use Publisher to create this publication.

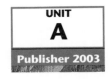
Defining Publication Software

Publisher is a **desktop publishing program**, a software program that lets you combine text and graphics, as well as worksheets and charts created in other programs, to produce typeset-quality documents for output on a computer printer, or for commercial printing. A document created in Publisher is called a **publication**. Table A-1 describes the types of publications you can create. ▚▚▞▞ You want to learn how to use Publisher so that you can generate professional-looking custom publications quickly and easily.

DETAILS

The benefits of using Publisher include the ability to:

- **Create professional publications**
  Publisher comes with a **Publication Gallery**, a collection of designs that let you choose the type of publication you want to develop, help you decide on its appearance, then suggest text and graphic image placement to complete the publication. The New Publication task pane and Publication Gallery create complete publications that you can modify easily to meet specific needs.

- **Use clip art**
  Artwork not only makes any publication appear more vibrant and interesting, but also helps to reflect and reinforce your ideas with visual images. Publisher comes with more than 15,000 pieces of artwork that can be incorporated into publications. In addition, other illustrations, sound files, video clips, and photographs can be imported into **Office Collections**, the artwork library that all Office applications share.

- **Create logos**
  Most organizations use a recognizable symbol, shape, color, or combination of these to attach to their name. This distinctive artwork, called a **logo**, can be created using Publisher's Design Sets, or by designing your own artwork and text. Figure A-1 illustrates a sample flyer created in Publisher that contains a logo formed by combining clip art and text.

- **Make your work look consistent**
  Publisher has many tools to help you create consistent publications that have similar design elements. You can use **design sets** to create different types of stylized publications. When creating work from scratch, you might, for example, want to have an information box in the lower-left corner on the back page of all Image Magic brochures. Using rulers and layout guides, you can create grids to help position graphics and text on a page. You can also save a publication as a **template**, a specially formatted publication with placeholder text that serves as a master for other, similar publications.

- **Work with multiple pages**
  Publisher makes it easy to work with multi-page publications. Pages can be added, deleted, and moved within a publication. Text that flows from one page to another can be connected with continued on and continued from notices.

- **Emphasize special text**
  Even great writing can be less than compelling if all the text looks the same. Using varied text styles to express different meanings and convey messages can add interest and help guide the reader's eye. You can use headlines to grab readers and lead them to stories of specific significance. You can use a sidebar to make a short statement more noticeable, or a pull quote to make an important point stand out and grab a reader's attention. Altering the appearance of text by making it bold, italicized, or underlined can emphasize the significance of text.

- **Publish to the Internet**
  Publisher contains design elements specifically for Web sites, making it easy to include links and graphics. Page backgrounds and animated GIFs add color and motion to your pages. A Web Publishing Wizard helps you make your Web site available to a local network drive, an intranet, or an Internet Service Provider for worldwide viewing.

FIGURE A-1: Sample flyer and logo

TABLE A-1: Common publications you can create in Publisher

publication type	example
Informational	Brochures, signs, calendars, forms
Periodical	Newsletters, catalogs
Promotional	Advertisements, flyers, press releases
Stationery	Letterhead, labels, business cards, envelopes, postcards, invitations
Specialty	Banners, airplanes, origami, resumes, award certificates, gift certificates

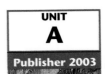

Starting Publisher 2003

To start Publisher, you click the Start button on the taskbar to access the Start menu. A slightly different procedure might be required for computers on a network, and those that use utility programs to enhance Windows. If you need assistance, ask your instructor or technical support person for help. When you start Publisher, the program displays a list of publication types and file options in the left pane, and a workspace in the right pane. The workspace may also display samples of publication types when you click a link in the left pane. ░░░░░ Before you can create the publication, you need to start Publisher and open a new document.

STEPS

1. **Locate the Start button ⟦ start ⟧ on the taskbar**
   The Start button is on the left side of the taskbar and is used to start programs on your computer.

QUICK TIP
Microsoft Publisher 2003 can be used with versions of Windows 2000 with Service Pack 3, Windows XP, or later.

2. **Click ⟦ start ⟧**
   Microsoft Office Publisher is located in the All Programs group, located near the bottom of the Start menu.

3. **Point to All Programs**
   All of the programs on your computer, including Microsoft Office Publisher, can be found in this area of the Start menu. Your All Programs menu might look different, depending which programs are installed on your computer.

TROUBLE
If you don't see the Microsoft Office Publisher icon, look in a folder called Microsoft Office or Office 2003, or ask your instructor or technical support person for help.

4. **Point to Microsoft Office**
   A submenu opens, listing all the Microsoft Office programs installed on your computer. You can see the Microsoft Office Publisher icon ▣ and the icons of other programs.

5. **Click the Microsoft Office Publisher 2003 program icon ▣, as shown in Figure A-2**
   Publisher opens and the New Publication task pane appears on the left side of the screen. The **task pane** is an area of the Publisher window that is used to organize design templates, color schemes, font schemes, and other layout tools in a visual gallery, which appears alongside your publication. The **New Publication task pane** lets you start a publication by design (by clicking a link in the New from a design section and browsing through the samples that appear in the right pane), start a new blank publication (by clicking a link in the New section), or open an existing publication (by clicking the More link in the Open section).

6. **Position ⤷ over Blank Print Publication in the New section of the task pane, but do not click**
   The pointer changes to 🖑 when positioned over Blank Print Publication, as shown in Figure A-3.

7. **Click Blank Print Publication in the New section of the task pane**
   A blank full-page publication appears on the screen.

8. **Click the Close button ⊠ in the task pane, then click the Close button ⊠ in any floating toolbars, if necessary**

FIGURE A-2: Start menu and All Programs menu

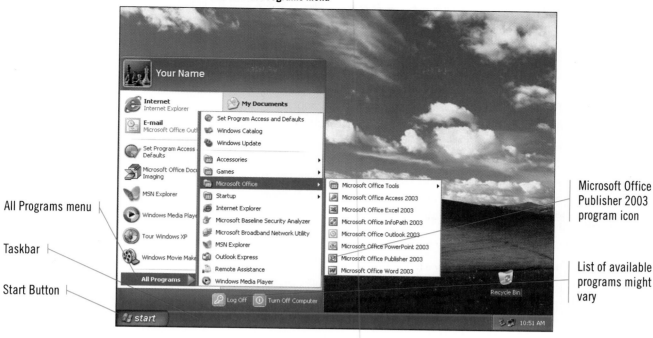

All Programs menu

Taskbar

Start Button

Microsoft Office Publisher 2003 program icon

List of available programs might vary

FIGURE A-3: Starting a Blank Publication

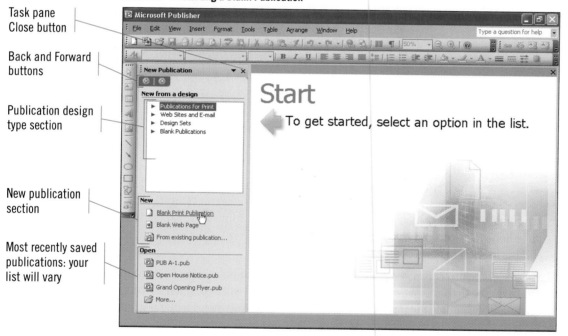

Task pane Close button

Back and Forward buttons

Publication design type section

New publication section

Most recently saved publications: your list will vary

Clues to Use

Using the New Publication task pane

When you first open Publisher, the New Publication task pane appears on the left side of the screen. It has three sections: New from a design, New, and Open. The New from a design section guides you through the creation of a new publication using a publication type, a design set, or different kinds of blank publications. The New section allows you to create new publications, and the Open section allows you to open a recently used publication, or to search for more existing publications. To close the task pane, click the Close button in the upper-right corner of the task pane. To open the task pane, click View on the menu bar, then click Task Pane.

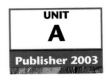

Viewing the Publisher Window

The area where a new or existing publication appears is called the **workspace**, which includes both the publication page and the scratch area. The workspace is where you actually work on a publication, and view your work. The workspace is bordered above and on the left by horizontal and vertical rulers that help you position text and graphics in your publications. The workspace is also bordered by horizontal and vertical scroll bars that allow you to view different areas of the workspace. You decide to take some time to get familiar with the Publisher workspace and its elements before working on the flyer. Compare the descriptions below to Figure A-4.

DETAILS

- The **title bar** is at the top of the window, and displays the program name (Microsoft Publisher), the type of publication (Print or Web), and the filename of the open publication. In Figure A-4, the filename is Publication1, a default name, because the file has not yet been named and saved. The title bar also contains a Control menu box, a Close button, and resizing buttons.

- The **menu bar** contains menus that list commands, organized in categories such as View and Format. As with all Windows programs, you can choose a menu command by clicking it with the mouse, or by pressing [Alt] plus the underlined letter in the menu name. A menu containing a down arrow at its lower edge contains additional commands. As you use Publisher, unused commands will be hidden, and only the frequently used commands will appear on the menu. To see these hidden commands, click the down arrow, or wait several seconds and the commands will appear. Once you select a previously hidden command, it will appear on the menu going forward. The Publisher Help feature can also be accessed by typing a question in the box on the right of the menu bar.

QUICK TIP
Any toolbar can be closed by clicking the Close button ✗ in its upper-right corner.

- The **toolbars** contain buttons for frequently used Publisher commands. The **Standard toolbar** is located just below the menu bar and contains buttons for the most frequently used Publisher commands. Place the pointer over each button to display the ScreenTip, a label that describes what each button does. To select a button, click it with the left mouse button. The face of any button has a graphic representation of its function; for instance, the Print button has a printer on its face. The **Objects toolbar** is on the left side of the screen next to the vertical ruler, and contains buttons used to insert the most frequently used objects (text boxes, clip art, geometric shapes, etc.) into Publications. The **Formatting toolbar** appears just above the horizontal ruler and contains buttons for often used text formatting commands such as bold, italics, or underlining. Toolbars can be opened or closed by clicking View on the menu bar, pointing to Toolbars, and clicking to select or deselect the particular toolbar.

- **Rulers** let you precisely measure the size of objects, as well as place objects in exact locations on a page. They can be moved from the edge of the workspace to more convenient positions. Your rulers may have different beginning and ending numbers, depending on the size of your monitor, the resolution of your display, and the positioning of the page on the workspace. The units of measurement displayed in rulers can be changed to show inches, centimeters, picas, or points.

- The workspace contains the currently displayed page and the scratch area. The **scratch area** is the gray area that surrounds the publication page, and can be used to store objects.

- The **status bar** is located at the bottom of the Publisher window. On the left side of the status bar are **page navigation icons**, which show you the number of pages in a publication, and are used to navigate from page to page. Click the icon for the page you want to view. In a multi-page publication, an icon is displayed for each page; the icon for the current page appears in light blue. The right side of the status bar shows the object status, which includes the size and position of selected objects.

FIGURE A-4: Blank Publication

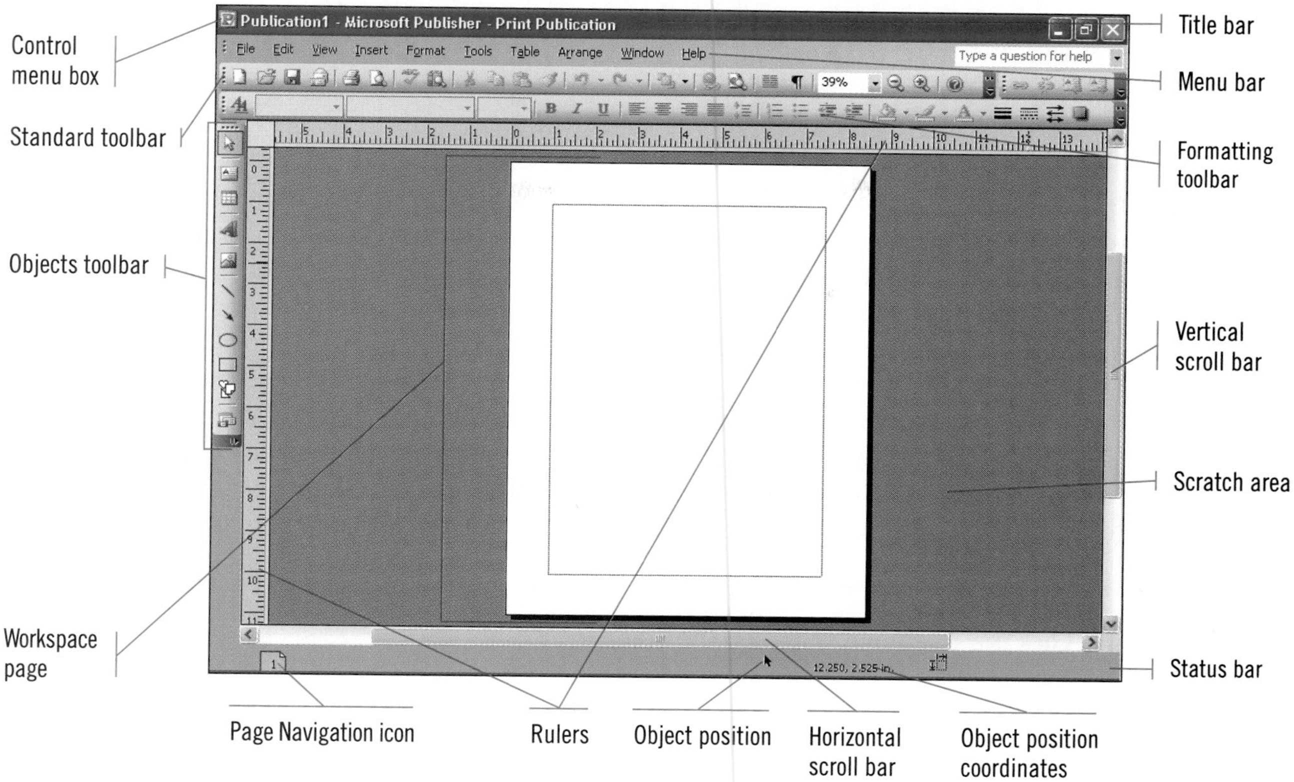

Control menu box

Standard toolbar

Objects toolbar

Workspace page

Publication1 - Microsoft Publisher - Print Publication

File   Edit   View   Insert   Format   Tools   Table   Arrange   Window   Help

Type a question for help

B   I   U

39%

Title bar

Menu bar

Formatting toolbar

Vertical scroll bar

Scratch area

Status bar

Page Navigation icon   Rulers   Object position   Horizontal scroll bar   Object position coordinates

12.250, 2.525-in.

Publisher 2003

Clues to Use

Using task panes

In addition to the New Publication task pane, seen in Figure A-5, you can use task panes for a variety of activities such as creating a new publication, changing color schemes, choosing font schemes, selecting a publication design, working with styles and formatting, and even doing a mail merge. You can turn the task panes feature on or off using the View menu on the menu bar, and move a task pane by clicking and dragging the title bar to a new location. You can move back and forth between open task panes by clicking the Forward or Back buttons in the upper-left corner of the task pane window. You can see more task pane options by clicking the Other Task Panes list arrow in the task pane title bar. You can also close the task pane by clicking the Close button in the upper-right corner of the task pane.

FIGURE A-5: New Publication task pane

New Publication

New from a design

▼ Publications for Print
► Web Sites and E-mail
► Design Sets
► Blank Publications

New

Blank Print Publication
Blank Web Page
From existing publication...

Open

Open House Flyer.pub
PUB A-1.pub
Open House Notice.pub
More...

Opening and Saving a Publication

Often a project is completed in stages: you start working on a publication, save it, and then stop to do other work or take a break. Later, you open the publication and resume working on it. Sometimes you open a file and save it under another name, either because you want to create a new publication by modifying one that already exists, or because you want to make changes to the document while preserving a copy of the original for safekeeping. Throughout this book, you will be instructed to open a file from the drive and folder where your Data Files are stored, use the Save As command to create a copy of the file with a new name, then modify the new file by following the lesson steps. Saving the files with new names keeps your original Data Files intact in case you have to start the lesson over again, or you wish to repeat an exercise. ████ Mike started the Image Magic flyer and gives you the file so that you can complete the document. You are ready to open the file and create a copy of it with a new name so that you can safely make changes.

STEPS

QUICK TIP

If you click the Views list arrow, then select Preview, the Preview pane shows a reduced image of the selected publication.

1. **Click the Open button 🗁 on the Standard toolbar**

   The Open Publication dialog box opens. A dialog box is a window that opens when more information is needed to carry out a command. A list of the available folders and publications appears.

2. **Click the Look in list arrow**

   A list of the available drives appears. The files that you need for these lessons are located where your Data Files are stored.

3. **Click the drive and folder where your Data Files are located**

   A list of the Data Files appears, as shown in Figure A-6.

TROUBLE

If you receive a message that the printer cannot be initialized, click OK to change to your default printer.

4. **Click the file PUB A-1.pub, then click Open**

   The file PUB A-1 opens. You could also double-click the filename in the Open Publication dialog box to open the file.

5. **Click File on the menu bar, then click Save As**

   The Save As dialog box opens.

6. **Make sure that the drive and folder where your Data Files are stored appear in the Save in list box**

   You should save all your files in the drive and folder where your Data Files are stored, unless instructed otherwise.

7. **Select the current filename in the File name text box if necessary, then type Open House Flyer**

   See Figure A-7.

QUICK TIP

Use the Save As command to create a new publication from an existing one. Use the Save command to store any changes made to an existing file on your disk.

8. **Click Save**

   The Save As dialog box closes, the file PUB A-1 closes, and a duplicate file named Open House Flyer is now open, as shown in Figure A-8. Changes made to Open House Flyer will not be reflected in the file PUB A-1. To save the publication in the future, you can click File on the menu bar, then click Save, or click the Save button 🖫 on the Standard toolbar.

FIGURE A-6: Open Publication dialog box

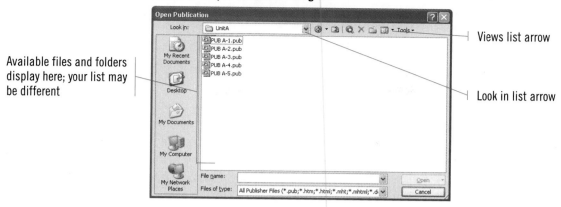

Available files and folders display here; your list may be different

Views list arrow

Look in list arrow

FIGURE A-7: Save As dialog box

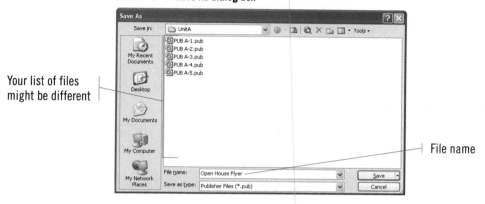

Your list of files might be different

File name

FIGURE A-8: Grand Opening Flyer publication

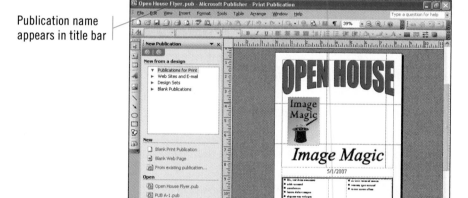

Publication name appears in title bar

Clues to Use

Using dialog box views

You may notice that the information in the Open and Save As dialog boxes varies depending on the view selected. There are eight views: Thumbnails, Tiles, Icons, List, Details, Properties, Preview, and WebView. The Thumbnails and Tiles Views show the file type and the name of the file. The List View displays the names of the contents of a given folder. The Details View displays the same information as the List View, but includes the size, the last date and time the file was saved, and the file type. The Properties View displays detailed information on the file size and when it was modified (when available). The Preview View displays an image of the file, although previews are not always available. The Thumbnail View shows the file type with the filename underneath. To select a different view, click the Views list arrow in a dialog box, then click the view you want.

Entering Text in a Text Box

In word processing, text is entered directly on a page and is the main element of a document. In desktop publishing, text forms part of the publication, along with images and graphic design elements. A **text box** is an object that can be resized and repositioned on a page. Once you type or paste text in a text box, you can easily manipulate the object relative to the graphics and other objects on a page, to achieve the best overall layout. **Point size** is the unit of measurement for fonts, and the space between paragraphs and text characters. There are 72 points in an inch. Because stories often continue onto another page, you can connect two or more text boxes, so the text flows logically from one to the next. You can select a text box by clicking anywhere within it. When selected, small hollow circles called **handles** appear at eight points around its perimeter. This publication also includes **placeholders**, which help you envision what type of information to include and where. **Ruler guides** are green horizontal and vertical lines that appear on the screen to help you position objects on a page, but do not print in the publication. ████████ You want to include the address of the new office space in the flyer, so you decide to create a text box to the right of the Image Magic logo to contain this information. You'll use ruler guides to position the text box just where you want it.

STEPS

1. **Click the** Text Box button 🔲 **on the Objects toolbar**
    The pointer changes to ╋.

2. **Position** ╋ **so that the object position coordinates are** 3.500, 4.000 in., **press and hold the** left mouse button, **drag** ╋ **to create a rectangle that has object size coordinates of** 4.000 × 2.750 in., **then release the mouse button**
    As you drag the text box, the coordinates on the status bar display the position of the pointer and object size. The ruler guides also help you position and size the text box correctly. When you release the mouse button, the text box appears as a selected object surrounded by handles, with the insertion point blinking in the upper-left corner, as shown in Figure A-9. Additional buttons appear on the Standard and Formatting toolbars when the text box is selected. This means that Publisher is ready for you to type text, and has made the relevant tools available to you.

    QUICK TIP
    You can also zoom in using the View menu or the Zoom In 🔍 button on the Standard toolbar.

3. **Press** [F9], **type** We are excited about our new office space. Here, we will offer expanded services in a professional atmosphere. Please join us at our Open House celebration on Tuesday, May 1, 2007, from 1 to 5 pm., **press** [Enter] **twice, type** Our new address is:, **press** [Enter], **type** 3444 Tramway Boulevard, **press** [Enter], **then type** Albuquerque, NM 87111

    TROUBLE
    Wavy red lines under typed text indicate words that may be misspelled. Correct any spelling errors you may have typed.

4. **Press** [Ctrl][A] **to select all the text in the box, click the** Font Size list arrow 10 ▾ **on the Formatting toolbar, then click** 16
    Enlarging the font size makes the text stand out so it is easier to read.

5. **Click anywhere on the** scratch area
    Clicking outside the text box deselects it. You could also press [Esc] twice to deselect the text box. Compare your screen to Figure A-10.

    QUICK TIP
    You can also zoom out using the View menu or the Zoom Out button on the Standard toolbar.

6. **Click the** Zoom list arrow 100% ▾, **then click** Whole Page
    The magnification adjusts so that the entire page is in view on the screen.

7. **Click the** Save button 🖫 **on the Standard toolbar**
    It is a good idea to save your work early and often in the creation process, especially before making significant changes to the publication, or before printing.

Text Box button

Object width appears on ruler

Text box

Placeholder text

Handles

Object position coordinates

Object size

FIGURE A-10: **Completed text in text box**

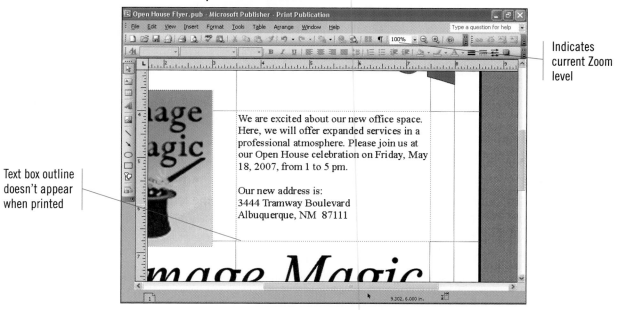

Indicates current Zoom level

Text box outline doesn't appear when printed

We are excited about our new office space. Here, we will offer expanded services in a professional atmosphere. Please join us at our Open House celebration on Friday, May 18, 2007, from 1 to 5 pm.

Our new address is:
3444 Tramway Boulevard
Albuquerque, NM 87111

Design Matters

Understanding objects

Objects are elements such as tables, text boxes, geometric shapes, clip art, and picture frames that can be resized, moved, joined, or organized so that one object appears to be in front of another. In addition, text boxes can be wrapped around other objects. The advantage to using text boxes is that the contents within the box can be easily moved anywhere within a publication. Figure A-11 shows text wrapped around a graphic image.

FIGURE A-11: **Text wrapped around a picture**

to market your product or service, and also create credibility and build your organization's identity among peers, members, employees, or vendors.

First, determine the audience of the newsletter. This could be anyone who might benefit from

You might consider purchasing a mailing list from a company.

If you explore the Publisher catalog, you will find many publications that match the style of your newsletter.

Next, establish how much time and money you can

Publisher 2003

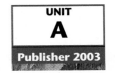

Viewing and Printing a Publication

Printing outputs a publication into paper form. When a publication is completed, you can print it to have a paper copy to reference, file, or send to others. You can also print specific pages from a publication that is not complete so that you can review it or work on it when you are not at a computer. Before you print a publication, you should use the **Print Preview** feature to make sure that it fits on a page and looks the way you want. You cannot make changes to your publication when in Print Preview, but it will allow you to see how it will look when printed. Publisher's Print Preview feature will show your publication in either grayscale or in color, depending upon the type of printer that is selected. Table A-2 provides printing tips. ▓▓▓▓▓ You want to print a copy of the Image Magic flyer to show Mike. First you want to view the document in Print Preview to check its overall appearance and see how it will look when it is printed.

STEPS

1. **Make sure the printer is on and contains paper**
   If a file is sent to print and the printer is off, an error message appears.

> **TROUBLE**
> If your selected printer is not a color printer, Print Preview may appear only in grayscale.

2. **Click the Print Preview button 🔍 on the Standard toolbar**

3. **If necessary, click the Color/Grayscale button 🎨 on the Print Preview toolbar to change the display to color**
   If your printer allows both black and white and color printing, you can change the display from black and white to color to see how it will appear using different printers. The page appears in color, as shown in Figure A-12. If there were multiple pages, you could preview them individually by clicking the Page Up 🔼 and Page Down buttons 🔽 on the Print Preview toolbar, or see as many as six pages at once by clicking the Multiple Pages button 🔠 on the Print Preview toolbar.

4. **Click the Close Preview button Close on the Print Preview toolbar**

5. **Click the Text Box button 🔲 on the Objects toolbar, position + so that the object position coordinates are 0.500, 8.000 in., press and hold the left mouse button, drag + to create a rectangular text box that has object size coordinates of 2.000 × 0.375 in., release the mouse button, press [F9], then type your name**

6. **Press [F9], then click the Save button 🖫 on the Standard toolbar**
   You should always save a publication before printing it.

> **QUICK TIP**
> You can also print using the Print button 🖨 on the Standard toolbar, but doing so will print all the pages of a publication.

7. **Click File on the menu bar, then click Print**
   The Print dialog box opens, as shown in Figure A-13.

8. **Make sure that the All option button is selected for print range, and that 1 appears in the Number of copies text box, then click OK**
   Review the publication to see if it printed as expected.

FIGURE A-12: Whole page in Print Preview window

Page Up button

Page Down button

Whole Page button

Multiple Pages button

Color/Grayscale button

FIGURE A-13: Print dialog box

Your printer may be different

Selects the printer

Indicates the number of printed copies

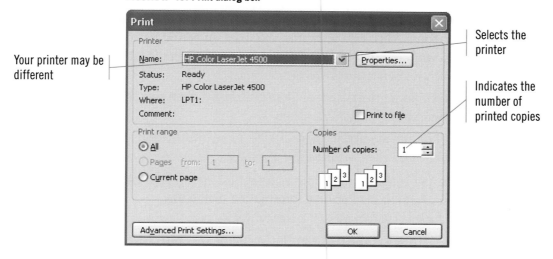

TABLE A-2: Publication printing tips

before you print	recommendation
Check the printer	Make sure that the printer is turned on and online, that it has paper, and that there are no error messages or warning signals
Check the printer selection	In the Printer section of the Print dialog box, select the correct printer from the Name list arrow to make sure that the correct printer is selected

Publisher 2003

GETTING STARTED WITH MICROSOFT OFFICE PUBLISHER 2003 **13**

Getting Help and Changing Personal Information

Publisher offers extensive **Help** features that give you immediate access to definitions, explanations, and useful tips. The Help window is displayed along the right side of the workspace and contains pages of documentation and examples to assist you in your work. When open, the window can be resized or moved for your purposes, and can remain on the screen so you can refer to it as you work. You can access Help any time while Publisher is open. Because you probably create publications for yourself, or your business or organization, Publisher makes it easy for you to store frequently used information about these entities. This feature, called **Personal Information Sets**, means that you won't have to enter this information each time. You can store up to four Personal Information Sets: for your primary and secondary businesses; another organization; and your home or family. The information in the Primary Business set is applied by default, but you can easily apply the information in any of the other sets. 🖳 You decide to use Help to find out about Personal Information and how it can be modified. You want to find out how to create a Personal Information Set for Image Magic that you can use to easily insert company information into publications.

STEPS

QUICK TIP
You can also display the Publisher Help task pane from any open task pane. To do this, click the Other task panes list arrow, then click Help.

1. **Click the** Type a question for help text box

   An alternative to using the Type a question for help text box is the Office Assistant. You can display the Office Assistant by clicking Help on the menu bar, then clicking Show Office Assistant. Type a question, statement, or work in the query box, then click Search.

2. **Type** How do I change Personal Information?, **then press** Enter

   The Search Results task pane displays topics about Personal Information, as shown in Figure A-14.

QUICK TIP
You can print the information in any Help window by clicking the Print button on the Publisher Help window toolbar.

3. **Click** Add, change, or remove personal information data, **the Microsoft Publisher Help window opens, click** Add or change information within a personal information set **from the Help window choices, then read about making modifications**

   Click the Show All arrow to read additional information.

4. **Click the** Publisher Help window Close button ⊠, **then click the** task pane Close button ✖

   The Help window and task pane are hidden.

TROUBLE
If Personal Information does not appear on the menu, click the down arrow at the bottom of the menu, or wait several seconds, and the command will appear.

5. **Click** Edit **on the menu bar, then click** Personal Information

   Any Personal Information Set can be modified, and the changes can be used in future publications.

6. **Click the** Select a personal information set list arrow, **then click the** Secondary Business information set **in the Personal Information dialog box**

   The information in the dialog box is for the current secondary business.

7. **Press** [Tab] **to select the** name **in the My name text box, type** Mike Mendoza, **press** [Tab], **then refer to Figure A-15 to enter the rest of the information in the Personal Information dialog box including job title, phone numbers, e-mail, and color scheme**

8. **Click** Update

   Clicking Update confirms your changes to the information set.

Search Results task pane

Type a question for help text box

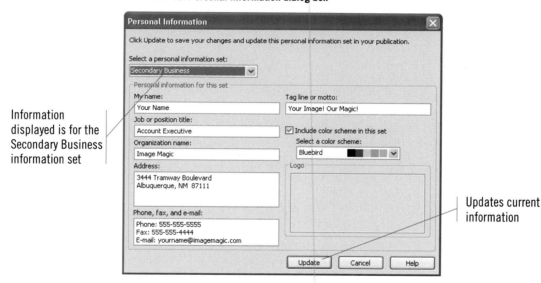

Information displayed is for the Secondary Business information set

Updates current information

Clues to Use

Using the Office Assistant

If the Office Assistant is displayed, click it to access Help. If it is not displayed, click Help on the menu bar, then click Show the Office Assistant. (You may need to install additional components in order to see the Office Assistant.) This feature provides help based on the text you type in the query box. To ask a question, click the Office Assistant. Type a question, statement, or word, then click Search. The Search Results Task Pane searches the database and displays any matching topics. The animated Office Assistant also provides Office Assistant Tips (indicated by a light bulb) on the current action you are performing. You can click the light bulb to display a dialog box containing relevant choices that you can refer to as you work. The default Office Assistant character is Clippit, but there are others you can choose. To change its appearance, right-click the Office Assistant, then click Options. Click the Gallery tab, click the Back and Next buttons until you find an Assistant you want to use, then click OK. (You may need to insert your Microsoft Office Publisher CD to complete this task.) Right-click the Office Assistant, then click Hide, to close it.

Publisher 2003

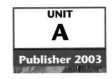

Closing a Publication and Exiting Publisher

When you finish working on a publication, you should save the file and close it. Closing a file puts away a publication so you can no longer work on it, but leaves Publisher running so you can work on other publications. When you complete all your work in Publisher, you want to exit the program. Exiting puts away any open publication files and returns you to the desktop, where you can choose to run another program. You finished adding the information to the Image Magic flyer and need to attend a meeting, so you close the publication and then exit Publisher.

STEPS

1. **Click File on the menu bar**
   The File menu opens. See Figure A-16.

2. **Click Close**

3. **If asked if you want to save your work, click Yes**
   Publisher closes the publication and a blank publication appears on the workspace.

> **QUICK TIP**
> To exit Publisher and close an open publication, click the Close button on the upper-right corner of the window. Publisher prompts you to save any unsaved changes before closing.

4. **Click File on the menu bar, then click Exit**
   You could also double-click the program control menu box to exit the program. Publisher closes, and computer memory is freed up for other computing tasks.

Clues to Use

Opening a file created in the Publication Gallery

When you open a file created with the New Publication task pane and the Publication Gallery, a specific task pane associated with that publication also opens. For example, when you open a newsletter you created using the New Publication task pane and the Publication Gallery, the Newsletter Options task pane opens. The specific task pane associated with the publication you created has options that make it easy to modify the publication.

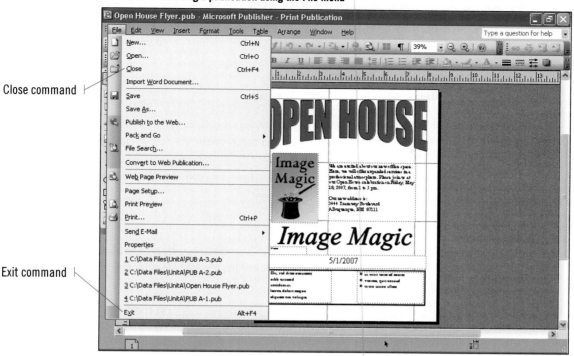

Close command

Exit command

Clues to Use

Microsoft Office Publisher World Wide Web site

You can get even more information about Microsoft Publisher by accessing the Microsoft Office Publisher Web site. This site is updated frequently, and offers tips, upgrades, sales promotions, and information on new developments in Publisher. By clicking on the blue underlined links, you'll be able to find additional information on the Microsoft product line. Figure A-17 shows the Web site for Microsoft Office Publisher. It may look different on your screen, because the site changes often. To find even more information, you can search the Internet using your favorite search engine for any sites about Microsoft Publisher. To visit the Publisher Web site, click the Help menu, then click Microsoft Office Online. When the Web site opens, click the Publisher link.)

FIGURE A-17: **Microsoft Office Publisher 2003 Web site**

Site address

Links to other Web pages

Publisher 2003

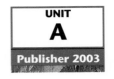
Capstone Project: Study Abroad Flyer

You have learned the basic skills necessary to modify an existing publication. You can open a file and save it under a different name. You know how to create a text box, insert text, zoom, and reduce the font size so you can add additional text. Once your work is complete, you can preview the flyer in both black and white and in color, then print it. ▓▓▓▓▓ Using the Publication Gallery, Mike started a flyer for the Community College Council that advertises a one-credit course in Mexico. He asks you to complete the project by adding contact information and then reviewing and printing the document.

STEPS

1. Start Publisher, click the Open button 🗁 on the Standard toolbar, open the file PUB A-2.pub from the drive and folder where your Data Files are located, then save the publication as Study Abroad Flyer

2. Close the task pane if necessary, click the Text Box button 🔲 on the Objects toolbar, then use ＋ to create a rectangular text box from 1" H/9" V to 5 1'2" H/10" V

3. Press [F9] to zoom in to the text box

4. Type For more information, contact:, press [Enter], type your name, press [Enter], then type Extension 3210

5. Press [Ctrl][A], click the Font Size list arrow 🔲10 🔽 on the Formatting toolbar, then click 16
   Compare your publication to Figure A-18.

6. Press [Esc] twice, press [F9] to zoom out, then click the Save button 🔲 on the Standard toolbar
   The overall design of the publication looks good.

7. Click the Print Preview button 🔲 on the Standard toolbar
   The publication appears on the screen as it will appear printed. You cannot see the outlines of text boxes, or other non-printing characters.

8. Click the Color/Grayscale button 🔲
   The view changes from black and white to color. Compare your publication to Figure A-19.

9. Close the Preview window, click the Print button 🖨 on the Standard toolbar, then exit Publisher

FIGURE A-18: Contact information inserted in Study Abroad Flyer

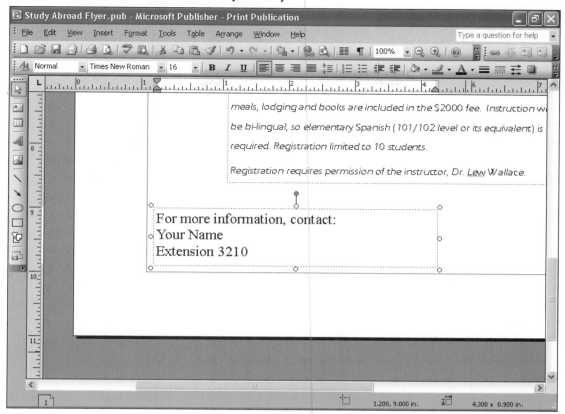

FIGURE A-19: Color Print Preview of Study Abroad Flyer

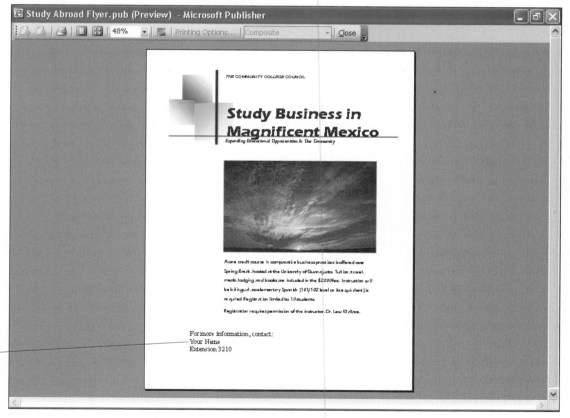

Your name should appear here

Publisher 2003

Practice

▼ CONCEPTS REVIEW

Label each of the elements in the Publisher window shown in Figure A-20.

FIGURE A-20

Match each of the terms or buttons with the statement that describes its function.

7. Handles
8.
9. Text box
10.
11. Status bar
12.

a. Used to save a publication to a disk
b. Small black circles surrounding an object
c. Shows size and position of selected object
d. Contains typed text
e. Opens an existing publication
f. Prints every page in the publication

Select the best answer from the list of choices.

13. A document created in Publisher is called a:
   a. Publication.
   b. Notebook.
   c. Booklet.
   d. Brochure.

14. **Which of the following is considered an object?**
   a. Text box
   b. Pictures
   c. Tables
   d. All of the above

15. **Which key is pressed to zoom into a selected area?**
   a. [F8]
   b. [F9]
   c. [F6]
   d. [F2]

16. **A template is:**
   a. A distinctive shape in a publication.
   b. A short statement placed off to the side to grab a reader's attention.
   c. An online artwork organizer.
   d. A publication that serves as a master for other publications.

17. **Which of the following statements about text boxes is false?**
   a. They can be connected to other frames.
   b. They can be resized.
   c. They aren't very useful.
   d. They can be moved.

18. **Which button is used to create a text box?**
   a.
   b.
   c. Times New Roman ▾
   d. 10 ▾

19. **Which is not a type of Personal Information set?**
   a. Primary Business
   b. Secondary Business
   c. Home/Family
   d. Colleague

20. **Each of the following is found in the status bar, except:**
   a. A selected object's position.
   b. The name of the current publication.
   c. Page icons.
   d. A selected object's size.

21. **Which feature is used to magnify the view?**
   a. Magnify
   b. Amplify
   c. Enlarge
   d. Zoom In

▼ SKILLS REVIEW

1. **Define publication software.**
   a. Identify five advantages of using a desktop publishing program.
   b. Name three Publisher features that you can use to create a publication.

2. **Start Publisher 2003.**
   a. Start Publisher.
   b. Open a new blank publication.
   c. Try to identify as many elements in the Publisher window as you can without referring to the unit material.

3. **View the Publisher window.**
   a. Identify as many elements in the Publisher window you can without looking back in the unit.
   b. Which toolbars are always visible?

4. **Open and save a publication.**
   a. Open the file PUB A-3.pub. If you get a message to initialize the default printer, click OK.
   b. Save the publication as **Sample Business Card** in the drive and folder where your Data Files are stored.
   c. Click the Business Card Options task pane Close button, if necessary.

FIGURE A-21

5. Enter text in a text box.

   a. Create a text box with the size coordinates 2.000 × 0.500 in. for your name, using Figure A-21 as an example. The top-left corner should be placed at 1.250, 0.500 in. (ruler guides were inserted to make this placement easier). Type your name using a 16 point font size or larger.

   b. Create a text box with the size coordinates 2.000 × 0.750 in. for your address, using Figure A-21 as a guide. The top-left corner should be placed at 1.250, 1.250 in. Substitute your address for the text shown using a 10-point text size.

   c. Save the publication.

6. View and print a publication.

   a. Zoom out.

   b. Zoom in.

   c. Use the Print button to print one copy of the publication.

7. Get Help and change Personal Information.

   a. Click the Type a question for help text box.

   b. Find information on text boxes. (*Hint*: Use keywords "text boxes," then read several of the search result topics.)

   c. Click the Print button above the Help window to print the information you find.

   d. Close the Help window.

   e. Hide the Office Assistant.

   f. Open the Personal Information dialog box.

   g. Select the Secondary Business information set.

   h. Change the Color Scheme for the Secondary Business to Wildflower.

8. Close the publication and exit Publisher.

   a. Save and close your publication.

   b. Exit Publisher.

▼ INDEPENDENT CHALLENGE 1

The Publisher Help feature provides definitions, explanations, procedures, and other helpful information. It also provides examples and demonstrations to show how Publisher features work. You need to add a page to a brochure you are working on for your new client, Mangez!, a French importer of baked goods and cheeses. Open any existing publication, and explore Help using the Office Assistant. Find out how to add a page to a publication. Print out the information.

Advanced Challenge Exercise

   ■ Display the Office Assistant, if necessary, using the Show the Office Assistant command on the Help menu. Click the Office Assistant, then type a question about how you can display the Measurement toolbar. (*Hint*: You may have to ask the Office Assistant more than one question.)

▼ INDEPENDENT CHALLENGE 2

Publisher can be used in many ways in business and education. If you were teaching a class, how could you use Publisher to your advantage as a teaching aid?

   a. Think of three types of publications you could create with Publisher that would be effective in a classroom.

   b. Sketch a sample of each publication.

▼ INDEPENDENT CHALLENGE 2 (CONTINUED)

c. Open a blank publication for each sample. Using text boxes, re-create your sketches. (These publications do not need to be fancy; they can just contain text boxes.) Your three publications should be named **Suggestion 1**, **Suggestion 2**, and **Suggestion 3**.

d. In a separate blank publication, use text boxes to explain why each of your suggestions would be an effective use of Publisher. Name this publication **Explanations**.

e. Be sure to include your name in a text box in each publication, then print each one.

f. Save and close the publications, then exit Publisher.

▼ INDEPENDENT CHALLENGE 3

You are selected as the Image Magic Employee of the Month. You're being honored because you always come up with creative ways of accomplishing tasks. When you are given your award, you are asked for ways to improve the certificate. To complete the certificate, more explanatory text about the recipient is needed.

FIGURE A-22

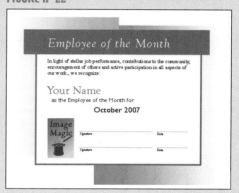

a. Start Publisher, if necessary, open the file PUB A-4.pub, then save it as **Image Magic Award** in the drive and folder where your Data Files are located. If you see a warning box, click Yes to install the wizard.

b. If necessary, close the task pane.

c. Use Zoom as needed. In the space above the Name of Recipient placeholder, insert a text box that contains an explanation of why you deserve this award.

d. Replace the Name of Recipient placeholder with your name.

e. Print the final publication.

f. Save your work, then compare it to the sample shown in Figure A-22.

Advanced Challenge Exercise

- Open the task pane, then switch to the Font Schemes task pane.
- Browse through the list of schemes, then click a Font Scheme of your choice. Observe the change in the publication.
- Save the modified publication as **Image Magic Award ACE**, then print a copy.

g. Close the publication, then exit Publisher.

▼ INDEPENDENT CHALLENGE 4

The World Wide Web is a rich resource for individuals and businesses. You examine the possibility of starting your own desktop publishing business. The advantages include: flexible hours, low start-up costs, having an outlet for artistic impulses, the ability to conduct business remotely over the Internet, contact with other business people, and being your own boss. On the negative side, you have no formal education in design. You decide to look on the Internet to learn something about design.

a. Start Publisher, if necessary, then open a new blank publication.

b. Save the publication as **Graphic Ideas** in the drive and folder where your Data Files are located.

c. Connect to the Internet, then use a search engine to go find information on design basics.

d. Click the topics listed to find articles on design basics.

e. Create text boxes in the blank publication and type brief descriptions of some of your findings.

f. Disconnect from the Internet, if necessary.

g. Complete your publication. Be sure to include your name.

h. Print the publication, then exit Publisher.

Publisher 2003

▼ VISUAL WORKSHOP

Open the publication PUB A-5.pub from the drive and folder where your Data Files are located, and add the text shown in Figure A-23 using the skills you learned in this unit. The font size in the text box is 16 point. Save the publication as Image Magic Gift Card. Be sure to include your name. Print the publication.

FIGURE A-23

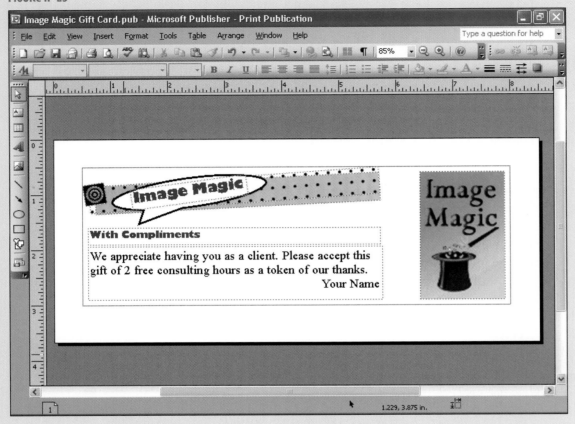

Creating a Publication

OBJECTIVES

Plan a publication
Design a publication
Create a publication using the task pane
Replace existing text
Add a graphic image
Add a sidebar
Use the Design Gallery
Group objects
Capstone Project: College Brochure

Now that you are familiar with the Publisher window and understand how to open and save a file, you are ready to create your own publication. It is important to think about the purpose and objectives of your publication, as well as your design goals, so that you can make effective layout decisions. Once you establish the message and layout of your publication, you must add text and graphics, as well as ensure objects are in the correct places. Mike Mendoza, your boss at Image Magic, has assigned you the task of designing a company newsletter. You decide to use Publisher to create this publication.

Planning a Publication

To create an effective publication, you should start with a planning session. Planning a publication involves at least three steps: determining what you want to achieve, deciding what information to include, and figuring out how to best present it. Knowing the goals of your publication helps you determine what form it should take. Keeping in mind the content of the message and your audience helps you to decide how the publication should be written, and how it should look. While there are many ways to plan a publication, it's best to start by determining its purpose. See Figure B-1. ▨▨▨▨ Your assignment is to create a one-page newsletter. Before starting, you answer these questions: Who is the audience? What is the message? What form should the message take?

DETAILS

Answering the following questions is the key to planning a successful publication:

- **What is the purpose of the publication?**

  Are you trying to inform, motivate, sell, inspire confidence, raise morale, solicit a vote, or solicit a contribution of time or money?

  In your discussions with Mike and other managers at Image Magic, you learn that the purpose of the company newsletter is to inform employees of news within the company and to publicize business and personal achievements.

- **What type of response do you want?**

  Do you intend this to be a one-way communication, or do you want feedback? If you do want feedback, what form should it take? Do you want volunteers, attendance at an event, and/or inquiries for additional information via phone or e-mail? For example, do you want visits to a Web site; registrations; contracts signed and returned; payments by check, cash or credit card; RSVPs, etc.?

  The Image Magic newsletter is intended to make employees feel important and included. It is primarily a one-way communication.

- **What are you going to do with the responses you receive?**

  If you solicit inquiries for additional information via mail or e-mail, but don't prepare a polite, informative response to send, you risk alienating your audience. If you solicit information, but neglect to gather it, interpret it, or fail to use it, you wasted time and effort, and lost an opportunity.

- **Who is the target audience?**

  The more narrowly you can define the characteristics of your target audience, the more you can tailor the content and appearance of the message to appeal to that group. For instance, a colorful comic book publication would be right for trying to educate fourth graders, but not appropriate for informing cardiologists of newly identified risk factors for heart disease.

  Some of the possible ways to identify a group are by age, sex, geography, reading level, educational background, first language, hobbies, nationality, ethnicity, religion, culture, political affiliation, employment, income level, taste in music and art, home ownership, and health or ill health.

  The Image Magic newsletter has a narrow audience. It will be read by employees and clients of the company. While their demographics vary, all share an interest in the Image Magic agency and its core service, advertising.

Design Matters

Developing design sense

Designing publications is a skill that can be learned through thoughtful practice and critical observation. Just as artists gather ideas from trips to museums, and musicians gather ideas from attending concerts, you can sharpen your design skills by looking at publications created by others. Start with a visit to a library or a magazine stand, observing the overall design of the publications.

Gauge your overall reaction to a publication, and judge for yourself what you find appealing and what you find distracting or offensive. Concentrate on how your eye moves across a page. What combinations of design elements (balance, color, consistency, contrast, and white space) are you drawn to, and what do you find unappealing?

FIGURE B-1: Planning process

Determine the following:
- What you want to achieve
- What you should include
- How to best present your ideas

Clues to Use

Including the facts

Probably the most daunting part of creating a new publication is the notion of what information is essential, and what is not. Space, of course, is a factor, but you should consider the following criteria:

- What information will the reader want? What questions is the reader likely to have? Your text should answer questions, not raise them.
- How much time does the reader have? Make sure the content is easy to read and scan, and that text is presented in 'bite-sized' chunks.

- Are there others in your organization who can provide guidance and ideas as you complete the planning stage?

There are many aspects to consider, and you should certainly get a consensus from your teammates. Take the time to hold one or more brain-storming sessions with all who will be involved in the development of the publication. It's easier to incorporate valuable feedback before beginning the design process, and saves time in the long run.

Designing a Publication

Just as form follows function in the old adage, planning should always precede design. The elements of design—unity, balance, color, consistency, contrast, and white space—should be combined to support the objectives of the publication. This is why design follows planning, because it must support the goals identified in the planning stages. After planning, you know that you want the newsletter to catch the eye of potential readers, be easy to read, and look professional to clients. You decide to include the company logo to identify the newsletter as belonging to Image Magic, and you want to call attention to specific text to be sure it is seen and understood. You also want the newsletter to display a tasteful sense of humor, so that it entertains readers and keeps them looking forward to the next issue.

DETAILS

- **View the document as a whole**

  The publication needs enough contrast and variety to be interesting, but must be consistent and logical so the reader can find the meaning without confusion or unnecessary effort.

- **Use placeholders for text and graphics to create an effective layout**

  Placeholder text and graphics are objects that are inserted into a publication to illustrate how the finished product will appear when replaced with more significant materials at a later time. Publisher uses placeholder text boxes and graphics extensively in the Publication Gallery, to demonstrate how the combined design elements in a finished publication will look.

- **Use graphics to add interest and present ideas**

  Use of artwork not only adds interest, but also is a means to communicate ideas and feelings that can reinforce text in a publication.

- **Use white space liberally**

  White space, also known as negative space, describes the open space between design elements. It can exist between elements of text (letters or paragraphs), in between and surrounding graphics, and between all other objects on the page. It is crucial for establishing spatial relations between visual items, and actually guides the reader's eye from one point to another. Without sufficient white space, text is unreadable, graphics lose emphasis, and there is no balance between the elements on a page. White space tells you where one section ends and another begins.

- **Prominently feature the company logo**

  The Image Magic logo appears on all its print material—letterhead, envelopes, business cards, and advertisements—to reinforce the identity of the company. It boosts morale for employees and associates to see the logo displayed with pride, and enhances clients' perception of the firm.

- **Emphasize certain text**

  Some text on a page should stand out. See Figure B-2. For example, **sidebars** are text related to the story but not vital to it. They are placed adjacent to the story to add emphasis and pique the interest of readers. Usually sidebars have a different background color, font, or point size to set them apart from the story.

FIGURE B-2: Sample newsletter

Masthead

Date and Issue Number

Graphic Image

Sidebar is a related story with formatting to add emphasis

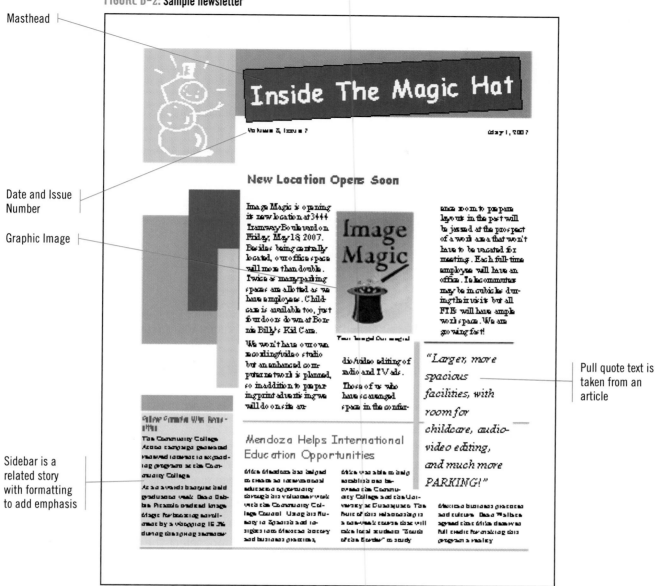

Pull quote text is taken from an article

Design Matters

Recognizing bad design

Thoughtful practice and critical observation are the keys to learning good design. But how can you recognize bad design? First, look at a publication from the reader's point of view, and try to identify what is of interest in the publication. If you don't spot something of interest right away, do you think the typical reader is going to pursue it or set it aside? Nothing discourages a reader more than long columns of dull gray type, unless it is long columns of dull gray type that are hard to read. Ornate type that might look stylish on the sample sheet in a well-lighted print shop may be very hard to read elsewhere. Is the artwork carefully chosen and well placed to generate interest, or is the publication too cluttered with fluff that will only distract the reader from the information you are trying to present? In a nutshell, "bad" design is anything that fails to capture or sustain a reader's interest.

Publisher 2003

CREATING A PUBLICATION **29**

Creating a Publication Using the Task Pane

The New Publication task pane makes it easy to create a new publication. This feature helps you get started by letting you choose among the New from a design, New, or Open options. The New from a design option is organized by Publications for Print, Web Sites and E-Mail, Design Sets, and Blank Publications. The Publications for Print option includes Quick Publications, Newsletters, resumes, and more. The Design Sets option includes Master Sets, Special Events Sets, Holiday Sets, and Restaurant Sets that are further organized by design schemes such as Accent Box, Accessory Bar, Arcs, Bars, Bubbles, etc. The choices you select help create the initial publication, and you take it from there. ▦▦▦▦ You use the New Publication task pane to create a newsletter.

STEPS

TROUBLE

If Publisher is already open but you don't see the New Publication task pane, click File on the menu bar, then click New. If the task pane does not appear on the left side of your screen, see your instructor or technical support person for help.

1. **Start Publisher**

   The New Publication task pane opens. The New from a Design list displays four main categories: Publications for Print, Web Sites and E-mail, Design Sets, and Blank Publications. You can click the arrow to the left of each category to open or close a list of subcategories.

2. **Click the Publications for Print category, if necessary, to open the subcategories list, then click Newsletters**

   The Publication Gallery displays different newsletter designs, as shown in Figure B-3.

3. **Scroll down if necessary, then click Borders Newsletter**

   The Newsletter layout appears in the workspace pane. The Newsletter Options task pane, where you can specify some features of your publication, opens on the left. The default choices of two-sided printing and no customer address are currently selected, as indicated by the borders surrounding these options in the task pane.

4. **Click the Close button on the Newsletter Options task pane**

   You now have a clear view of the newsletter in the workspace.

TROUBLE

If your name and personal information don't appear in this dialog box, enter it before proceeding with this step.

5. **Click Edit on the menu bar, click Personal Information, select the Secondary Business set if necessary, click the Select a color scheme list arrow, click Bluebird, then click Update**

   The Bluebird color scheme provides an array of bright colors. The newsletter appears in the workspace, as shown in Figure B-4.

6. **Click the Save button 🖫 on the Standard toolbar, click the Save in list arrow, locate the drive and folder where your Data Files are located, select the text in the File name text box if it is not highlighted, type IM Newsletter, then click Save**

FIGURE B-3: New Publication task pane and Publication Gallery

Publication types in the Publications for Print category

Newsletters option

Publications in the Publications Gallery

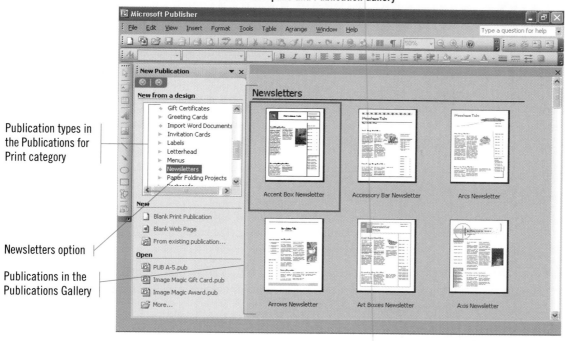

FIGURE B-4: Newsletter with the Bluebird color scheme

Your zoom percentage might be different

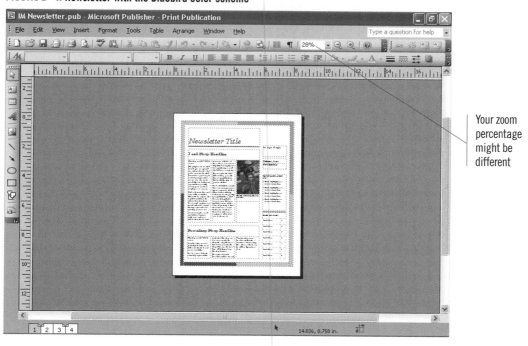

Clues to Use

Publication Gallery options

The Publication Gallery is a visual directory of more than 1600 different publications. It is organized into four sections: Publications for Print, Web Sites and E-mail, Design Sets, and Blank Publications. To switch between them, click the arrow for the category you want. Each selection offers a variety of choices within its particular category.

Brochures, for example, are available in many different styles and layout schemes. Labels can be created for computer disks, binders, audiocassettes, videocassettes, and CD case liners. Publications created using the Publication Gallery can be easily modified.

Replacing Existing Text

One of the benefits of using the Publication Gallery is that your new document contains preformatted place-holders that suggest content for your publication. In order to replace these placeholders with your own content, you must first select the existing text in a text box. You can then either type directly in the text box, or can insert a document created with a word processor, such as Microsoft Word. ▰▰▰ You need to replace the placeholders in the newsletter with text for the Image Magic newsletter. Mike Mendoza has provided you with a Word document to use for the lead story.

You can zoom in or out whenever you need to. Zooming doesn't affect the printed publication in any way.

1. **Press [F9]**

   Zooming into the selected text can help you get a closer look at specific objects. You can zoom by clicking the Zoom button [100% ▾], which always displays the Zoom factor, or clicking the Zoom In 🔍 and Zoom Out 🔍 buttons.

2. **Click the Lead Story Headline text box at 2"H/2¾V, as shown in Figure B-5**

   Handles surround the selected text box, and its position and size appear on the status bar. The Formatting toolbar appears below the Standard toolbar.

3. **Press [Ctrl][A] to select the placeholder text Lead Story Headline, then type New Location Opens Soon**

   The placeholder text is deleted with the first keystroke of the new text.

4. **Click the placeholder text in the column below the new heading to select it**

   Clicking placeholder text, instead of the text box surrounding it, selects all the text, so there is no need to press [Ctrl][A].

If you receive an error message saying that Publisher can't import the specified format because this feature is not installed, click OK to install it. If necessary, insert the requested CD, then follow the instructions. If you need further assistance, ask your instructor or technical support person.

5. **Click Insert on the menu bar, click Text File, locate the drive and folder where your Data Files are located, click the file PUB B-1.doc, then click OK**

   You might have to use the scroll buttons to see the new text. Compare your newsletter to Figure B-6. Instead of using the menu bar to insert text from a document file, you could right-click placeholder text, point to Change Text, then click Text File.

6. **Press [F9], then click the Save button 💾 on the Standard toolbar**

FIGURE B-5: Selected text box

Handles surround selected text box

Lead story headline placeholder text

Lead story placeholder text

Placeholder graphic

Upper-left corner coordinates of the selected text box

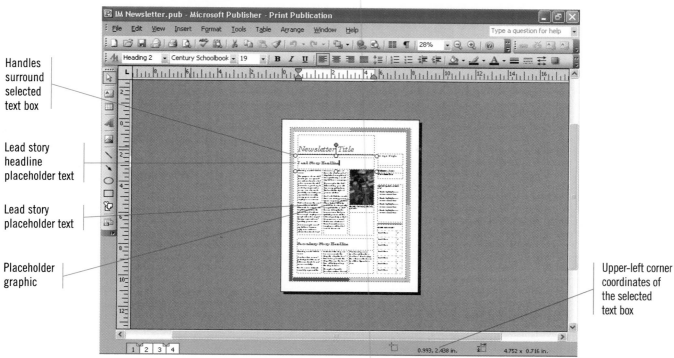

FIGURE B-6: Word document text in newsletter

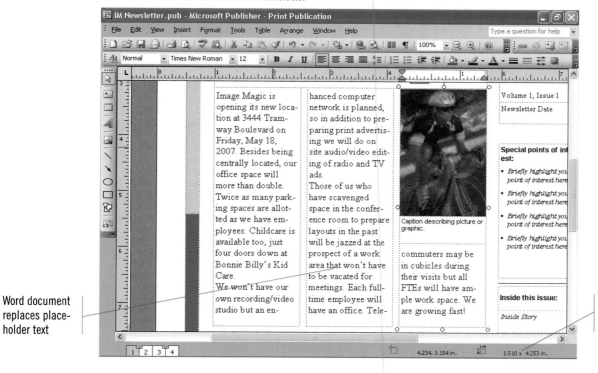

Image Magic is opening its new location at 3444 Tramway Boulevard on Friday, May 18, 2007. Besides being centrally located, our office space will more than double. Twice as many parking spaces are allotted as we have employees. Childcare is available too, just four doors down at Bonnie Billy's Kid Care.
We won't have our own recording/video studio but an en-

hanced computer network is planned, so in addition to preparing print advertising we will do on site audio/video editing of radio and TV ads.
Those of us who have scavenged space in the conference room to prepare layouts in the past will be jazzed at the prospect of a work area that won't have to be vacated for meetings. Each full-time employee will have an office. Tele-

Caption describing picture or graphic.

commuters may be in cubicles during their visits but all FTEs will have ample work space. We are growing fast!

Volume 1, Issue 1
Newsletter Date

Special points of interest:
- *Briefly highlight your point of interest here*
- *Briefly highlight your point of interest here*
- *Briefly highlight your point of interest here*
- *Briefly highlight your point of interest here*

Inside this issue:

Inside Story

Word document replaces placeholder text

Dimensions of the selected text box

Clues to Use

Resizing a frame

A frame—whether it is a text box or contains an object—can be resized. Once a frame is selected, you can change its size by placing the mouse pointer over a handle, then dragging the handle. The pointer may change to ↔, ↕, ↗, or ↘, depending on which handle you place the pointer on. If, for example, the Text in Overflow button **A ▪▪▪** appears at the end of a selected frame, it may be possible to resize the frame, enabling the text to fit.

Adding a Graphic Image

Artwork can express feelings and ideas that words just can't capture. A picture, a piece of clip art, a graph, or a drawing is called a **graphic image**, or simply a **graphic**. Artwork can also be scanned into your computer, created using drawing programs or a digital camera, or purchased separately on a disk or online. **Clip art** is a term for graphic images that can be used free of charge or for a fee. Clip art is usually supplied on a disk or over the Web. Publisher comes with thousands of pieces of clip art. Table B-1 lists some of the common graphic image formats that can be used with Publisher. ░░░░ You have decided to include the Image Magic logo in the newsletter. Luckily, you already have this image in electronic format. You decide to place this logo near the graphic image placeholder of the bicyclist, so first you need to delete that placeholder.

STEPS

1. **Click the** graphic image placeholder

   Handles surround both the placeholder clip art and the caption beneath it, indicating that both are selected. Underneath the selection is the Ungroup Objects button 🔳, which indicates that you selected objects that were purposely grouped together so that they can be treated as one unit.

2. **Press** [Delete]

   The graphic image and caption text box placeholders disappear, and the text box expands to replace them. If the graphic image were inserted here, it would replace the current graphic. It would be the same size as the current one, and in the same location.

3. **Click** Insert **on the menu bar, point to** Picture, **then click** From File

   The Insert Picture dialog box opens. It opens to the My Pictures folder by default.

4. **Click the** Look in list arrow, **locate the drive and folder where your Data Files are stored**

QUICK TIP

You can change the view in the Insert Picture dialog box to Preview so that it shows you a sample of the images available in the folder.

5. **Click the** Views list arrow 🔳, **click** Preview, **click** Imlogo **as shown in Figure B-7, then click** Insert

   The Image Magic logo appears.

6. **Select the** Imlogo graphic image **if necessary, use** ⬚ **to drag it until the upper-left corner of the image is at coordinates** 4.250, 4.125 in., **then press** [F9]

   The repositioned image is near the upper-left portion of the column, as shown in Figure B-8.

7. **Place the pointer over the lower-right handle of the image so it turns to** ⬚, **press and hold** [Shift], **click the** left mouse button, **drag** + **down and to the right until the image has dimensions** 1.484 × 2.375 in., **release** [Shift], **then release the mouse button**

   The top-left corner of the image is now at coordinates 4.250, 4.125 in., and has dimensions 1.484 × 2.375 in., as shown in Figure B-9. Placing the pointer over a handle and then dragging the frame edge resizes an image. As you drag the pointer, the status bar reflects the object's size and position, using the ruler coordinates. To preserve an image's scale while increasing or decreasing its size, press and hold [Shift] while dragging the frame edge. The top-right corner of the image will change position, but the upper-left corner remains fixed in place.

8. **Press** [F9], **then click away from the logo to deselect it**

9. **Click the** Save button 💾 **on the Standard toolbar.**

FIGURE B-7: Insert Picture dialog box

Available graphic images appear here

Preview of selected file

Displays recognized picture file formats

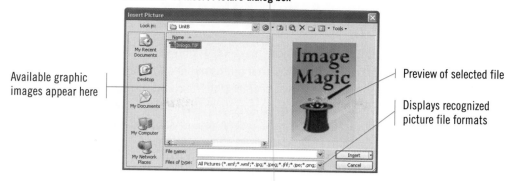

FIGURE B-8: Repositioned graphic image

Selected image has not yet been resized

Upper-left coordinates change as object is moved

Object's dimensions do not change as it is moved

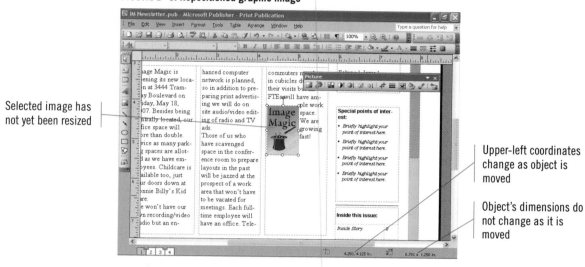

FIGURE B-9: Resized graphic image

Object's coordinates

Object's new dimensions

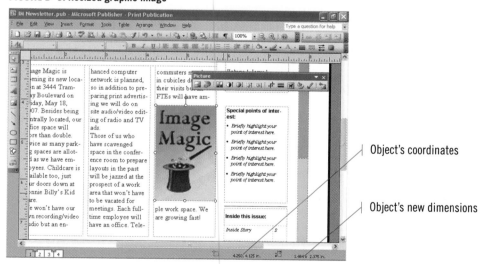

TABLE B-1: Common graphic image formats

graphic image	extension	graphic image	extension
Bitmap	.BMP	Tagged Image File Format	.TIF
PC Paintbrush	.PCX	JPEG Picture Format	.JPG or .JPEG
Graphics Interchange Format	.GIF	Windows Metafile	.WMF
Encapsulated PostScript	.EPS	CorelDraw	.CDR

Adding a Sidebar

Information not vital to a publication can make interesting reading when placed in a sidebar. A **sidebar** is a short news story containing supplementary information. You can place it alongside or below a feature story. It can use the same font size as regular body text, but it may look better in a larger size or a different font. Adding a border or shading can dramatize sidebars. You want to add a brief story to the newsletter about the success of a recent Image Magic ad campaign. You decide to use the sidebar placeholder in the third column to insert this existing text. You also want to experiment with some formatting effects, to draw greater attention to the sidebar.

STEPS

1. **Click inside the sidebar placeholder, as shown in Figure B-10, then press [Ctrl][A] to select the text**

   Handles appear around the sidebar.

2. **Press [F9], click Insert on the menu bar, click Text File, click the file PUB B-2.doc from the drive and folder where your Data Files are located, then click OK**

   The new text appears in the text box. Notice the changes to the formatting. The inserted Word document is not italicized, and the font size changed to fit the text in the frame. The heading is bold, and is now in the Arial font.

3. **Press [Esc] to deselect both the text and the text box, leaving the sidebar selected**

4. **Click the Shadow Style button ▣ on the Formatting toolbar, click Shadow Style 1 ▣, then press [Esc] to deselect the frame**

   Compare your work to Figure B-11. A gray shadow is behind the white background containing the text.

5. **Click the scratch area to deselect the sidebar**

   The sidebar is deselected.

6. **Click the Save button ▣ on the Standard toolbar**

7. **Press [F9]**

   Looking at the full-page image, you can see that all the text fits nicely inside the frame.

FIGURE B-10: Sidebar placeholder selected

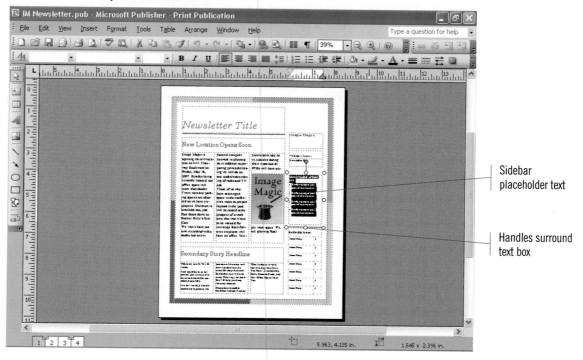

Sidebar placeholder text

Handles surround text box

FIGURE B-11: Sidebar with shadow

Current zoom level

Sidebar with shadow

Design Matters

Using templates

Have you ever stared at a blank piece of paper or a blank screen and just didn't know where to begin? You can use a template as a starting point, particularly if you are just beginning in design. Just browsing through the Publication Gallery can spark your creativity and get you started down the path to creating your own masterpieces. Believe it or not, there are occasions when even the best designers use templates. You can use a template if you just need a routine expense form or an invoice, if your client can't afford a "one-of-a-kind design," or just to save time. The important thing to remember about using a template is to choose one that is appropriate to the publication. A bad choice will require too many alterations and the advantages of using a template will be lost.

Using the Design Gallery

The Design Gallery contains a wide variety of preformatted design objects you can insert to assemble a publication quickly. These can include ads, calendars, coupons, logos, mastheads, pull quotes and more. A **pull quote** is an excerpt pulled from the text and set next to it, usually in a different typeface. The purpose of a pull quote is to draw attention to the story from which it is quoted. Pull quotes should be short enough to read easily, but long enough to capture interest. They should be on the same page as the story and placed close to it. The wording is not always an exact quote from the article, but should be an accurate reflection of the content. ▓▓▓▓ You want to insert a pull quote near the article on the company's new location. Because the Image Magic newsletter is a one page publication, you do not need a Table of Contents, so you decide to replace that placeholder with the pull quote.

STEPS

1. **Click the** Table of Contents **at 7.000, 7.000 in., click** Edit **on the menu bar, then click** Delete Object

2. **Click the** Design Gallery Object button ▦ **on the Objects toolbar**
   The Design Gallery opens. The Design Gallery is organized into three tabs: Objects by Category, which lets you select the type of object to add to a publication; Objects by Design, which helps you organize your objects with a uniform design; and My Objects, for special objects you create and save.

3. **Click the** Objects by Category tab **if necessary, click** Pull Quotes **in the Categories list, click** Borders Pull Quote, **then click** Insert Object
   You select the Borders Pull Quote because you want the pull quote to have a plain design. It is often best to use less ornate design elements, to avoid distracting the reader. The pull quote placeholder appears on the first page of the publication, as shown in Figure B-12. Note that the Wizard Button appears underneath the pull quote ◣. It indicates that the object is a Smart Object and is associated with a wizard. If you wished to replace this object with another similar object from the Design Gallery, you could click on the button to return to the Design Gallery to pick another design.

4. **Place the pointer over the upper-left edge of the pull quote so it changes to** ⬉, **drag the upper-left corner to** 6.005, 6.800 in., **then press [F9]**
   The pull quote sits just below the sidebar. Compare your pull quote text box to Figure B-13.

5. **Click the** pull quote text **to select it, then type** "Twice as many parking spaces are allotted as we have employees. Childcare is also available."
   When the pull quote is selected, the horizontal ruler becomes active, just as with any text box.

6. **Use the lower-right handle to resize the pull quote so its dimensions are** 1.917 × 3.063 in.

7. **Press [Ctrl][A] to select the text, click** Format **on the menu bar, point to** AutoFit Text, **then click** Best Fit
   Compare your pull quote to Figure B-14.

8. **Press [F9], then click the** scratch area **to deselect the pull quote**

9. **Click the** Save button ▦ **on the Standard toolbar**

FIGURE B-12: Pull quote added

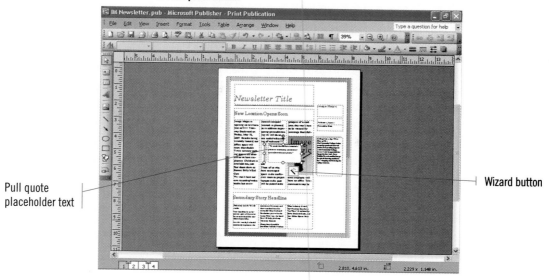

Pull quote placeholder text

Wizard button

FIGURE B-13: Repositioned pull quote placeholder

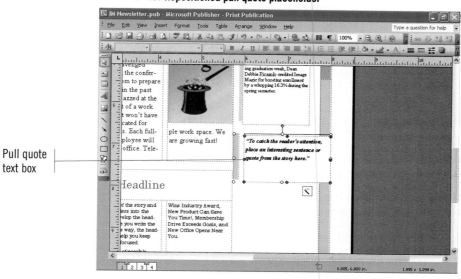

Pull quote text box

"To catch the reader's attention, place an interesting sentence or quote from the story here."

FIGURE B-14: Pull quote after AutoFit

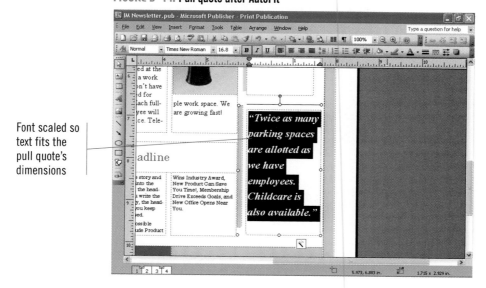

Font scaled so text fits the pull quote's dimensions

"Twice as many parking spaces are allotted as we have employees. Childcare is also available."

Grouping Objects

Once many objects are positioned on a page, you may find that you want to move one or more of them. Moving a single object is as simple as selecting it, then dragging it to a new location. But it gets more complicated when more than one object is involved, and you want them to retain their relative positions. **Grouping**, or defining several objects as one object, is an easy way to move multiple items. Later, you can always ungroup them, turning the combined objects back into individual objects, for individual modifications. You want to place a caption under the Image Magic logo. To change the size of the caption text box, you need to ungroup the objects, make the modifications, then regroup the logo and caption.

STEPS

1. **Click the** Image Magic logo, **press** [F9], **then press** [Esc]

2. **Click the** Text Box button ⬚, **draw a text box whose upper-left corner is at** 4.250, 6.125 in., **and whose dimensions are** 1.500 × 0.313 in.

3. **Type** Your Image! Our Magic! **in the text box, press** [Ctrl][A], **click the** Bold button **B** **on the Formatting toolbar, click** Format **on the menu bar, point to** AutoFit Text, **then click** Best Fit
   The new caption appears beneath the logo and is now in a Century Schoolbook font.

4. **With the text box still selected, press and hold** [Shift], **click the** Image Magic logo, **then release** [Shift]
   The Group Objects button ⬚ appears beneath the two selected objects, as shown in Figure B-15. Notice that both objects have handles surrounding them.

5. **Click** ⬚, **position** ⬚ **over the object, then drag the upper-left corner of the object to** 4.250, 3.667 in.
   You notice that the handles changed to a single set of handles surrounding both the combined objects. Compare your newsletter to Figure B-16.

6. **Press** [Esc], **scroll up to the text box whose top-left corner is at** 6.50, 2.50 in., **click inside the** text box, **press** [Ctrl][A], **type** Your Name, **then press** [Esc] **twice**

7. **Press** [F9], **then click the** Save button ⬚ **on the Standard toolbar**

8. **Click** File **on the menu bar, click** Print, **click the** Current page option button, **then click** OK
   A copy of the publication is printed.

9. **Click** File **on the menu bar, then click** Exit

FIGURE B-15: Preparing to group objects

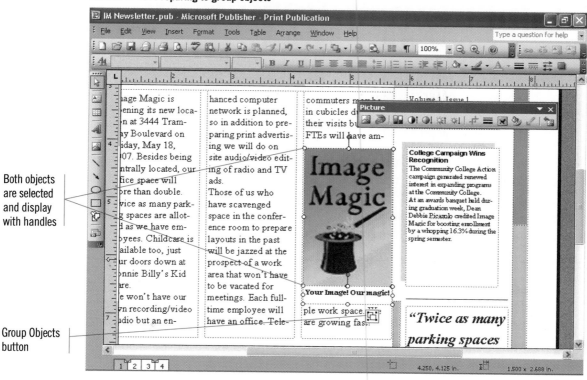

Both objects are selected and display with handles

Group Objects button

FIGURE B-16: Grouped and repositioned objects

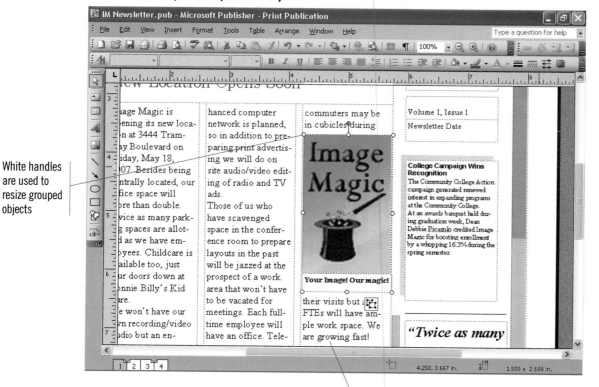

White handles are used to resize grouped objects

Text automatically fills the space left by the moved object

Publisher 2003

Capstone Project: College Brochure

You have learned the skills necessary to plan, design, and create a new publication. You can find and open an existing file using the New Publication task pane and Publication Gallery, and save it under a different name. Using buttons on the Objects toolbar, you can create a text box, and add graphic images and sidebars, and using the Design Gallery, you can insert objects that enhance your publication. Once objects are placed in your publication, you can group them so they can be treated as a single object. ▄▄▄▄ Camelback Community College is one of Image Magic's local clients. You have been asked to create a brochure that promotes their courses. For the purposes of drafting the design, you decide to use the Image Magic Personal Information Set as placeholder text. Once it has ben approved, you can update it with the college's information.

STEPS

1. **Start Publisher, click** Brochures **from the Publications for Print category in the New from a design list, click** Informational, **click** Blends Informational Brochure, **then save the publication to the drive and folder where your Data Files are located as** Camelback Brochure

2. **Click** Edit **on the menu bar, click** Personal Information, **select the** Secondary Business **information set, use the Sunset color scheme, then click** Update

3. **Click the** Product/Service Information placeholder, **type** Camelback University, **press** [Esc] **twice, then close the task pane**

4. **Click the placeholder beneath the Camelback University text box at** 8.500, 4.000 in., **press** [Ctrl][A] **to select the text, then type** An Education You Can Use!

5. **Click the** Design Gallery Object button ▦ **on the Objects toolbar, click** Pull Quotes **under Categories, click** Blends Pull Quote, **click** Insert Object, **then move the pull quote to** 4.109/3.290 in., **if necessary**

   See Figure B-17.

6. **With the pull quote still selected, press** [Shift], **click the object at** 5.250, 5.000 in., **then click the** Group Objects button ▣

   The objects are grouped, as shown in Figure B-18.

7. **Position the pointer over the grouped object, when the pointer changes to** ⊹⊱ **click and drag the grouped objects until the coordinates are** 4.250, 2.000 in., **then release the mouse button**

   The grouped objects are now on the center panel of the brochure.

8. **Click the** placeholder text **in the pull quote, replace it with** Your Name, **press** [Ctrl][A], **click** Format **on the menu bar, point to** AutoFit Text, **click** Best Fit, **then press** [Esc] **three times**

   Compare your publication with Figure B-19.

9. **Save the publication, print the first page, then exit Publisher**

FIGURE B-17: Inserted Design Gallery object

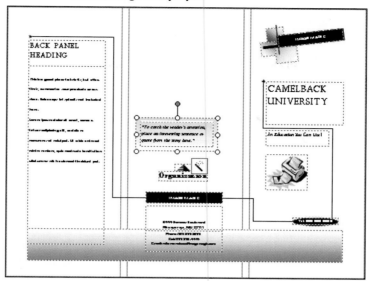

FIGURE B-18: Grouped objects

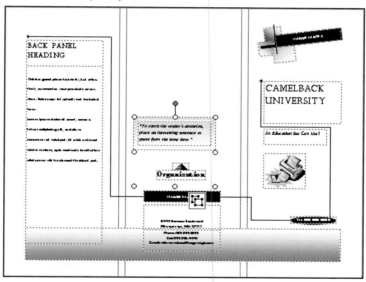

FIGURE B-19: Objects moved and text replaced

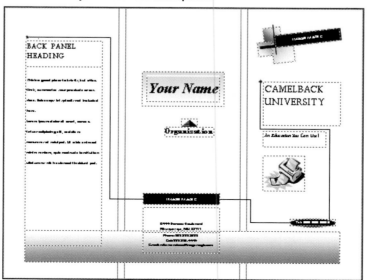

Publisher 2003

Practice

▼ CONCEPTS REVIEW

Label each of the elements of the Publisher window shown in Figure B-20.

FIGURE B-20

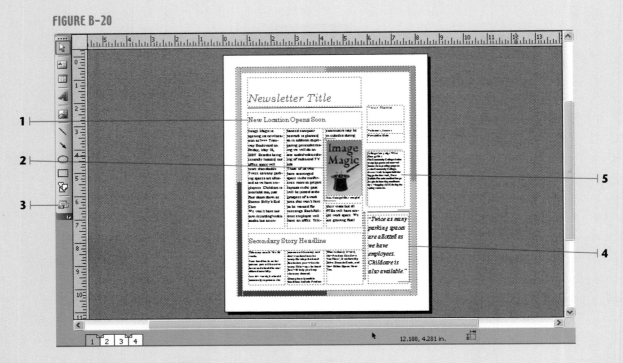

Match each of the terms or buttons with the statement that describes its function.

6.
7.
8. **New Publication option**
9.
10. **Publication Gallery**
11. **Graphic image**

a. Can be used to create an ad or logo, for example
b. A visual directory containing different publications
c. Resizes a frame vertically
d. Creates a text box
e. Artwork stored in an electronic file
f. Displays different shadows

Select the best answer from the list of choices.

12. **Paraphrased information that invites you to read a story is called a:**
   a. Placeholder.
   b. Sidebar.
   c. Pull quote.
   d. Side quote.

13. **Which pointer is used to change the location of an object?**
   a. I
   c. (pointer icon)
   b. (hand icon)
   d. ↔

14. **Which of the following statements about graphic images is false?**
   a. Scanned artwork can be used in Publisher.
   b. Artwork created in drawing programs can be used in Publisher.
   c. You can use only the artwork that comes with Publisher.
   d. You can use any electronic artwork in Publisher, as long as it's saved in a format that Publisher recognizes.

15. **Which menu is used to access the AutoFit text feature?**
   a. Edit
   c. Tools
   b. Format
   d. Arrange

16. **Which of the following statements about a pull quote is false?**
   a. It should entice you to read the article.
   b. It should be short and easy to read.
   c. It does not have to be identical to the text in the article.
   d. It should be on a different page from the actual text.

17. **Which of the following extensions does not indicate a common graphic image format?**
   a. .GFX
   c. .CDR
   b. .TIF
   d. .GIF

18. **Which button is the Design Gallery button?**
   a. (button icon)
   c. (button icon)
   b. (button icon)
   d. (button icon)

19. **Maintain the scale of an image while resizing a graphic image by pressing:**
   a. [Esc].
   c. [Alt].
   b. [Shift].
   d. The right mouse button.

20. **Group objects by holding and pressing [Shift], clicking each object, then clicking:**
   a. (button icon)
   c. (button icon)
   b. Tools on the menu bar, then Group Objects.
   d. Objects on the menu bar, then Group.

▼ SKILLS REVIEW

1. **Planning a publication.**
   a. Name the three steps involved in planning a publication.
   b. Identify the questions you should ask as part of planning a publication.

2. **Designing a publication.**
   a. Name as many elements of design, such as consistency, as you can.
   b. Identify at least three guidelines of good design, such as viewing the document as a whole.

3. **Create a publication using the task pane.**
   a. Start Publisher, then select Newsletters from the New from a design, Publications for Print list in the New Publication task pane.
   b. Create a publication that has the following options: Floating Oval Newsletter, two-sided printing, and no placeholder for the customer address. Use the Personal Information Set of your choosing, or enter information for address, phone number, and other pertinent information.
   c. Change to the Monarch color scheme. In the Page Content section of the task pane, change to two columns. (*Hint*: You can change the number of columns by clicking Page Content in the task pane, then clicking the 2 Columns option.)
   d. Save this publication as Mock-up Newsletter to the drive and folder where your Data Files are stored.

4. **Replace existing text.**
   a. Close the task pane.
   b. Click the Lead Story Headline placeholder, then zoom in.
   c. Replace the placeholder text with the following text: Making the Most of Your Workspace
   d. Select the lead story text, then delete it.
   e. Insert the Word file PUB B-3.doc from the location where your Data Files are stored.
   f. Read the article, then zoom out, then save the publication.

5. **Add a graphic image.**
   a. Select the graphic image placeholder and its caption, then delete them.
   b. Insert the picture file **Imlogo.tif** from the drive and folder where your Data Files are located.
   c. Press and hold [Shift], resize the image to 1.563 × 2.500 in., then reposition it so that the upper-left corner is at 6.000, 5.000 in., then save the publication.
6. **Add a sidebar.**
   a. Select the sidebar placeholder in the left column above the Table of Contents, then select the text within it.
   b. Zoom in to view the Special Points of Interest placeholder text in the sidebar, then delete the text.
   c. Insert the Word file PUB B-4.doc from the drive and folder where your Data Files are located.
   d. View and read the sidebar, zoom out so you can see the entire publication, then deselect the sidebar.
   e. Save the publication.
7. **Use the Design Gallery.**
   a. Click the Design Gallery Object button on the Objects toolbar, then click Pull Quotes.
   b. Add a Floating Oval pull quote, then zoom in to view the pull quote.
   c. Move the pull quote so the upper-left corner is at 2.500, 4.500 in.
   d. Replace the placeholder with: *"Work shouldn't hurt. If you feel pain while sitting at your workstation, stop what you are doing."*
   e. Select AutoFit Text on the Format menu, then click Best Fit.
   f. Zoom out so you can see the entire publication, deselect the pull quote, zoom in, then save the publication.
8. **Group objects.**
   a. Press and hold [Shift], then select both the volume and newsletter date text boxes in the left column.
   b. Group the two selected objects.
   c. Move the grouped object so the top-left corner of the combined object is at 0.500, 2.500 in.
   d. Ungroup the objects, deselect the objects, then replace the Newsletter Date text with **Your Name**.
   e. Save your work, print the first page of the publication, then exit Publisher.

▼ INDEPENDENT CHALLENGE 1

You volunteered to help the local Rotary Club design a flyer for its upcoming fund-raiser, a Fun Run. The organization is trying to raise money for victims of earthquakes in Central America. The funds will go toward medicine, building materials, food, clothing, and transportation costs for the material and some volunteers.

   a. Start Publisher if necessary, then create a flyer using the Charity Bazaar Fund-raiser Flyer design.
   b. Save the publication in the folder where your Data Files are stored as **Fun Run Flyer**.
   c. Change the Color Scheme to Monarch if necessary, then accept the default options on the Flyer Options task pane.
   d. Modify the Charity Bazaar text placeholder to say **Rotary Fun Run**, replace the five bulleted items with five of your own good reasons to attend this event, then include your name somewhere on the flyer.
   e. Make up the necessary information, such as the location of the fund-raiser, the address of the Rotary Club, and the date and time of the event, to make sure all the text in the flyer relates to the Fun Run event.

Advanced Challenge Exercises

   ■ Try resizing at least two of the frames within the flyer.
   ■ See how the pointers change during resizing, and how the text reflows.

   f. Save and print the publication, then close the publication and exit Publisher.

▼ INDEPENDENT CHALLENGE 2

You are a regular at the Come and Get It luncheonette. They ask you to help create a menu for their new take-out division. Use the New Publication option to create this menu, and replace the existing text with your own.

   a. Start Publisher if necessary, then create a take-out menu by choosing the Gingham Take-Out Menu. You may be prompted for the installation CD.
   b. Save the publication to the drive and folder where your Data Files are located as **Take-Out Menu**.

▼ INDEPENDENT CHALLENGE 2 (CONTINUED)

c. Change the Color Scheme to Wildflower, and accept the default options for Customer Address.

d. Modify the placeholder company name and information for the Come and Get It establishment.

e. Replace the placeholder text under the restaurant's name with a description of the food served at this establishment.

f. Include your name as the contact person for take-out orders.

g. Make sure all the text in the flyer relates to the take-out menu.

h. Make up at least two menu items. (*Hint*: Click the Page 2 icon to access the second page.)

i. Group two objects on the menu and move them.

j. Save the publication, print the publication, then exit Publisher.

▼ INDEPENDENT CHALLENGE 3

The tenants in your rental property just gave you 30 days notice, so you must find new tenants. You need to create a sign in which you can describe the house in order to attract new tenants.

a. Start Publisher if necessary, then use the Publications for Print subcategory in the New from a design list to create a sign using the For Rent Sign. You may be prompted for the installation CD.

b. Save the publication to the drive and folder where your Data Files are located as **For Rent Sign**.

c. Replace the bulleted items with your descriptions of the house for rent.

d. Modify the telephone number placeholder using your number or a ficticious number.

e. Create a text box under the telephone number that says **Call Your Name for more information**.

f. Select the text containing your name, then make the font size 18 points. (*Hint*: Resize the text box to fit the text if necessary, and resize the telephone number text box if you think it improves the overall design.)

Advanced Challenge Exercises

■ Use a command on the Format menu to change the publication design to a different For Rent sign. Make sure you add any elements necessary so that the new design contains the same information.

g. Save the publication, print the publication, then exit Publisher.

 ## ▼ INDEPENDENT CHALLENGE 4

You are asked to create a Web page for your school's Publisher class. You will use the New Publication task pane and the Publication Gallery. This site should discuss what topics are covered in the class.

a. Connect to the Internet and go to your school's Web site.

b. Print out the home page and the page for the department offering this Publisher course. You can use these materials as a reference throughout this project.

c. Start Publisher if necessary, then use the New Publication task pane and the Publication Gallery to create a Web site for your Publisher class.

d. The Web page should consist of one page, using a style, color scheme, and background that complement the school's existing Web site.

e. Save your publication as **Publisher Class Web Page** to the drive and folder where your Data Files are located.

f. Create a text box contact information. Add a telephone number and a fax number, and add Your Name as part of a ficticious e-mail address.

g. Replace the text placeholders with your own text, based on the topics that are covered in this class. (*Hint*: Consult your class syllabus and the materials you printed from your school's Web site.)

h. Save and print your publication, then exit Publisher.

Use the New Publication task pane and Publication Gallery to create the informational postcard shown below. Save the publication as **IM Postcard** to the drive and folder where your Data Files are located. Use the Borders Informational Postcard layout, the quarter-page format, and show only the address on the other side of the card. Add the Imlogo graphic image, apply the Wildflower color scheme, and replace the placeholder text and add new text in text boxes, as necessary, using Figure B-21 as a guide. Add a text box to the publication with your name, then print the page.

FIGURE B-21

Working With Text

OBJECTIVES

Use layout guides

Use ruler guides

Format a text box

Add bullets and numbering

Check spelling

Modify a Design Gallery Object

Paint formats

Add a table

Capstone Project: College Brochure

Publisher has many powerful tools to help you design and lay out text with confidence. You can use layout guides and rulers to assure that your layout is accurate and consistent. You can check spelling and apply formatting so that the finished text looks professional. And you can add objects such as tables to organize text more effectively. 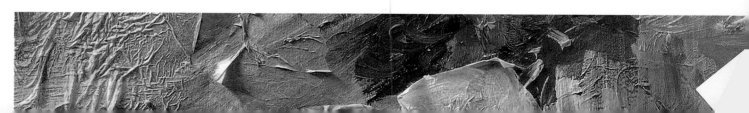 Your current assignment is to design a flyer that will be used to promote an upcoming Image Magic Professional Design Seminar. You want the flyer to be colorful and informative, and to grab people's attention.

UNIT
C

Publisher 2003

Using Layout Guides

Elements in a well-designed publication achieve a balanced and consistent look. This balance and consistency occurs only with careful planning and design. **Layout guides** and **margin guides**, horizontal and vertical lines visible only on the screen, help you accurately position objects on a page and across pages in a publication. Layout guides are created on the **Master Page**, a background that is the same for pages within a publication that are defined by a specific master page. For example, each initial page in a newsletter might have a similar layout, as might an editorial page and the final page, so you might want these pages to share the same master page. [image] Your assignment is to create a flyer for an upcoming design seminar. You decide to use a publication from the Publication Gallery, then set up the layout guides to help plan for future placement of objects in the publication. You also want to experiment with a different color scheme.

STEPS

1. **Start Publisher, click** Publications for Print, **click** Flyers **in the New from a design list, click** Informational, **then click** Bars Informational Flyer **in the Informational Flyers list**

   A new publication based on this template opens, and the Flyer Options task pane opens as well.

> **QUICK TIP**
> Color schemes are listed in alphabetical order.

2. **Click** Edit **on the menu bar, click** Personal Information, **click** Secondary Business, **click the** Select a color scheme list arrow, **click** Floral, **then click** Update

3. **Click the** Close button **on the Flyer Options task pane, then save the publication to the drive and folder where your Data Files are located as** Design Seminar Flyer

   The task pane is not necessary for the remainder of your work on this design.

> **QUICK TIP**
> In this book, ruler coordinates are given as follows: 4" H / 5" V. This refers to the intersection of 4" on the horizontal ruler and 5" on the vertical ruler, and is where you should click.

4. **Right-click the** graphic placeholder **containing the photograph at** 4" H / 5" V, **then click** Delete Object

   A dialog box opens, asking if you want to change to a design that does not include a graphic placeholder.

5. **Click** Yes, **right-click the remaining text box at** 3.10" H / 3.5" V, **then click** Delete Object

   The image and text box are deleted from the flyer. When selecting an object, you can click anywhere within its borders, but coordinates are provided to make it easy to locate each specific object.

6. **Click** Arrange **on the menu bar, then click** Layout Guides

   The Layout Guides dialog box opens. You use the Layout Guides dialog box to change the margin dimensions.

7. **If necessary, click the Margin Guides tab, then verify that the Left, Right, and Top margins are each set at** 0.5", **and the Bottom margin is set at** 0.66", **as shown in Figure C-1**

   The top and bottom margins are small enough to allow lots of information to be placed on each page. Layout guides create a grid to help you line up design elements, such as images and text boxes, on the page.

> **QUICK TIP**
> You can type a value in each margin guide text box, or use the arrows (to the right of each text box) to change the settings.

8. **Click the** Grid Guides tab, **click the** Columns up arrow **until** 3 **appears in the text box, click the** Rows up arrow **until** 3 **appears in the text box, click the** Add center guide between columns and rows check box **as shown in Figure C-2, then click** OK

   The pink lines represent the column guides, and the blue lines represent the column guide margins. The guides appear on the screen, as shown in Figure C-3, but do not print on the page.

9. **Click the** Save button [icon] **on the Standard toolbar**

FIGURE C-1: Margin Guides tab of Layout Guides dialog box

Creates right- and left-hand pages

Margin settings

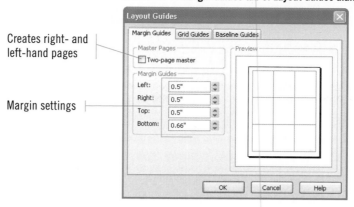

FIGURE C-2: Grid Guides tab of Layout Guides dialog box

Changes the number of columns and rows

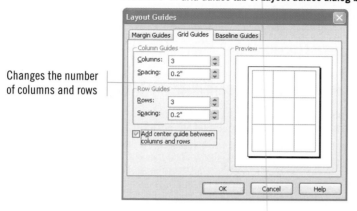

FIGURE C-3: Layout guides in publication

Initial zero point for the horizontal and the vertical ruler

Layout guides

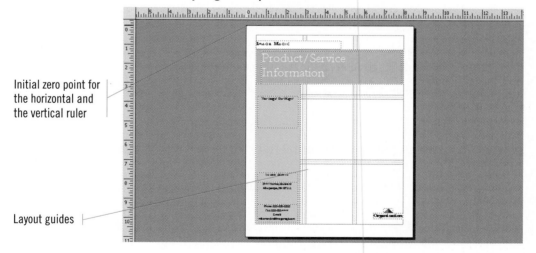

Publisher 2003

Design Matters

Understanding mirrored layout guides

In a publication with both left and right pages (such as a bound book or magazine), you can use **mirrored guides** so that facing pages have opposite margins and layout guides. This can make your material easier to read and more consistent in appearance. When you click the Two-page master check box, the names of the Left and Right margin guides become Inside and Outside margin guides. A bound publication should have larger inside margins to allow for the space taken up by the binding. You can switch the layout guides from the Master Page by pressing [Shift] and pointing to a layout guide. The pointer changes to either ÷ or +‖+. Drag the guide to any location, using the vertical and horizontal rulers for exact measurements. You can also return layout guides to their original locations by clicking the Undo button on the Standard toolbar before performing any other action.

Using Ruler Guides

Publisher lets you create individual page guides, called ruler guides. These are useful when you have set layout guides for a specific page type, but want to lay out elements differently on one particular page. **Ruler guides** work just like layout guides but appear in the foreground of an individual page or selection of pages, whereas layout guides appear on the background of each page, or selected pages, in the publication. Functionally, layout guides and ruler guides are the same, and neither prints on the publication. Ruler guides are green horizontal and vertical lines that are dragged from the rulers into the workspace, and can make it easy to position a text box or graphic image in a specific location. The location of zero, the **zero point**, on both the vertical and horizontal rulers can be moved, giving you the flexibility to make precise measurements from any point on the page. ▧▧▧ You want to move each ruler's zero point so you can measure distances from a specific point on a page, and add ruler guides to make it easier to position a graphic image on the first page. First, you move the vertical ruler closer to the page.

STEPS

1. **Position ⇖ over the vertical ruler, press and hold [Shift], when the pointer changes to ◀▶, press and hold the left mouse button, drag the vertical ruler to the left edge of the publication, then release [Shift] and the left mouse button**

   The ruler is repositioned, as shown in Figure C-4. When you move a ruler, the zero point does not change; the ruler simply moves closer, making it easier to locate positions. You don't need to move the horizontal ruler because it sits just above the top of the page. Currently, the horizontal and vertical zero point is set at the top-left edge of the page.

TROUBLE

You can reset the zero point to its default settings by double-clicking each ruler, or by double-clicking the Move Both Rulers button.

2. **Position ⇖ over the Move Both Rulers button ▢ at the intersection of the horizontal and vertical rulers, when the pointer changes to ↘ press and hold [Shift], right-click ▢, drag ↘, to ½" H / ½" V, release the mouse button, then release [Shift]**

   You changed the horizontal and vertical zero point to the start of the left and top margins. This makes it easy to determine exact measurements from the top-left margin.

3. **Position ⇖ at the top-left corner of the margin guides**

   The coordinates in the object position on the status bar are 0.000, 0.000 in.

QUICK TIP

Use the horizontal ruler to position a vertical ruler guide; use the vertical ruler to position a horizontal ruler guide.

4. **Position the pointer anywhere over the vertical ruler, drag ◀‖▶ to 3" H, then release the mouse button**

   A green vertical ruler guide appears on the screen at the 3" horizontal mark.

5. **Position the pointer over the horizontal ruler, drag ▼▲ to 3" V, then release the mouse button**

   After looking at the new horizontal ruler guide, you realize its position is too high for the text box you plan to add.

6. **Position the pointer over the horizontal ruler guide at 3" until it changes to ▼▲, drag the ruler guide to 3¾" on the vertical ruler, then release the mouse button**

   The ruler guides will be helpful when a text box is added.

7. **Place ⇖ on the vertical ruler, then drag ◀‖▶ to create a vertical ruler guide at 5½" H**

8. **Place ⇖ on the horizontal ruler, then drag ▼▲ to create three horizontal ruler guides: at 6¼" V, 7" V, and 8¾" V**

   Compare your ruler guides to those shown in Figure C-5.

9. **Click the Save button ▣ on the Standard toolbar**

FIGURE C-4: **Moving a ruler**

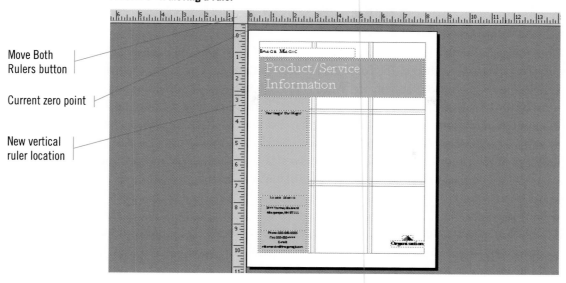

Move Both
Rulers button

Current zero point

New vertical
ruler location

FIGURE C-5: **Horizontal and vertical ruler guides added**

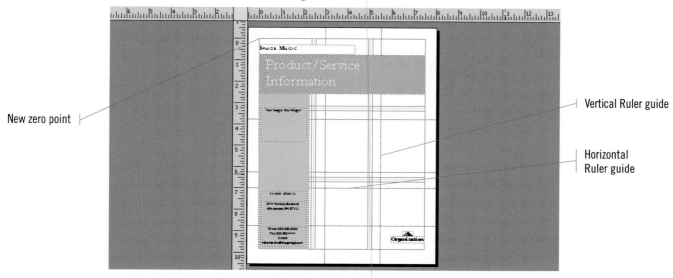

New zero point

Vertical Ruler guide

Horizontal
Ruler guide

Design Matters

Choosing measurement tools

Publisher provides different ways to measure the dimensions and positions of objects. The Object Position and Object Size coordinates on the status bar are always visible, but it can be difficult to place and size objects using them. The **Measurement toolbar** is a direct way to precisely position and size objects to one $\frac{1}{1000}$ of an inch accuracy. To open the Measurement toolbar, shown in Figure C-6, click View on the menu bar, point to Toolbars, then click Measurement. This toolbar lets you control horizontal position, vertical position, width, height, rotation, tracking, text scaling, kerning, and line spacing. Another option for positioning items is the Format dialog box for a selected object, such as a text box, picture, etc. This dialog box has tabs that let you position and size the item, but requires you to shift from one tab of the dialog box to another. The horizontal and vertical rulers have the advantage of

being the closest tools to the publication, and they are moveable so they can be even closer.

FIGURE C-6: **Measurement toolbar**

Measuremer ▼ ×	
x	0"
y	0.292"
⊡	4.313"
↧	0.426"
∠	0.0
⇄	125%
⟨A⟩	100%
AW	0pt
A↕	1sp

Publisher 2003

Formatting a Text Box

Once you add a text box to a page, you can move or resize it. You can add and format a border in any available color or line width you choose. The Formatting toolbar contains buttons for the commands most commonly used to improve a text box's appearance. When adding a text box or other object to a page, ruler guides can be helpful—either by providing a visual reference, or by literally pulling objects so they align exactly. To create this magnetic effect, you turn on the Snap To command. This feature pulls whatever you're trying to line up toward the ruler, guide, or object.  You want to add a text box that describes how to best use logos. You decide to place the text box using the ruler guides and Snap To feature, and then enhance it with formatting attributes. To begin, you move the vertical ruler out of the way.

STEPS

1. **Position the pointer over the vertical ruler, press and hold [Shift], when the pointer changes to ←→, drag the vertical ruler to the left edge of the workspace, then release [Shift]**
   The vertical ruler is now out of the way.

2. **Click the flyer heading placeholder text at 1" H / 1" V, type Professional Design Seminar, then press [Esc] three times**
   The new heading appears in the text box, and the text box is deselected.

3. **Click Arrange on the menu bar, point to Snap, then click To Ruler Marks and To Guides if these options do not already contain a check mark**
   A check mark next to a menu option indicates that it is selected, or activated. Clicking the option again turns it off.

4. **Click the Text Box button ⧈ on the Objects toolbar**
   The pointer changes to +.

5. **Drag + from approximately 3" H / 3¾" V to 5" H / 6¼" V**
   The text box automatically snaps to the ruler and layout guides.

   > **TROUBLE**
   > A text box must be selected before you can modify it.

6. **Right-click the text box, click Format Text Box, click the Line Color list arrow, then click the blue (sixth from left) color box**
   A sample of the color appears in the Format Text Box dialog box, as shown in Figure C-7. Because you selected a color scheme in the Personal Information dialog box, those colors are presented on this palette to help you retain design consistency in the publication. You could click More Colors from the Line Color drop down list if you wanted to work outside the color scheme.

7. **Click the Weight up arrow until 4 pt appears in the text box, then click OK**
   The text box that you placed on the page using the ruler guides appears with the thick blue border, as shown in Figure C-8.

8. **Click the Save button ⧈ on the Standard toolbar**

FIGURE C-7: **Format Text Box dialog box**

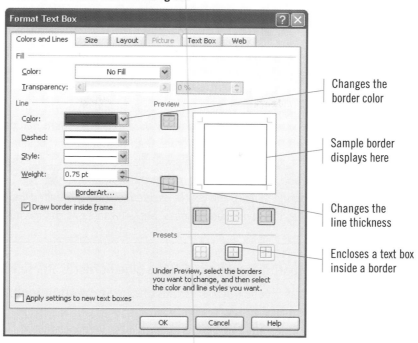

Changes the border color

Sample border displays here

Changes the line thickness

Encloses a text box inside a border

FIGURE C-8: **Text box with thick, blue border**

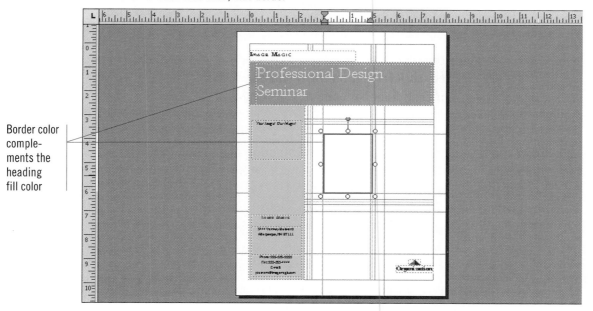

Border color complements the heading fill color

Design Matters

Making use of margins

When you think of **margins**, you probably think of the space surrounding the four edges of a page. The term also applies to the space that surrounds any boundary, so each design object, including columns, tables, and text boxes, have their own margins. Margins are often used to create **white space**, the designer's term for space on a page that is not covered with printed or graphic material. The addition of white space is critical for clarity because without it the page looks cluttered and is difficult to read.

Publisher 2003

Adding Bullets and Numbering

When you need to display information in a list, you can add emphasis to the items by formatting them with bullets or numbers. A **numbered list** is generally used to present items that occur in a particular sequence, while items in a **bulleted list** can be in any order. Both numbered and bulleted list formats can be applied either before or after the text is typed. You can switch back and forth between numbers and bullets, trying different styles of numbers and bullets until you arrive at the right format. ▓▓▓ You want the information in the text box to be large enough to read, and you've decided to add a numbered list in the text box you just created. You may not like the way the numbered list looks, but you can easily change this to a bulleted list.

1. **Make sure that the text box with the blue border is still selected, then press** [F9]

2. **Click the** Font Size list arrow `10 ▾` **on the Formatting toolbar, click** 16, **type** Why use a logo?, **then press** [Enter]
   The heading, which is not part of the numbered list, is entered first.

3. **Click the** Numbering button ▤ **on the Formatting toolbar**
   1. appears in the text box.

4. **Type** Customers look for it., **press** [Enter], **type** It distinguishes your firm from others., **press** [Enter], **then type** It is an element of marketing
   Compare your text with Figure C-9. To apply numbers or bullets to existing text, or to change from numbers to bullets, or back again, you first must select the text you want to format.

5. **Drag** Ⅰ **to select the text from** Customers **to** marketing. **so that the three numbered sentences are selected, click Format on the menu bar, then click** Bullets and Numbering
   The Bullets and Numbering dialog box opens and the Numbering tab displays. You can change the appearance of a numbered list, convert it to a bulleted list, or change the appearance of the bullets by using this dialog box.

6. **Click the** Bullets tab **in the Bullets and Numbering dialog box**
   Available bullet options appear in the Bullets and Numbering dialog box, as shown in Figure C-10. To enhance any list, you can change the appearance of the bullets. Publisher lets you use a variety of characters as bullets, as well as change the size (measured in points) of the bullets.

7. **Click the** diamond bullet, **click** OK, **then press** [Esc] **twice**
   Compare your work with Figure C-11. The numbered list has been converted to a bulleted list.

8. **Press** [F9]
   You can see the full page, and see that the bulleted list fits nicely on the page.

9. **Click the** Save button ▤ **on the Standard toolbar**

FIGURE C-9: Numbered list in a text box

Numbering button

Numbers created automatically

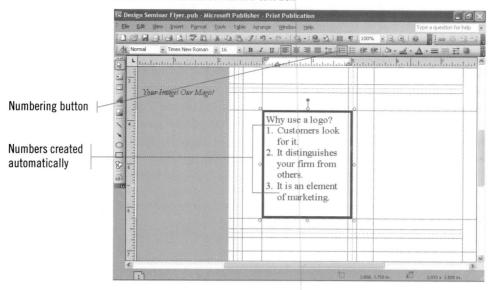

FIGURE C-10: Bullets tab of Bullets and Numbering dialog box

Bullet types

Sample list

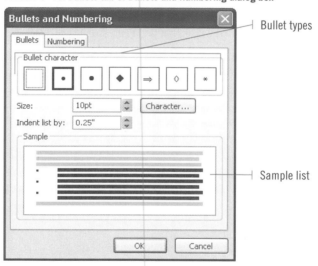

FIGURE C-11: Numbered list changed to a bulleted list

Diamond bullets

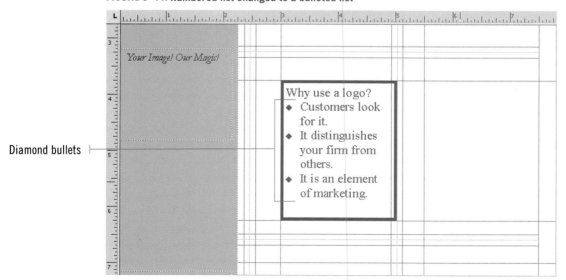

Checking Spelling

Spelling errors can ruin the most beautifully designed and well-written publication by distracting the reader from the message. Fortunately, using the **Spelling Checker** helps you to correct misspelled words before the reader sees them. The Spelling Checker is available only if a text box is selected. You can then check spelling using the Tools menu, or by right-clicking text, pointing to Proofing Tools, then clicking Spelling. Spelling errors are shown immediately as you type, indicated by a wavy red underline. You can add correctly spelled personal or industry-specific words not already in the dictionary as you work. You need to add information to the flyer about the guest speaker for the seminar. Mike has provided you with a text file containing this information. Once you create a text box for this information, you can insert the text file and check for any spelling errors.

STEPS

1. **Click the** Text Box button **on the Objects toolbar, drag** + **from 5½" H / 3¾" V to the margin guide at 7½" H / 6¼" V, then press** [F9]

   The text box appears on the page. Text placed in a text box is sometimes referred to as a **story**.

TROUBLE

If you receive an error message saying that you do not have the correct converter installed, see your instructor or technical support person.

2. **Click** Insert **on the menu bar, click** Text File, **locate the drive and folder where your Data Files are located, click the file** PUB C-1.doc, **then click** OK

   The text stored in the document file PUB C-1 is inserted into the text box, as shown in Figure C-12. This text contains misspelled words that you want to correct.

3. **Click** Tools **on the menu bar, point to** Spelling, **then click** Spelling

   The Check Spelling dialog box opens, as shown in Figure C-13. The first incorrect word found is "prievious." Publisher checks its dictionary to determine a word's spelling and places a suggestion in the Change to text box, so you don't have to click a suggestion.

QUICK TIP

To check the spelling of an individual word, click anywhere within the word, then press [F7].

4. **Click** Change

   The Spelling feature advances to the next misspelled word, "ebent." This word is incorrect and should be "event."

5. **Click** event **in the Suggestions list, then click** Change

QUICK TIP

To choose not to accept a suggestion, click Ignore. You can also add words Publisher identifies as misspellings, such as proper names, to the dictionary by clicking Add.

6. **Accept the suggestions for the remaining misspelled words:** gaols, Leeder, prestigous, **and** Desing

   The Spelling feature finished checking the text box.

7. **Click** No **in the dialog box prompting you to check other text boxes in your publication, click** OK, **then press** [Esc] **twice**

   Compare your corrected text to Figure C-14.

8. **Press** [F9], **then click the** Save button **on the Standard toolbar**

FIGURE C-12: Spelling errors in text

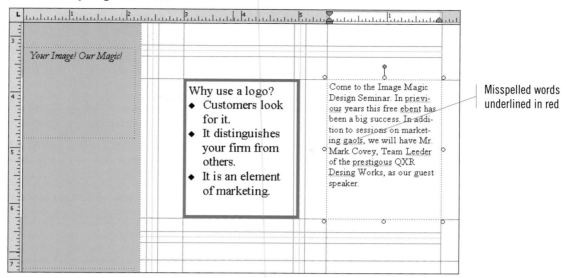

Misspelled words underlined in red

FIGURE C-13: Check Spelling dialog box

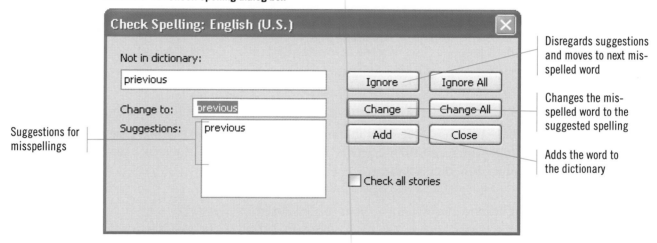

Suggestions for misspellings

Disregards suggestions and moves to next misspelled word

Changes the misspelled word to the suggested spelling

Adds the word to the dictionary

FIGURE C-14: Corrected spelling

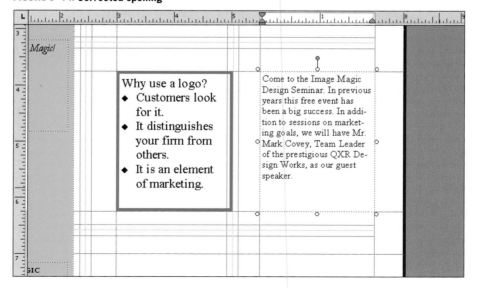

Modifying a Design Gallery Object

In addition to all the choices you can make using the New Publication task pane, you can also insert and modify individual objects from the Design Gallery. These **Design Gallery Objects** contain text or graphic images and can be edited for size, shape, and content. Beneath each Design Gallery Object is a Click to edit options button. Clicking this button (whose name varies with the type of Design Gallery Object that was inserted) opens a list of additional editing options. This feature offers an easy way to change the content of a publication while ensuring accuracy and consistency. You want to draw attention to the information about the guest speaker, so you decide to add a Design Gallery Object just above this information. First, you add a ruler guide to help place this new object.

STEPS

1. **Position** over the horizontal ruler, drag to 3" on the vertical ruler, then release the mouse button

    You can add ruler guides at any time during the design process to make positioning objects easier.

2. **Click the** Design Gallery Object button on the Objects toolbar, click Attention Getters **in the Categories list, click the** Arrowhead Attention Getter **if necessary, then click** Insert Object

3. **Place** over the Attention Getter object, use to drag the object to 5½" H / 3" V, **then press** [F9]

    Text within a Design Gallery Object can be modified, and you can use the AutoFit Text feature to fill the text box.

4. **Select the text** Free Offer **in the Design Gallery Object text box, type** Special, **press** [Enter], **type** Guest, **press** [Enter], **type** Speaker, **press** [Ctrl][A], **then click the** Bold button **on the Formatting toolbar**

    Compare your work with Figure C-15.

5. **Click the** Click to edit options for this Attention Getter button

    The Attention Getter Designs task pane opens. You can use this task pane to apply a different design to the selected Smart Object.

6. **Click** Corner Starburst **in the Attention Getter Designs task pane**

    The Corner Starburst is substituted for the Arrowhead and the text you typed is inserted in the new object.

7. **Place** over the selected object's right-center handle, then drag to 7½" H

    Compare your work with Figure C-16. The width of the Attention Getter is now consistent with the width of the text.

8. **Close the task pane, then press** [Esc]

9. **Click the** Save button on the Standard toolbar

FIGURE C-15: Design Gallery Object positioned and new text inserted

Bold button

Design Gallery Object

Click to edit options for this Attention Getter button

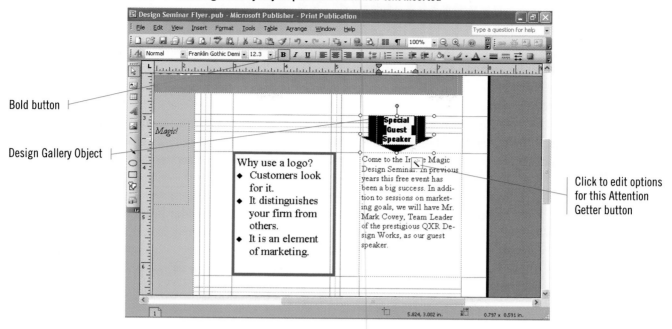

FIGURE C-16: Design Gallery Object replaced and resized

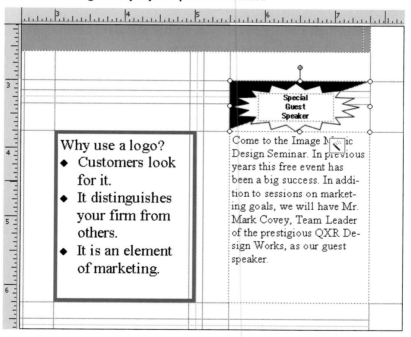

Why use a logo?
♦ Customers look for it.
♦ It distinguishes your firm from others.
♦ It is an element of marketing.

Clues to Use

Nudging an object

You can use the keyboard arrow keys to move a selected object, a technique called **nudging**. This is helpful for moving an object a relatively small distance because the object only moves in the direction of the key you are pressing. Each time you press an arrow key, the object moves a fraction of an inch (0.13") in the direction of the key you

pressed. You can change the distance an object is nudged by clicking Tools on the menu bar, clicking Options, clicking the Edit tab. Select the Arrow keys nudge object by text box to edit the default nudging distance, then click OK.

WORKING WITH TEXT **61**

Painting Formats

As you have learned, toolbar buttons can be used to apply object formatting or text attributes such as bold, italic, and underlining, as well as to increase or decrease font size. If you are applying the same formatting combinations to text in different locations in your publication, this process can get repetitive. To help you apply formats with consistency and without difficulty, you can use the Format Painter button on the Standard toolbar. Once you have applied formatting attributes, you use this feature to apply the formatting to other text. ▰▰▰▰ You want to spruce up the text about using a logo so that it stands out. Once you find a formatting combination you like, you want to paint the formatting to selected text.

STEPS

1. **Use the scroll bars to center the text box with the blue border in the work area**

    To draw attention to certain words in each sentence, you want to apply specific formats. One method of formatting is to use buttons on the Formatting toolbar.

TROUBLE

If the text wraps, enlarge the text box slightly by dragging the middle right sizing handle slightly right.

2. **Select the text Why use a logo?, then click the Bold button B on the Formatting toolbar**

3. **Click Format on the menu bar, click Font, click the Color list arrow, click the maroon (second from left) color box, then click the Small caps check box**

    Compare the Font dialog box to Figure C-17. You can add as many attributes as you want by clicking the check boxes in this dialog box, but some are mutually exclusive. For example, Small caps and All caps cannot be selected at the same time.

4. **Click the Shadow check box, then click OK**

5. **Click the Format Painter button 🖌 on the Standard toolbar, position ᗔI in the text box, then click and drag ᗔI over Customers**

    You can double-click 🖌 to apply the same formatting to more than one location. To turn off the feature, press [Esc].

6. **Double-click 🖌, drag ᗔI over firm, drag ᗔI over marketing, then press [Esc]**

    You think the maroon color of the newly formatted bulleted text and small caps are too distracting.

TROUBLE

Once you save your work, you cannot undo the steps you performed.

7. **Click the Undo button 🔄 three times, then press [Esc] twice**

    Your formatting of the text box is now complete. Compare your work to Figure C-18.

8. **Press [F9], then click the Save button 💾 on the Standard toolbar**

FIGURE C-17: **Font dialog box**

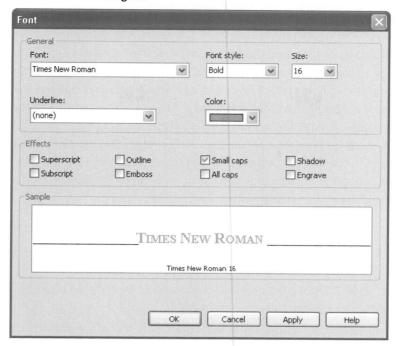

FIGURE C-18: **Formatting applied**

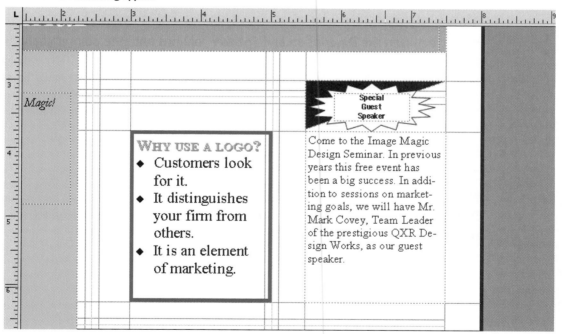

Design Matters

Creative deletion

Identifying poor design is an important skill, but mere recognition is not enough. Once a design flaw is identified, you have to either fix it or delete it. Not only is there nothing wrong with deleting flawed design elements, creative deletion is actually one of the most important skills a designer can learn. It is particularly important to be able to edit your own work. Look for elements that either detract from or fail to support the publication's message. If the element detracts or is unnecessary, it should be changed or deleted in favor of a constructive design element or more white space.

UNIT C

Publisher 2003

Adding a Table

Some information is more easily communicated in a table because its organization allows for quick reference. A **table** is a collection of information formatted in a grid of columns and rows. To create a table, you first need to determine how many columns and rows you need. You can always change the size of the table and the number of columns and rows if necessary. Publisher comes with 23 different table formats from which you can choose. To enter text in a table, you can type directly in the cells of the table, pressing [Tab] to move from cell to cell. You can also navigate the cells in a table using the arrow keys. You need to include information in the flyer about the agenda for the seminar, including the title, description, and speaker for each. You decide to organize this information in a table. The table needs to contain six rows and three columns to hold all the necessary information.

STEPS

1. **Click the Insert Table button on the Objects toolbar, then drag + from 3" H / 7" V to 7½" H / 8¾" V**

   The Create Table dialog box opens, as shown in Figure C-19. The available table formats contain combinations of formatting attributes, borders, and shading.

2. **Scroll down the Table format list, click List with Title 2, click the Number of rows down arrow until 6 appears in the text box if necessary, click the Number of columns down arrow until 3 appears in the text box, then click OK**

   The table appears in the table frame.

3. **Press [F9], type Session Title, press [Tab], type Description, press [Tab], then type Speaker**

4. **Place I between the Description and Speaker columns until the pointer changes to +||+, press and hold [Shift], drag +||+ to 6½" H, release the mouse button, then release [Shift]**

   When first created, table columns are all the same width. When you place the pointer between column boundaries of a selected table, it changes to +||+. Changing the boundary width changes the size of the table; however, you can change the width of a column but retain the table size by holding [Shift] while dragging to the new width.

5. **Enter the table data using Figure C-20 as a guide**

6. **Click outside the table to deselect it, then press [F9] to zoom out**

   You are pleased with the progress of the flyer.

7. **Click the Save button on the Standard toolbar, click the Print button on the Standard toolbar, then exit Publisher**

> **QUICK TIP**
> You can move a selected table using the pointer. You can resize a table by clicking and dragging when the pointer is positioned over any of the handles.

> **QUICK TIP**
> Use ÷ to change row height.

> **QUICK TIP**
> Press [Tab] at the end of the last cell in a table to insert a new row in the table. Press [Enter] in any cell to insert lines within the row.

FIGURE C-19: **Create Table dialog box**

Sample of
selected table

Available table formats

Recommended use of
selected format

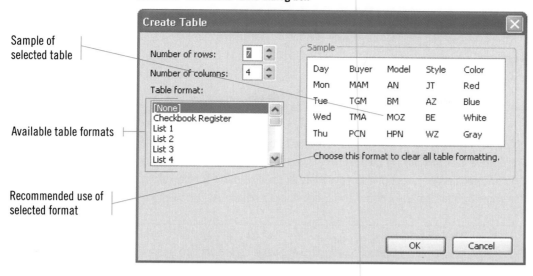

FIGURE C-20: **Completed table**

Six rows

Three columns

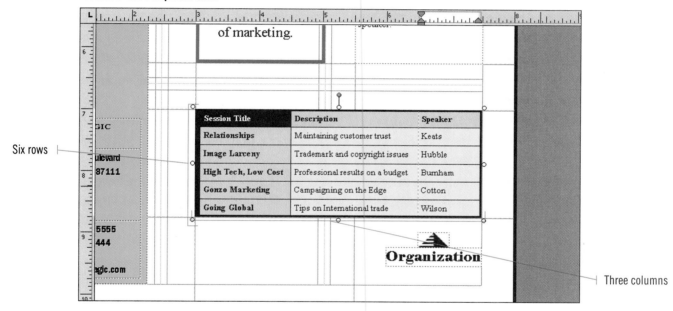

Session Title	Description	Speaker
Relationships	Maintaining customer trust	Keats
Image Larceny	Trademark and copyright issues	Hubble
High Tech, Low Cost	Professional results on a budget	Burnham
Gonzo Marketing	Campaigning on the Edge	Cotton
Going Global	Tips on International trade	Wilson

Clues to Use

Using AutoFormat

An existing table's design can be changed using the AutoFormat feature. The **Table AutoFormat** feature looks similar to the Create Table dialog box, except that it contains only table formats. Open the Auto Format dialog box by clicking Table on the menu bar, then clicking Table AutoFormat. Choose a new Table format, then click OK, and the new table format will replace the old. Figure C-21 shows the Numbers 3 format in the Auto Format dialog box. In order to use AutoFormat, you must select a table.

FIGURE C-21: **Auto Format dialog box**

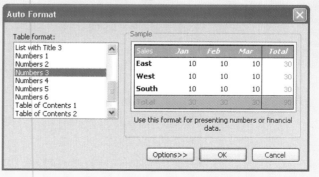

Capstone Project: College Brochure

You have learned how to change layout and margin guides and how to use ruler guides. You have also learned to format a text box, and add and modify bullets, numbering, and Design Gallery Objects. Additionally, you now know how to paint formats, add a table, and check spelling. ▪▪▪▪▪ You have been asked to create a flyer promoting the Camelback Community College Library Book Sale. The sale will feature the library's Great Books collection, so you want to call attention to this information in the flyer. The flyer needs to emphasize information about the great books available at the sale.

STEPS

1. **Start** Publisher, **click** Publications for Print, **click** Flyers **in the New from a design list in the New Publication task pane, click** Sale, **click** Book Sale Flyer **in the Publication Gallery, then save it to the drive and folder where your Data Files are located as** Book Sale Flyer
   The template you selected from the Publication Gallery has the right tone for the flyer.

2. **Change to the** Secondary Business Personal Information Set, **then change the color scheme to** Reef

3. **Click the** Book Sale placeholder, **then change it to read** Library Book Sale

4. **Click** Arrange **on the menu bar, click** Layout Guides, **change all the margin guides to** 0.4", **change the grid guides to** 3 Columns **and** 3 Rows, **then click** OK

5. **Click the** Design Gallery Object button 🖼 **on the Objects toolbar, click** Attention Getters, **click** Flag Attention Getter, **click** Insert Object, **drag the object to** ½" H, ½" V, **then close the task pane**

6. **Press** [F9], **resize the selected object to** 2¾" H × 1½" V **by dragging the lower-right handle, click the** Free Offer text, **type** Great Books, **press** [Ctrl][A], **click** Format **on the menu bar, click** Font, **click the** All caps check box, **click** OK, **press** [F9], **then press** [Esc] **three times**
   Making the Attention Getter larger and changing the text will help the reader decide immediately if he or she is interested in reading further.

7. **Click the text box at** 7" H / 5" V, **click** Format **on the menu bar, click** Bullets and Numbering, **click the** diamond bullet, **increase the bullet point size to** 15 pt, **then click** OK

8. **Click the text box at** 7" H / 8" V, **replace the text with the name of your school, click the text box at** 7" H / 9" V, **replace the text with your school's address, then change the text** Organization **in the logo to** Rotary Club

9. **Save the publication, print the first page, compare your work to Figure C-22, then exit Publisher**

FIGURE C-22: Completed publication

Practice

▼ CONCEPTS REVIEW

Label each of the elements of the Publisher window shown in Figure C-23.

FIGURE C-23

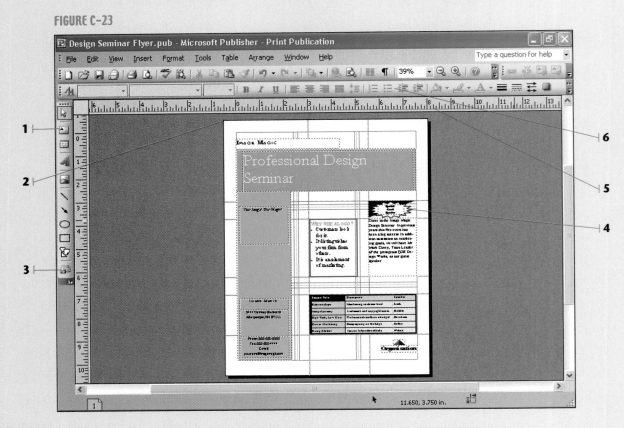

Match each of the buttons with the statement that describes its function.

7. ⊣‖⊢
8. ⟊Ⅰ
9. ◹
10. ▣
11. ⊡
12. **B**

a. Inserts a table
b. Click to edit options button
c. Paints formatting attributes
d. Opens the Design Gallery
e. Makes text bold
f. Changes a column's width

Select the best answer from the list of choices.

13. To maintain a table's size, resize a column while holding the _____ key.
   a. [Shift]
   b. [Alt]
   c. [Ctrl]
   d. [Esc]

14. Modify a Design Gallery object by:

a. Clicking any element within it.

b. Using a command on the Edit menu.

c. Clicking Arrange on the menu bar.

d. Clicking the Click to edit options button for the object.

15. Ruler guides are:

a. Blue.

b. Green.

c. Pink.

d. Red.

16. Each of the following is true about layout guides, except:

a. Objects can snap to them.

b. They are only visible onscreen.

c. They appear on a Master Page.

d. They appear in the foreground.

17. The Spelling feature in Publisher:

a. Identifies misspelled words.

b. Finds all spelling and grammatical errors.

c. Gets rid of the blue wavy lines.

d. Cannot check words in a table.

18. Each of the following buttons is used for formatting text, except _____.

a.

b.

c.

d.

19. You can draw a table frame when the pointer turns to _____.

a.

b.

c.

d.

20. Which of the following is not a font attribute?

a. Bold

b. Snap

c. Italics

d. Shadow

▼ SKILLS REVIEW

1. Use layout guides.

a. Start Publisher, click Flyers in the Publications for Print category of the New Publication task pane, then click Event.

b. Use the Company Picnic Flyer, the Secondary Business Personal Information Set, and the Shamrock color scheme, close the task pane, then save the file to the drive and folder where your Data Files are located as **Company Picnic Flyer**.

c. Use the Arrange menu to open the Layout Guides dialog box.

d. Change the margin guides if necessary to 0.5 left, 0.5 right, 0.5 top, and 0.66 bottom.

e. Use the Layout Guides dialog box to create three columns and three rows of grid guides in this publication.

f. Save your work.

2. Use ruler guides.

a. Move the vertical ruler closer to the page.

b. Create horizontal ruler guides at ¼" V, 1" V, 7⅞" V, and 9½" V. Create vertical ruler guides at ½" H, 4" H, 5¾" H, and 7" H.

c. Save your work.

3. Format a text box.

a. Move the vertical ruler back to the left side of the screen.

b. Click the text box at 2" H / 5" V, then zoom in to view the text box.

c. Create a 4 pt green border around the text box, zoom out so you can see the full page, then deselect the text box.

d. Save your work.

▼ SKILLS REVIEW (CONTINUED)

4. Add bullets and numbering.

  a. Select the text box at 5" H / 5" V, then zoom in to view the text box.

  b. Replace the text under the Highlights heading with the following information, pressing [Enter] after each activity to create a bulleted list: **Volleyball, Live music, Sack race, Softball, Pie-eating contest**.

  c. Change the bullet style to a 12 pt open arrow, zoom out, then save the publication.

5. Check spelling.

  a. Select and zoom in to the text box at 2" H / 5" V, then replace the existing text in the box with the file PUB C-2.doc from the drive and folder where your Data Files are located.

  b. Correct the spelling of the selected text. (*Hint*: You should find four spelling errors.) Do not check the spelling in the rest of the publication.

  c. Zoom out so that you can see the entire publication, deselect the highlighted text if necessary, then save the publication.

6. Modify a Design Gallery Object.

  a. Click the Design Gallery Object button on the Objects toolbar, click the Attention Getters category, then insert the Chevron Attention Getter.

  b. Move and resize the object so that the upper-left edge has the coordinates 5 ¾" H / ¼" V and the dimensions are 1¼" H x 1" V, then zoom in to the object.

  c. Change the text to **Too Much Fun**!

  d. Click the Click to edit options button for the object, change the design to Double Slant, then close the Attention Getter Designs task pane.

  e. Zoom out, then save the publication.

7. Paint formats.

  a. Select the bulleted list and zoom in.

  b. Select the text **Volleyball** and format it using the Engrave effect and orange color.

  c. Use the Format Painter to paint **Live music** with the same formatting.

  d. Double-click the Format Painter button on the Standard toolbar.

  e. Paint the formatting to the following text: Sack race, Softball, and Pie-eating contest.

  f. Zoom out so that you can see the entire page, then save your work.

8. Add a table.

  a. Resize the three text boxes above the Time text box so that their right edges end at 4" H. Delete the border element between the text boxes.

  b. Create a table from 4" H / 7⅞" V to 7¾" H / 9½" V, using the List 3 format.

  c. Create six rows and three columns. Click Yes to create a table larger than the selected area.

  d. Zoom in, then enter the following text for the three column headings: **Activity**, **Contact**, and **Extension**.

  e. Enter the information in Table C-1, then resize the columns so the left edge of the Extension column begins at 6¾" H.

  f. Zoom out so that you can see the full page.

  g. Deselect the table, then save your work.

  h. Make sure your name appears as the Contact Person.

  i. Print the publication, then exit Publisher.

TABLE C-1

Activity	Contact	Extension
Volleyball	Lucy McMannus	4828
Live music	Frank Etherton	4689
Sack race	Roger Hubbard	5220
Softball	Gail Farnsworth	1096
Pie-eating contest	Greta Tolkmann	3117

▼ INDEPENDENT CHALLENGE 1

The firm of Top-Drawer Law Associates has hired you to design a postcard that invites people to a promotion party.

a. Start Publisher if necessary, use the New Publication task pane and the Publications for Print category in the New from a design list to select the Blends Informational Postcard, use the color scheme of your choice, save it as **Promotion Announcement** to the drive and folder where your Data Files are located, then close the task pane.

b. Change all four margin guides to .25".

c. Delete the text box containing placeholder text for a business tag line that is just under the upper margin.

d. Move the zero points to the top-left margin, then add a vertical ruler guide at 1" and a horizontal ruler guide at ⅛".

e. Move the Product/Service Information text box so that the upper-left corner is at ⅛" V / 1" H, create a 2 pt Accent 1 red border around it, then type **TOP-DRAWER LAW ASSOCIATES ANNOUNCE**.

f. Align all of the text boxes so their left sides are on the vertical ruler guide.

g. Select the text box that starts **Place text here** and insert the text found in PUB C-3.doc.

h. Use the Spelling Checker to correct any errors in the text.

i. Type the firm's name in the text box found at 1" H / 2 ⅜" V, then modify text and formatting to create a meaningful invitation.

j. Create text that has bold and italic formatting, then use the Format Painter to copy formats for the text.

k. Add a text box that includes your name, save and print the publication, then exit Publisher.

▼ INDEPENDENT CHALLENGE 2

The seminar you are teaching in London on International Business Leadership is about to end. At the conclusion, you would like to present each attendee with a certificate of completion.

a. Start Publisher, if necessary, use the Publications for Print category in the New from a design list in the New Publication task pane to select Award Certificates, choose the Plain Paper option, the Celtic Knotwork Certificate, and the color scheme of your choice. Complete any additional installation processes, if necessary.

b. Save the publication as **International Leadership Certificate** to the drive and folder where your Data Files are located, then close the task pane.

FIGURE C-24

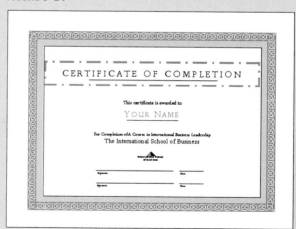

c. Move the zero points to the top-left margin.

d. Replace the Name of Recipient with your name, then change the words "Certificate of Appreciation" to **CERTIFICATE OF COMPLETION**.

e. Format the Certificate of Completion text box border so it is a 5 pt, red solid line.

Advanced Challenge Exercise

■ Change the red solid line to a long dash dot line. Compare your publication to Figure C-24.

f. Format the **Name of Recipient** text using the formatting of your choice.

g. Change "Organization" in the logo to **International School of Business**.

h. Modify any other existing text to create a meaningful certificate of completion.

i. Save and print the publication, then exit Publisher.

▼ INDEPENDENT CHALLENGE 3

The local music appreciation society asks you to design a program for its upcoming festival.

a. Start Publisher if necessary, then use the New Publication task pane to create a Music Program. Save the publication as **Music Program** to the drive and folder where your Data Files are located, then close the task pane.

b. On page 2, delete the existing table (for The Singers) and replace it with a 3-column, 8-row table with the format of your choice.

c. Make up the names of the singers, the songs they will sing, and the type of music (for example, opera, folk, or jazz).

d. Replace the **Conductor's Name** text with your name.

e. Replace any existing text on all pages with information that creates a meaningful music program.

f. Format text using at least two attributes, then use the Format Painter to copy the formatting to other text.

g. Use the Spelling Checker to correct any errors in the text.

h. Save and print pages two and three of the publication, compare your publication to Figure C-25, then exit Publisher.

FIGURE C-25

▼ INDEPENDENT CHALLENGE 4

Your keen mind, artistic tastes, and desire to make money are leading you to pursue business opportunities that involve designing publications. To become more credible, you decide to learn more about different fonts.

a. Connect to the Internet, then using your favorite search engine or Web site (such as google.com or about.com), search for information on choosing fonts and typefaces.

b. Use the New Publication task pane to create any style of flyer, then save it as **Different Font Flyer** to the drive and folder where your Data Files are located.

c. Create a heading that uses and names your favorite font.

d. Add a text box that contains a bulleted list that uses and names five other fonts that you find easy to read.

e. Add a text box that discusses the differences between serif and sans serif fonts.

f. Format the text to illustrate both sans serif and serif fonts.

g. Add a prominently placed text box with your name in a clearly readable font and point size.

h. Use your judgment to delete any objects that do not contribute to the design of your publication.

i. Add a colorful border to the text boxes.

Advanced Challenge Exercise

■ Change the appearance of the bullets in the list.

j. Use the Spelling Checker to correct any errors in the text, then save and print the publication.

k. Compare your publication to Figure C-26, then exit Publisher.

FIGURE C-26

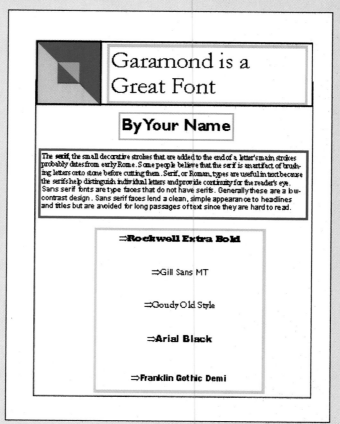

Use the New Publication task pane to create an Estate Sale Flyer. Save this publication as **Estate Sale Flyer** to the drive and folder where your Data Files are located. Use Figure C-27 as a guide. Use the Sunset color scheme and replace all text as shown in the figure. Include your name on the flyer. Save and print the flyer.

FIGURE C-27

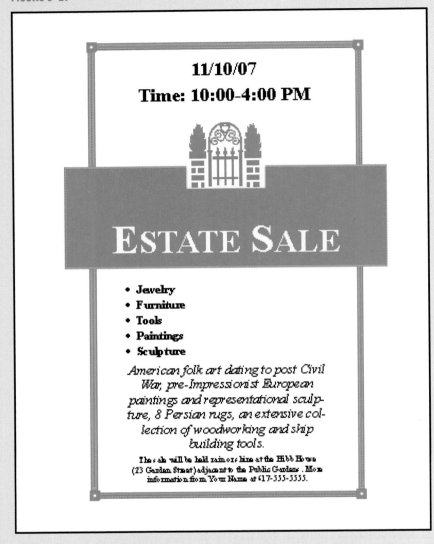

11/10/07
Time: 10:00-4:00 PM

ESTATE SALE

- Jewelry
- Furniture
- Tools
- Paintings
- Sculpture

American folk art dating to post Civil War, pre-Impressionist European paintings and representational sculpture, 8 Persian rugs, an extensive collection of woodworking and ship building tools.

The sale will be held rain or shine at the Hibb House (23 Garden Street) adjacent to the Public Gardens. More information from Your Name at 617-555-5555.

Working with Graphic Objects

OBJECTIVES

Insert and resize clip art

Copy and move an object

Crop an image

Align and group images

Layer objects

Rotate an image

Use drawing tools

Fill shapes with colors and patterns

Capstone Project: Flower Show Web Page

Artwork is much more than decoration. At its best, it expresses ideas and feelings that words cannot. In practical terms, artwork can be used to grab a reader's attention and clarify themes and messages in a publication. Proper positioning of graphic objects can relieve the monotony of text, add emphasis to the written word, and separate subjects. You have been asked to take over work on a flyer for a veterinary hospital fundraiser. The client wants the flyer to be inviting and friendly, with lots of graphics. Your first task is to choose appropriate artwork; the text will be added later.

Inserting and Resizing Clip Art

The Insert Clip Art task pane makes it easy to dress up any publication with images. There is so much clip art available, online and from commercial sources, that you can almost always find an image to represent a topic or round out a theme. With the Insert Clip Art task pane, you can use the Search feature to locate specific artwork by keyword or topic. The Clip Organizer contains pictures, motion clips, and sounds, and is not limited to the artwork that comes with Publisher. You can customize the Clip Organizer by adding any electronic image you wish. You are ready to search for artwork for the fundraiser flyer. You want to find art representative of a veterinary hospital setting, and then resize it to fit your design for the flyer.

STEPS

1. **Start Publisher, open the file** PUB D-1.pub **from the drive and folder where your Data Files are located, click** File **on the menu bar, click** Save As, **then save the file as** Fundraiser Flyer

2. **Click the** Picture Frame button **on the Objects toolbar, then click** Clip Art
   The Clip Art task pane opens. It contains options that allow you to limit your search to specific collections, and search for different types of media, such as clip art, photographs, movies, and sounds, arranged by content.

3. **Click the** Search for text box, **delete any existing text if necessary, type** animal, **click the** Results should be list arrow, **click checkboxes as necessary so that** Clip Art **is the only checkbox that contains a check mark, then click the** list arrow **again to close the list**

4. **Click the** Search in list arrow, **click checkboxes as necessary so that** My Collections **and** Office Collections **are the only checkboxes that contain check marks, click** Go, **then click the** list arrow **again to close the list**
   The results of the search appear, as shown in Figure D-1.

TROUBLE
If you do not have the images used in this unit, choose appropriate alternatives in the Microsoft Clip Organizer.

5. **Position** ⌕ **over the** second image in the first row, **click the** down arrow **on the right side of the image, click** Preview/Properties, **verify that** j0216724.wmf **is the filename, then click** Close

6. **Right-click the selected** image, **click** Insert, **then click the** Close button **on the Clip Art task pane**
   The floating Picture toolbar opens in the program window.

TROUBLE
If the Picture toolbar blocks your view, you can move it out of the way by clicking and dragging its title bar.

7. **Press** [F9], **position** ⌕ **over the** clip art **until the pointer changes to** ⛶, **click the** clip art, **drag** ⛶ **so that the object's upper-left corner is at the guides intersection at** 2¾" H / 3¾" V, **then release the mouse button**
   Compare the repositioned clip art to Figure D-2.

8. **Place** ⌕ **over the** lower-right corner frame handle **until the pointer changes to** ⤡, **press and hold** [Shift], **drag** ⤡ **to the guides intersection at** 5¼" H / 6⅞" V, **then release** [Shift]

9. **Click the** Save button **on the Standard toolbar**

FIGURE D-1: Clip Art task pane with search results

Image
j0216724.wmf

Pictures found
in the search

Link
connects to
the Web for
additional
clips

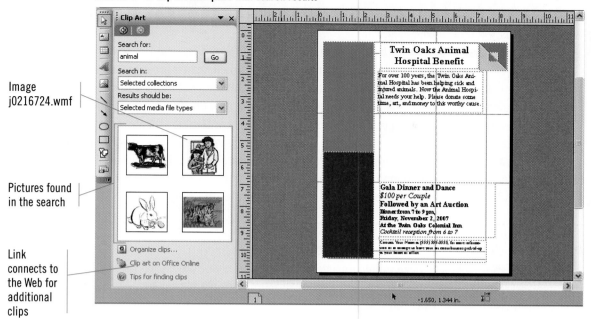

FIGURE D-2: Clip art picture inserted and repositioned

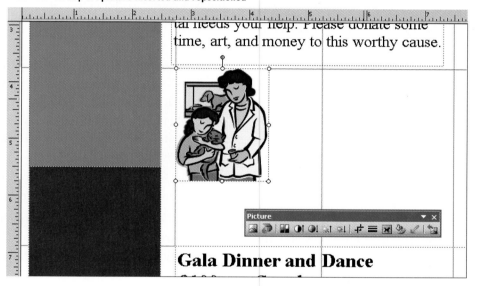

Design Matters

Browsing Office Online Clip Art and Media

If you have access to the Internet, you can add to the Microsoft Clip Organizer from Microsoft Office Online Clip Art and Media. This site, located at office.microsoft.com/clipart/default.aspx, offers a constantly changing selection of artwork. Figure D-3 shows some of the choices offered at this Web site, although it will look different when you view it, as it changes constantly. This site lets you constantly update your clip art so you always have new, exciting types of artwork to include in your publications. You can download clip art, photographs, sounds, and video clips from this Web site.

FIGURE D-3: Microsoft Office Oline Clip Art and Media

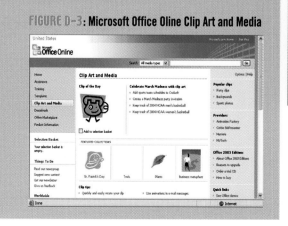

Copying and Moving an Object

You can move and copy images in a publication quickly and easily. By copying artwork, you can create interesting effects with duplicated images. You can also use copied images for experimentation in manipulating their colors, contours, cropping, dimensions, and orientations, without changing the design of your original publication. For example, you can manipulate an image to create a mirror image. A mirror image shows two identical images with one flipped, so that it appears as though you are viewing the object in a mirror. When you copy an image, the copy is held temporarily in the Windows **Clipboard**, a temporary storage area for copied or cut items. ⬛⬛ You want to create a mirror image using the image you just inserted. You are also considering using the image in another location in the publication. You decide to accomplish these tasks by using the Clipboard to copy and move the image.

STEPS

1. **Right-click the selected object, then click Copy**

   Although it looks as though nothing happened, the clip art object was copied to the Clipboard. Once an image is on the Clipboard, you can paste it repeatedly, using any pasting method.

2. **Right-click again, then click Paste**

   A copy of the object appears overlapping the original object, as shown in Figure D-4. The newly copied image is selected and is on top of the original image. This copy appears slightly offset from the original image's location.

3. **Position ⬚ over the selected copy until it changes to ⬚, then drag the selected object so the upper-left corner is at 5¼" H / 3¾" V**

4. **Press [F9], position the pointer over the selected object until it changes to ⬚, press and hold [Ctrl], press and hold [Shift], then drag ⬚ so that the upper-left corner is on the scratch area at 9" H / 3¾" V, release the mouse button, release [Shift], then release [Ctrl]**

   The second copy of the clip art is placed in to the right of the original object, but off the page. You now have three images, two below the upper text box, and one on the scratch area. The **scratch area** is a convenient place to store design elements while working on the overall design of a publication.

5. **Right-click the selected object, then click Cut**

   The second copy is no longer visible, and because no image is selected, the Picture toolbar closes.

6. **Click the image whose upper-left corner is at 5¼" H / 3¾" V, click Arrange on the menu bar, point to Rotate or Flip, then click Flip Horizontal**

   The copy is flipped, as shown in Figure D-5, and you can see the original image next to the flipped copy. You decide you do not like its appearance.

7. **Right-click the flipped copy, click Delete Object**

   The mirrored image is no longer visible. Deleted items are not sent to the Office Clipboard.

8. **Click the Save button 🖫 on the Standard toolbar**

Copy appears on top of the original clip art

FIGURE D-5: **Flipped image**

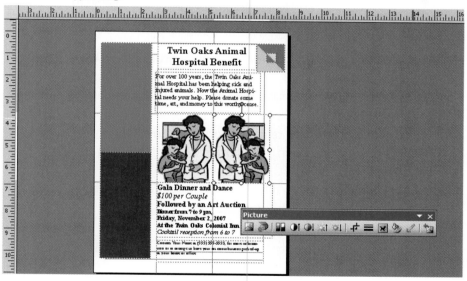

Clues to Use

Using the Office Clipboard

The Office Clipboard lets you copy and paste multiple items, such as text, images, or tables, within or between Microsoft Office applications. The Office Clipboard can hold up to 24 items copied or cut from any Office program. You choose whether to delete the first item from the Clipboard when you copy the 25th item. The collected items remain in the Office Clipboard and are available to you until you close all open Office programs. You can scroll through the Clipboard task pane, shown in Figure D-6, to choose an item to paste; clicking the item inserts it at the current location of the cursor. You can specify when and where to show the Clipboard task pane by clicking the Options list arrow at the bottom of the Clipboard task pane.

FIGURE D-6: **Clipboard task pane**

2 of 24 - Clipboard

Paste All   Clear All

Click an item to paste:

For over 100 years, the Twin Oaks Animal Hospital has been helping sick and inj...

Cropping an Image

Even when you find the perfect image for a publication, you may find that it needs some modification to fit perfectly on the page. Perhaps a part of a picture's contents interferes with the publication's message or contains too much white space. When this happens, you can trim, or **crop**, portions of the artwork to modify it to fit your needs. A graphic image can be cropped vertically, horizontally, or both. Even though they are not visible, the cropped portions of an image are still there—they are just concealed, so you can make them visible again if you change your mind. ▄▄▄▄▄ You want to add a photographic image to the flyer, and crop it so that it better suits your design.

STEPS

1. **Click Insert on the menu bar, point to Picture, click From File, locate the drive and folder where your Data Files are stored, click the file PUB D-2.tif, click Insert, then move the image so that the upper-left corner is at 9" H / 1" V on the scratch area**

   A photograph of kittens is placed on the scratch area, as shown in Figure D-7.

2. **Scroll if necessary so you can see the entire image, click the Crop button 🔲 on the Picture toolbar, position 🔭 over the upper-left corner handle, when the pointer changes to ⌐ click the upper-left handle, then drag ⌐ to approximately 3" V**

   The Crop button stays selected until you turn it off, so you can continue cropping until you are finished. The surplus white space on the left edge will be concealed later.

3. **Click the lower-right handle, drag ⌐ to approximately 15" H, press [Esc] to deselect the cropping tool**

   The cropped image is much smaller, but it still needs to be resized so that it will fit next to the existing artwork on the page.

   QUICK TIP
   To crop both edges simultaneously and equally, click the Crop button, press and hold [Ctrl], then drag ⌐.

4. **Click the photo image to select it, position 🔭 over the lower-right corner handle, when it changes to ↘ press [Shift], then drag ↘ until the right border of the image is at 11½" on the horizontal ruler**

   The resized image now has a width of 2½" and can be placed on the page.

5. **Click the cropped and resized image, then drag it using 🔭 so that the upper-left corner is at 2¾" H x 4½" V**

   The cropped image is directly on top of the clip art for now, but you will move it later. Compare your image to Figure D-8.

6. **Click the Save button 🔲 on the Standard toolbar**

FIGURE D-7: Image before cropping

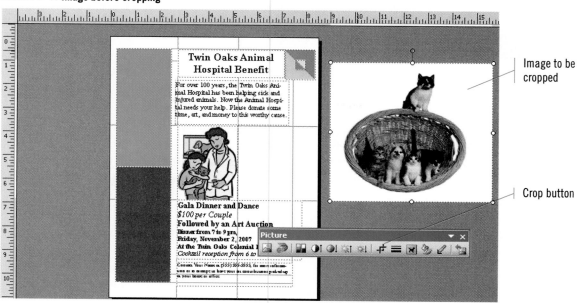

Image to be cropped

Crop button

FIGURE D-8: Image cropped, resized, and placed on page

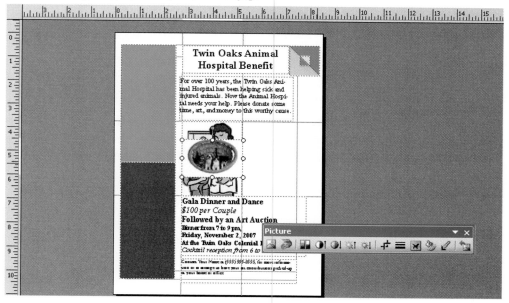

Design Matters

Cropping creatively

Cropping is used to remove portions of an image that do not support the publication's design. How do you decide what images should be cropped and how they should be cropped? Look for elements that either interfere with or fail to carry the publication's message. Just as with text or other objects, if a part of the image is distracting or unnecessary, it should be changed or deleted in favor of a beneficial design element. Often, it is white space in a photo or in clip art that should be cropped. If white space is needed, it can be added with a margin around the art.

Aligning and Grouping Images

Once you insert clip art, you can align multiple images so that the layout of the publication looks clean and balanced. Alignment helps guide the reader's eye across the page by avoiding isolated patches of white space that might be distracting. Artwork can be aligned from left to right or from top to bottom. You can group images to work with them more easily. A **group** is a selection of multiple images that you can move or resize as one unit. When you finish working with objects as a group, you can **ungroup** them to work with them individually again. ▩▩▩▩ You want to align the main text boxes and the two images in the flyer so that the overall appearance is neater. You also want to experiment with grouping the images to flip them as a single object on the page to see if this would improve your design.

STEPS

QUICK TIP

Pressing and holding [Shift] lets you select multiple objects.

1. **With the cropped image still selected, press and hold** [Shift], **click the** text boxes **at** 6" H / 3" V **and** 6" H / 8" V, **then release** [Shift]
   Two text boxes and the image should be selected, as shown in Figure D-9.

2. **Click** Arrange **on the menu bar, point to** Align or Distribute, **then click** Align Right
   The text boxes and the photo image are lined up on the right edge, as shown in Figure D-10.

3. **Press** [Esc] **to deselect the objects**

4. **Press** [Shift], **click the cropped** photo image, **use** 🕃 **to drag the photo image until its** bottom-left corner **is at** 5" H / 6⅞" V, **then release** [Shift]
   Holding [Shift] while you move an object moves it in a straight line, either vertically or horizontally. The images are aligned along their bottom edges, and the text boxes are perfectly aligned with the photo image along their right edges.

5. **With the photo image still selected, press and hold** [Shift], **click the** clip art image **to select it, release** [Shift], **then click the** Group Objects button ▣
   The two selected objects can now be manipulated as a single selected object.

6. **Click** Arrange **on the menu bar, point to** Rotate or Flip, **then click** Flip Horizontal
   Compare your work with Figure D-11. You don't like this change. The space above the kittens' heads is unusable white space, and the publication seems unbalanced with the objects reversed.

7. **Click the** Undo button ↺

8. **Click the** Ungroup Objects button ▤, **then press** [Esc]
   The objects are deselected and the Picture toolbar is no longer visible.

9. **Click the** Save button ▣ **on the Standard toolbar**

Clues to Use

Scanning artwork

If you have a favorite photo or piece of artwork that does not exist in electronic form, you can convert it to a digital computer file with a scanner. A variety of scanners are available in either handheld, sheetfed, or flatbed format. You can scan text, line art, or full-color images with amazing accuracy, enabling you to use virtually any image in publications. Every scanner comes with its own imaging software. With the camera or scanner in place and the software installed, Publisher lets you scan directly into a publication by clicking Insert on the menu bar, pointing to Picture, then clicking From Scanner or Camera.

FIGURE D-9: Three objects selected

Object 1

Object 2

Object 3

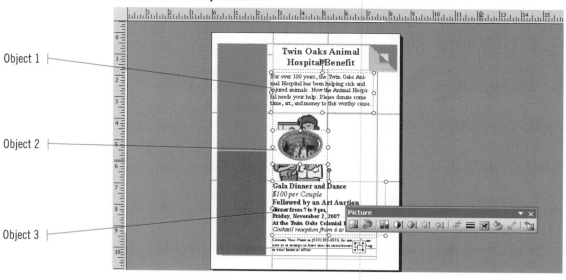

FIGURE D-10: Objects aligned right

Selected objects
right-aligned

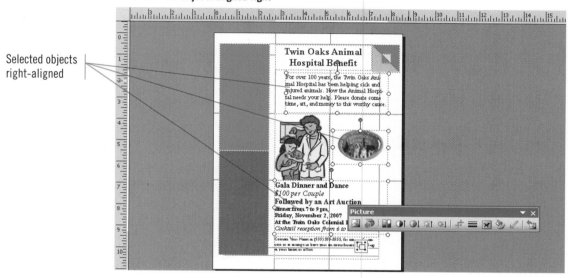

FIGURE D-11: Grouped objects flipped horizontally

Objects flipped
horizontally
along the
vertical axis

Ungroup button

Overlap from the
photo image covers
part of the clip art

Layering Objects

When positioning objects, you might want some images to overlap, or appear as if they were in front of others. This layering effect can be used with any type of object. Sometimes you will want text to display on top of a shape, or one object to overlap another object to partially conceal it. You might want to superimpose a text box in front of one object or a collection of objects. You can send an image **to the back** so that it appears to be underneath an object, or bring it **to the front** so it appears to be on top of an object. You want to experiment with layering and manipulating objects to improve the look of the flyer.

STEPS

1. **Click the** clip art image **at 4" H / 5" V, press [F9], then click the** Bring to Front button **on the Standard toolbar**

   The clip art image of the Animal Hospital now overlaps the photograph, as shown in Figure D-12. You think the images look better with this amount of overlap because it reduces the white space separating the two images. You think the design might be improved by reversing the clip art image.

2. **Click** Arrange **on the menu bar, point to** Rotate or Flip, **then click** Flip Horizontal

   The overlap is maintained when the image is flipped. Flipping the clip art image lines up the subjects of the image in a strong diagonal that guides the eye from the upper-left to the lower-right. It also changes the apparent view of the veterinarian from one animal to all the animals and the little girl.

   TROUBLE
   You may have to use the vertical scroll bar to see 3¼" V.

3. **Click the** AutoShapes button **on the Objects toolbar, point to** Callouts, **click the** Oval Callout **(third shape in the first row), then drag** + **from 5¼" H / 3½" V to 8" H / 4¾" V**

   The image of the kittens now has a cartoon balloon to which you can add a caption. One of the effects of inserting a callout can be movement of some text in the upper text box to accommodate the object.

4. **Type** They are even nice to dogs!, **press [Ctrl][A], click** Format **on the menu bar, point to** AutoFit text, **then click** Best Fit

5. **Click the** AutoShape **to select it, position the pointer over the** yellow handle, **then drag** ▷ **to just above the head of the left-most kitten, at approximately 5⅞" H / 5¾" V**

   The callout is positioned so that it appears to originate from the kitten's mouth, as shown in Figure D-13.

6. **Click the** Save button **on the Standard toolbar**

Bring to Front button

List arrow displays
additional layering
options

The complete image
is visible

FIGURE D-13: Clip art flipped, callout added to photo

Oval callout

Design Matters

Using the Bring Forward and Send Backward commands

By creatively using the Format AutoShape and Format Text dialog box
commands and the Bring to Front and Send to Back buttons, you can
superimpose text boxes on all kinds of objects and shapes. Without
these features, the shapes could be distracting and easily obscure the
text, making it unreadable. Figure D-14 shows a text box in front of
one and behind another geometric shape. This effect is achieved using
the Bring Forward and Send Backward commands on the Arrange
menu. Unlike Bring to Front and Send to Back, these commands move
an image forward or back only one layer at a time.

FIGURE D-14: Layered text box and shapes

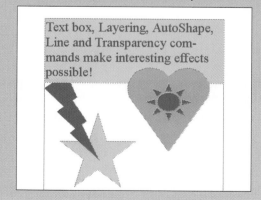

Publisher 2003

Rotating an Image

The **rotation** of an image—measured in degrees from a vertical plane—can be changed by dragging the green rotation handle on a selected object or using menu commands. Rotating images and other objects can change and guide the reader's focus and create visual interest. You can rotate a selected object in 90-degree increments by using the Rotate commands found on the Arrange menu, or in specific degree increments by choosing the Format *item* (where item stands for AutoShape, Text box, Table, etc.) command on the short-cut menu and making selections in the dialog box that opens. You can rotate an object around a point on its base by pressing [Ctrl] while dragging the green rotation handle. You want to rotate the cartoon balloon, then change the position of the callout so it looks like a different kitten is speaking. This will help to catch the reader's attention and further lighten the tone of the publication, to create a sense of fun.

STEPS

1. **Make sure the callout is still selected, click the green rotation handle ↕ on the callout, then drag ↻ to the right until it is at 6¾" H / 3¼" V**

   The AutoShape is rotated to the right, as shown in Figure D-15.

2. **Right-click the callout, click Format AutoShape, then click the Size tab**

   The Size tab in the Format AutoShape dialog box is shown in Figure D-16. Using this dialog box lets you rotate an image a specific number of degrees giving you more precise control over the rotation.

3. **Select the contents of the Rotation text box, type 2, then click OK**

   The AutoShape is rotated two degrees clockwise. The object coordinates and object dimensions remain unchanged for a rotated object.

4. **Click the callout, then drag the yellow handle over the second kitten from the left (at approximately 6⅛" H / 5¾" V), then press [Esc]**

   Compare your image with Figure D-17.

5. **Press [F9], then click the Save button 🖫 on the Standard toolbar**

Design Matters

Using the Measurement toolbar

The Measurement toolbar lets you precisely move and resize graphic images or text boxes, and fine-tune text. To display the Measurement toolbar, click View on the menu bar, point to Toolbars, then click Measurement. You can adjust text point size, distance between characters, and line spacing using this toolbar, as well as an object's height, width, length, and rotation. This toolbar is context-sensitive, so the available options vary based on the type of object that is selected.

FIGURE D-15: Object rotated with handle

Rotation handle

FIGURE D-16: Size tab of Format AutoShape dialog box

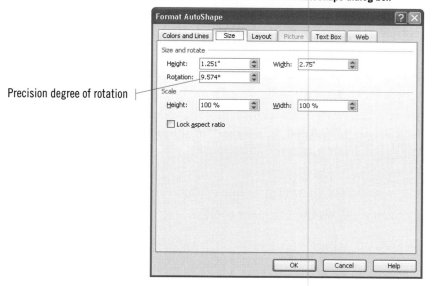

Precision degree of rotation

FIGURE D-17: Precisely rotated object

Using Drawing Tools

Publisher has a variety of drawing tools that you can use to create your own geometric designs. The Objects toolbar contains five drawing tools that let you draw lines, arrows, ovals, rectangles, and add AutoShapes. Any shape drawn on a page can be moved, resized, or formatted to meet your design specifications. Like objects, shapes created with drawing tools can be flipped as well as rotated. Creating a shape is easy. You click the button for the tool you want to use, click where you want to start the shape, and drag to create the size you need. You want to add a geometric design to the gray rectangle at the lower-left corner of the page. You begin by drawing a border to frame the design and make it stand out.

STEPS

1. **Click the** Rectangle button ▢ **on the Objects toolbar**

2. **Drag** + **from** ½" H / 8¼" V **to** 2¼" H / 10" V, **then press** [F9]
   The box is layered on the gray rectangle and has the dimensions 1¾" × 1¾".

3. **Click the** AutoShapes button 🔧 **on the Objects toolbar, then point to** Basic Shapes
   The Basic Shapes menu opens, as shown in Figure D-18.

4. **Click the** heart, **then drag** + **from the upper left corner of the box at** ½" H / 8¼" V **to the lower right corner of the box at** 2¼" H / 10" V
   The heart is inside the box you just created.

QUICK TIP

If you want to repeat a designed shape with the identical dimensions, create one with all the formatting attributes you want, then copy and paste it.

5. **Click** 🔧, **point to** Basic Shapes, **click the** heart, **then drag** + **to create a slightly smaller heart shape from** ¾" H / 8½" V **to** 2" H / 9¾" V

6. **Right-click the selected** heart, **click** Format AutoShape, **click the** Line Color list arrow, **click** Accent 2 (RGB (255, 204, 102)) color box **(third from the left), then click** OK
   The smaller heart shape is now outlined with a gold border.

7. **Click the** rectangle, **then click** [Delete]
   You like the heart shape without the framing rectangle. Compare your work to Figure D-19.

8. **Click the** Save button 🖫 **on the Standard toolbar**

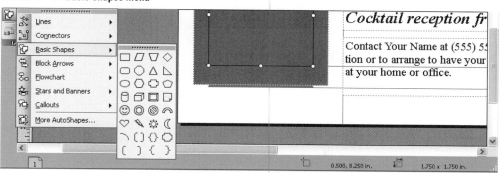

FIGURE D-19: **Design created with drawing tools**

New color
appears

Design Matters

Drawing perfect shapes and lines

Sometimes you want to draw an exact shape or line. To draw a square, click the Rectangle button ⬜ then press and hold [Shift] as you drag ✛. Press and hold [Shift] to create a circle using the Oval button ⭕. Press and hold [Shift] to create a horizontal, vertical, or 45-degree angle straight line using the Line button ◣ (this method draws a line at 15 degree increments). To center an object at a specific location, click the tool to create the object, place the pointer where you want the center of the object to be, then hold [Ctrl] as you drag the mouse. Remember to always release the mouse button before you release [Ctrl] or [Shift].

Filling Shapes with Colors and Patterns

Colors and patterns enhance overall design and help you create elegant original graphics. Drawn shapes can be left with their default attributes—displaying whatever background exists—or you can fill them using a variety of colors and patterns. When choosing background colors, it's often effective to use the standard palette of colors for the current publication. These include a Main color, two or more Accent colors, and colors for hyperlinks that might be included in the publication. ░░░░ You want to add color and patterns to the shapes in your publication. You begin by adding color to the callout and one of the hearts.

STEPS

1. **Select the** smaller heart shape, **press** [F9], **press** [Shift], **click the** callout shape **at 7" H / 4" V, release** [Shift], **click the** Fill Color list arrow ⬛ **on the Formatting toolbar, then click the Accent 2 (RGB (255, 204, 102)) color box**
   Gold is added to the small heart shape and the callout, making them stand out.

2. **Press** [Esc], **right-click the** large heart, **click** Format AutoShape, **click the** Fill Color list arrow, **click the** Accent 1 (RGB (51, 153, 255)) color box **(second from the left), then click** OK
   You don't like the gold color for the small heart shape.

3. **Right-click the** small heart, **click** Format AutoShape, **click the** Fill Color list arrow, **then click** More Colors
   The Colors dialog box opens.

4. **Click the** red color box (third box from the left in the bottom row, as seen in Figure D-20), **click** OK **to close the Colors dialog box, then click** OK **to close the Format AutoShape dialog box**
   A yellow outline still surrounds the small heart.

5. **Press** [F9], **click the** Line Color list arrow ✏ **on the Formatting toolbar, then click the** red color box **(beneath the gray line)**
   The red was added to your palette for this publication; however, it will not be added to the palette in subsequent publications.

6. **Right-click the selected** red heart, **click** Format AutoShape, **select the text in the** Transparency text box, **type** 15, **click** OK, **then press** [Esc]
   The smaller heart is now paler.

7. **Right-click the** blue heart shape, **click** Format AutoShape, **click the** Fill Color list arrow, **then click** Fill Effects

8. **Click the** Pattern tab, **click the** second box from the left in the first row, **click** OK **to close the Fill Effects dialog box, click** OK **to close the Format AutoShape dialog box, then press** [Esc]
   Compare your work to Figure D-21.

9. **Make sure your name displays in the** text box **at 4" H / 10" V, press** [F9], **then deselect any objects**
   Compare your work with the completed flyer in Figure D-22.

10. **Click the** Save button 🖫 **on the Standard toolbar, click the** Print button 🖨 **on the Standard toolbar, then exit Publisher**

FIGURE D-20: Colors dialog box

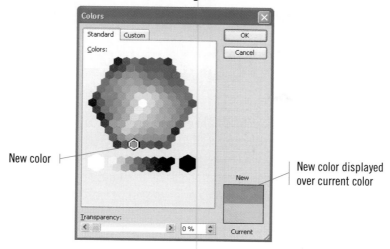

New color

New color displayed over current color

FIGURE D-21: Re-colored objects with pattern

FIGURE D-22: Completed flyer

Capstone Project: Flower Show Web Page

You have learned the skills necessary to insert, resize, and rotate clip art. You can copy and move objects, and crop, align, and group objects. You have used drawing tools and added fill colors and patterns to drawn shapes. Now you will use your new skills to add and manipulate artwork on a Web site. ▅▅▅▅▅ Image Magic was contracted to create a Web Page for an annual flower show. Mike is heading up this project and has some preliminary work on a design, and has asked you to improve on his work by adding images. Because the Web page is advertising a flower show, you decide to start by looking for photos and clip art related to flowers.

STEPS

QUICK TIP

Throughout this lesson, press [F9] to zoom in or out as necessary, to facilitate working with the publication.

1. Start Publisher, open the file PUB D-3.pub from the drive and folder where your Data Files are located, then save it as Flower Show Web Page

2. Click the Picture Frame button 🖼 on the Objects toolbar, then click Clip Art 🖼

3. Click the Search for text text box, type flowers, click the Search in list arrow, click My Collections and Office Collections if necessary to select them, click the Results should be list arrow, click Clip Art and Photographs to select them if necessary, click the list arrow again to close the list, then click Go

   Your search finds two objects, as shown in Figure D-23.

4. Insert the picture of the white roses (*Hint:* The filename is j0281904.wmf), then close the Insert Clip Art task pane

5. Move the picture so that the upper-left corner is at 1½" H / 6" V

6. With the object still selected, click the Copy button 📋, click the Paste button 📋, then position the pasted image so that its upper-left corner is at 3½" H / 6" V

7. Click Arrange on the menu bar, point to Rotate or Flip, then click Flip Horizontal

   Flipping the copy creates an attractive mirror image.

8. Create a text box at ¼" H / 3" V, type your name, then modify the font and point size so that the text is readable

   Compare your work to Figure D-24.

9. Click the Save button 💾 on the Standard toolbar, click File on the menu bar, click Print, select the Current page button, click OK, then exit Publisher

FIGURE D-23: Results of clip art search

Your search results may vary

FIGURE D-24: Completed Web Page

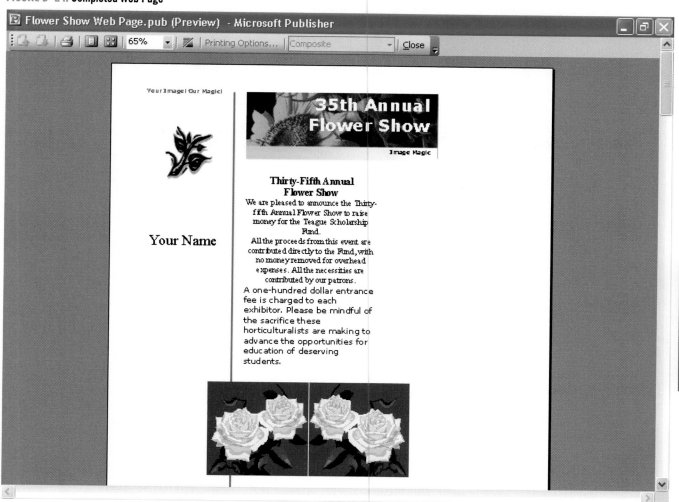

Practice

▼ CONCEPTS REVIEW

Label each of the elements of the Publisher window shown in Figure D-25.

FIGURE D-25

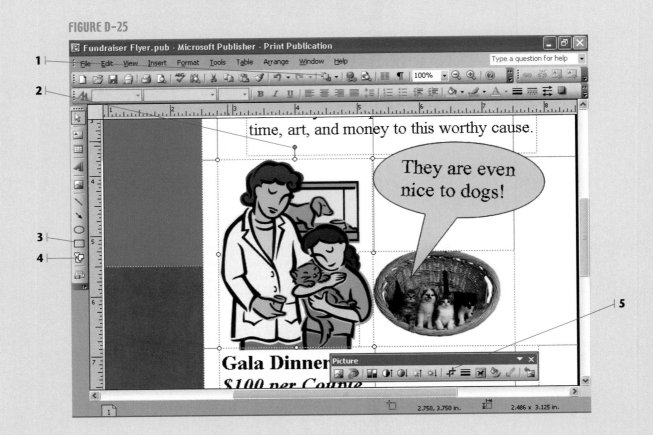

Match each of the buttons with the statement that describes its function.

6.
7.
8.
9.
10.
11.

a. Contains clip art
b. Brings an object to the front
c. Conceals part of an image
d. Colors a line or border
e. Fills an object with color
f. Creates a custom shape

Select the best answer from the list of choices.

12. Create a square using the Rectangle button by holding while dragging $+$.
    a. [Ctrl]
    b. [Alt]
    c. [Shift]
    d. [Esc]

13. You can do each of the following with clip art, except:
    a. Crop.
    b. Italicize.
    c. Flip.
    d. Rotate.

14. To create a circle, click _____, then press and hold [Shift] while dragging the pointer.
    a.
    b.
    c.
    d.

15. Which pointer is used to insert an AutoShape?
    a.
    b.
    c. $+$
    d.

16. Which pointer is used to copy an object without placing a copy on the Clipboard?
    a.
    b.
    c.
    d.

17. Which button is used to add colors and patterns to objects?
    a.
    b.
    c.
    d.

18. Rotate an object clockwise in 90-degree increments by clicking:
    a. Flip Horizontal.
    b. Free Rotate.
    c. Rotate Left.
    d. Rotate Right.

19. Which button cannot be used with clip art?
    a.
    b.
    c.
    d.

20. To resize an object, maintaining its scale while dragging, press and hold _____.
    a. [Shift]
    b. [Alt][Shift]
    c. [Ctrl]
    d. [Alt]

▼ SKILLS REVIEW

Throughout this exercise, zoom in and out whenever necessary.

1. **Insert and resize clip art.**
   a. Start Publisher.
   b. Open the file PUB D-4.pub from the drive and folder where your Data Files are located, then close the task pane.
   c. Save the file as **Family Reunion Postcard**.
   d. Use the Microsoft Clip Organizer to search My Collections and Office Collections for clip art and photographs using the word **home**. Locate the black-and-white image of a house in the top row, second from the left in the Clip Art task pane (filename: j0185604.wmf).
   e. Insert the image in the lower left corner of the publication so that the upper-left corner is at ½" H / 3" V (the clip art's dimensions should be approximately 1" H × 1" V), then close the task pane.
   f. Press and hold [Shift], then reduce the size of the image by positioning the pointer over the lower-right handle, then dragging until the lower-right corner is at 1¼" H / 3¾" V. The image should now be approximately ¾" H × ¾" V.
   g. Save the publication.

2. **Copy and move an object.**
   a. Copy the selected image, then paste the image anywhere on the publication.
   b. Move the newly pasted copy so that the upper-left corner is at 4¼" H / 3" V.
   c. Flip the copy horizontally, then deselect it. (*Hint*: The image's chimneys will be on opposite sides.)
   d. Save the publication.

3. **Crop an image.**
   a. Move the image of the flowers from the upper-right corner of the publication so that the upper-left corner of this image is at 2" H / 2" V.
   b. If the Picture toolbar is not visible, click View on the menu bar, point to Toolbars, then click Picture.
   c. Click the Crop button on the Picture toolbar. Crop the top edge of the image using the center cropping handle, hiding ⅛" of the image so that the top-left corner is now at 2" H / 2 ⅛" V, then press [Esc].
   d. Save the publication.

4. **Align and group images.**
   a. Press and hold [Shift], select the two clip art images of the house, then select the image of the flowers.
   b. Right-click, point to Align or Distribute, then click Align Bottom.
   c. Right-click, point to Align or Distribute, then click Distribute Horizontally.
   d. Save the publication.

5. **Layer objects.**
   a. Copy the object at 1" H / 3½" V, then paste and drag the copy so that its upper-left corner is at 1" H / 2¾" V.
   b. Send the copied object behind the original object.
   c. Copy the object at 4½" H / 3½" V, paste it, then drag the copy so that its upper-left corner is at 3¾" H / 2¾" V.
   d. Send the copied object behind the original object.
   e. Save the publication.

6. **Rotate an image.**
   a. Flip the image of the flowers horizontally.
   b. Right-click the image of the flowers, click Format Picture, use the dialog box to change the rotation to 300 degrees. (*Hint*: Use the Size tab in the Format Picture dialog box.)
   c. Deselect the image, then save the publication.

7. Use drawing tools.

a. Click the AutoShapes button on the Objects toolbar, point to Basic Shapes, then click the heart (sixth row down on the left).

b. Draw the heart so that its upper-left corner is at 4½" H / ¼" V and it has the dimensions ¾" H x ¾" V.

c. Create a copy of this shape, paste the copy, then drag it so that the upper-left corner is at 4 ¼" H / ¼" V (the two hearts should overlap).

d. Save the publication.

8. Fill shapes with colors and patterns.

a. Add a red fill color to both heart shapes.

b. Select the right heart, then change the fill transparency to 30%.

c. Create a text box with the upper-left corner at ½" H / 2¼" V with the dimensions 2" H × ½" V, then insert your name, using AutoFit Text to adjust the point size as necessary.

d. Save and print the publication, compare your screen to Figure D-26, then exit Publisher.

FIGURE D-26

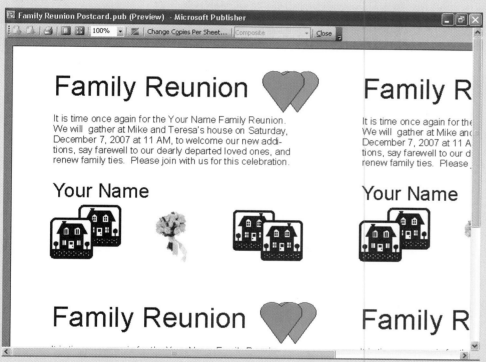

▼ INDEPENDENT CHALLENGE 1

You have decided to market yourself more effectively in the business world. Your first priority is designing a new business card. You want to create a card that reflects your interests and personality.

a. Start Publisher, if necessary, use the Scallops Business Card (Plain Paper) from the Publication Gallery, with Landscape orientation, include a logo placeholder, one card in the center of the page, then close the task pane.

b. Save the publication as **New Business Card Design** to the drive and folder where your Data Files are located.

c. Enter and use any appropriate information about yourself in the Primary Business Personal Information Set, change the logo so it reads **Image Magic**, then change the color scheme to Redwood.

FIGURE D-27

d. Use at least three drawing tools to create an interesting series of shapes in the upper-right corner of the business card. Change the fill color and fill effects of at least two shapes.

Advanced Challenge Exercises

■ Use [Shift] to create a perfectly round or square shape.

■ Insert a piece of clip art downloaded from the Microsoft Office Online Clip Art and Media. Compare your publication to Figure D-27.

e. If desired, rotate and layer the artwork.

f. Save and print the publication, then exit Publisher.

▼ INDEPENDENT CHALLENGE 2

A local clothing store is planning a new sales promotion to increase their sale of gift certificates. The manager of the store asks you to use your design skills to create a gift certificate that is attractive and eye-catching.

a. Start Publisher, then use the Mobile Special Gift Certificate found in the Publication Gallery. Complete any necessary installations, if prompted.

b. Save the publication as **Gift Certificate** to the drive and folder where your Data Files are located.

c. Enter appropriate information in the Secondary Business Personal Information Set, change the logo so it reads **Image Magic**, then change the color scheme to Reef.

d. Use the Microsoft Clip Organizer to search My Collections and Office Collections for clip art and photographs using the word **maps**, then insert the globe (filename: j0335112.wmf) at approximately 0" H / 2" V.

e. Add an AutoShape of your own choosing.

f. Make at least two copies of the AutoShape, resize them, then place them according to your own sense of design.

g. Add different fill colors to the AutoShapes.

h. Type your name in the Authorized by text box.

i. Save and print the publication, then exit Publisher.

▼ INDEPENDENT CHALLENGE 3

You want to spruce up your work area. A customized calendar is just what you need to help organize and add visual interest to your surroundings.

a. Start Publisher, if necessary, then use the Full Page Blocks Calendar from the Publication Gallery for the next month of this year. Complete any necessary installations, if prompted.

b. Save the publication as **Next Month's Calendar** to the drive and folder where your Data Files are located.

c. Enter appropriate information about yourself in the Primary Business Personal Information Set.

d. Change the color scheme to one of your own choosing.

e. Click Change date range on the task pane and change the range to start and end next month, then close the task pane.

f. Add clip art of your choosing to the calendar.

Advanced Challenge Exercises

- Download and insert at least one piece of artwork from Microsoft Office Online Clip Art and Media.
- Crop the new artwork.
- Add objects created with drawing tools, and add color and patterns, if appropriate. If necessary, resize any drawn objects.

g. Save and print the publication, then exit Publisher.

▼ INDEPENDENT CHALLENGE 4

There are many sources on the Web for clip art. Some require payment to use an image, while other images are free to download. You need to find some free clip art that relates to your favorite hobby.

a. Connect to the Internet, then use your browser and favorite search engine to find free clip art sites. Some possible free clip art sites are: www.free-clip-art.com, www.clipartconnection.com, and www.graphicsfree.com.

b. Print out the home page from at least two of the sites you found. Take note of any restrictions regarding use of graphic images.

c. Right-click any of the free clip art images that appeals to you, then download it by choosing the Save picture as command in the shortcut menu. Save it to the drive and folder where your Data Files are located using the artwork's default name.

d. Start Publisher, use the Publication Gallery to create a single-page Quick Publication using any design you choose, then save the publication to the drive and folder where your Data Files are located as **My Clip Art**.

e. Replace a placeholder with a downloaded file, add appropriate text (if necessary) to describe the artwork, then add your name somewhere on the page.

f. Format the artwork by cropping any undesirable elements, then copy or align images if necessary to enhance the publication.

g. Save and print the publication, then exit Publisher.

Use the elements found in PUB D-5.pub to create the party invitation seen in Figure D-28. Save this publication as **Party Invitation** to the drive and folder where your Data Files are located. Make sure your name appears on the publication, then save and print it.

FIGURE D-28

Promotion Party

The pleasure of your company is requested in celebration of the promotion of Your Name to Campaign Manager.

30 November 2007
7:30 PM

Smith River Restaurant
214 River View Road
Santa Fe, NM 87504

Enhancing a Publication

OBJECTIVES

Define styles
Apply and modify a style
Change a format into a style
Create columns
Adjust text overflows
Add Continued on/from notices
Add drop caps
Create reversed text
Capstone Project: Solar System Newsletter

Text in a publication should be easy to read. Professionals advise using no more than two fonts per page because too many fonts make a page look busy and detract from the message. Instead, you can add visual interest by formatting fonts in different sizes, with bold, italic, or other effects. To further enhance readability, consider formatting story text in one or more columns, instead of running text in a single block between the page margins. If you are working on a story that is too long to fit on one page, you can use additional text boxes to continue it elsewhere in the publication. Publisher has tools to help map and link the text boxes to create a cohesive publication. Mike Mendoza has asked you to work on *Route 66 Traveler*, a quarterly newsletter for an Image Magic client. You begin by revising styles and formatting in the newsletter, so that it has a strong, consistent design, and is enjoyable to read.

Defining Styles

You can maintain consistent formatting, even in multi-page publications, by using styles. A **style** is a defined set of text and formatting attributes, such as font, font size, and paragraph alignment. As a reader moves from page to page, consistent styles make it easy to recognize what is an article headline, what is pull-quote text, and so on. The Styles and Formatting task pane contains all of the styles specific to a particular publication, and displays each style exactly as it will look. You can create your own styles and modify those that already exist. These new styles apply only to the publication for which they are created, but they can also be imported into other publications. By naming a style, you can make it available for further use. When naming a style, it is important to make it descriptive to distinguish it from other styles that exist. █████ You want to define a new style for the body text in the newsletter. You want the body text to be easy to read and to complement other text in the publication.

STEPS

1. **Start Publisher, open the file** PUB E-1.pub **from the drive and folder where your Data Files are located, then save it as** Route 66 Traveler

QUICK TIP

You can also open the Styles and Formatting task pane by clicking the list arrow on any open task pane, then clicking Styles and Formatting.

2. **Click the** Styles and Formatting button 🔢 **on the Formatting toolbar**
   The Styles and Formatting task pane opens, as shown in Figure E-1.

3. **Click** Create new style **on the task pane**
   The New Style dialog box opens, as shown in Figure E-2. In this dialog box, you can change the font and font size, modify the alignment of indents and lists, change the line and character spacing, adjust the tabs, and even modify the appearance of the horizontal rules.

4. **Type** 66 Body Text **in the** Enter new style name text box, **then click the** Font button

QUICK TIP

Choose font sizes and styles carefully. Text that is too large looks awkward; text that is too small or too ornamental is distracting and hard to read.

5. **Click the** Font list arrow, **click** Times New Roman, **click the** Size list arrow, **click** 14, **then click** OK **to close the Font dialog box**
   The 66 Body Text style consists of the Times New Roman font, which is a very common type style for the body text of documents because it is easy to read, with a point size of 14.

6. **Click** Paragraph, **click the** Alignment list arrow, **click** Right, **then click** OK **to close the Paragraph dialog box**
   The sample in the New Style dialog box indicates how the new style will look, as shown in Figure E-3.

7. **Click** OK
   The New Style dialog box closes and the 66 Body Text style appears in the list of existing styles in the task pane.

8. **Click the** Save button 💾 **on the Standard toolbar**

FIGURE E-1: Styles and Formatting task pane

Styles and Formatting button

Available styles are listed alphabetically

Create new style button

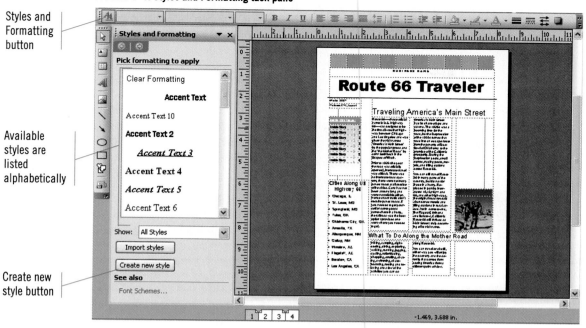

FIGURE E-2: Create New Style dialog box

Buttons change style properties

Sample shows alignment of text

Sample of currently selected style

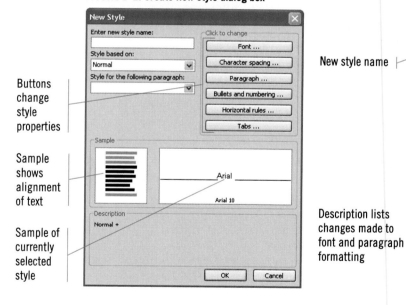

FIGURE E-3: Style changes appear in New Style dialog box

New style name

Description lists changes made to font and paragraph formatting

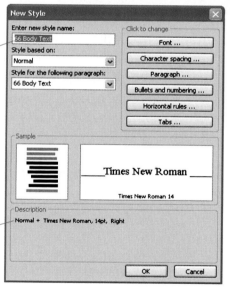

Design Matters

Choosing fonts

Font types generally fall into one of two categories: serif fonts and sans serif fonts. **Serifs** are small decorative strokes added to the end of a letter's main strokes. Serif, or roman, types are useful for long passages of text because the serifs help distinguish individual letters and provide continuity for the reader's eye. Times New Roman and Courier are two popular serif fonts. **Sans serif** fonts are typefaces that do not have serifs. Examples include Arial or Helvetica. Sans serif faces lend a clean, simple appearance to headlines and titles but are avoided for long passages of unbroken text because they are more difficult to read than serif fonts.

Applying and Modifying a Style

Applying a style is easy. You simply select the text you want to format, then click the style in either the Style list on the Formatting toolbar or the Pick formatting to apply list in the Styles and Formatting task pane. Because any style can be modified, you have the freedom to change the appearance of all the text assigned to a specific style within a publication. Once you define a style, you can apply it to text so that your publication develops a consistent look with similar attributes, or you can change the style, and the newly modified style will be applied automatically. ▰▰▰ You decide that the font size for the style you created is too large, so you want to modify it. Then you will be ready to apply the modified style to a story. Mike has provided you with a Word document containing a story for the publication, so you can insert the document instead of typing the story from scratch.

STEPS

1. **Click the** text box at 3" H / 5" V, **press** [Ctrl][A], **then click the** Zoom In button 🔍 **until** 50% **appears in the Zoom box on the Standard toolbar**
   You can see the task pane and the top and bottom of the text box.

2. **Click** 66 Body Text **in the Pick formatting to apply list in the task pane, then press** [Esc] **twice**
   The selected text was converted to the 66 Body Text style.

3. **Position** ⬚ **over** 66 Body Text **in the Pick formatting to apply area of the task pane (do not click the style), click the** 66 Body Text list arrow, **then click** Modify
   The Modify Style dialog box opens.

4. **Click the** Font button, **click the** Size list arrow, **click** 12, **then click** OK
   The font size for 66 Traveler changes from 14 point to 12 point, and the change appears in the sample.

5. **Click the** Paragraph button, **click the** Alignment list arrow, **click** Left, **then click** OK
   The Paragraph dialog box closes. The modified text size and alignment appears in the Modify Style dialog box, as shown in Figure E-4.

6. **Click** OK
   The Modify Style dialog box closes. Any new or existing text that has the 66 Body Text style applied to it will show the modified 66 Body Text style, as shown in Figure E-5.

7. **Click the** Save button 💾 **on the Standard toolbar**

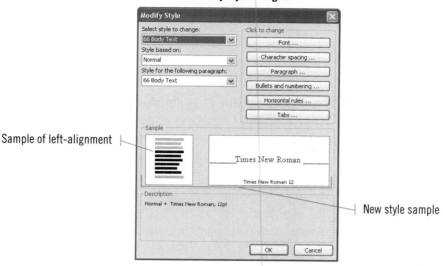

Sample of left-alignment

New style sample

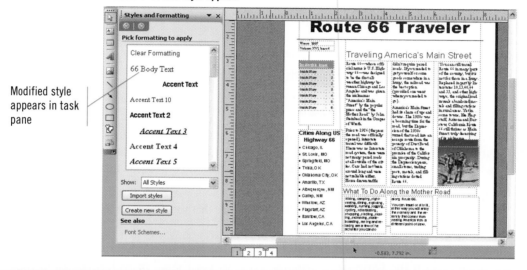

Modified style appears in task pane

Design Matters

Adjusting spaces between characters

Sometimes words on the page don't look quite right: they may seem packed too close together or spread too far apart. This is particularly true of typefaces at 14 points and larger. Adjusting the spacing between specific character pairs, or **kerning**, can make large text look better and be easier to read. Publisher automatically kerns characters with point sizes of 14 and larger, but you can kern any characters you choose by selecting the character pair(s) to be adjusted, clicking Format on the menu bar, then clicking Character Spacing. Using the Character Spacing dialog box, you can change scaling, the width of the text characters, and tracking, the distance between text characters, in addition to kerning, and the point size where automatic kerning begins, as shown in Figure E-6.

FIGURE E-6: Character Spacing dialog box

Publisher 2003

UNIT
E
Publisher 2003

Changing a Format into a Style

You can create a style from formatted text even if you don't know all the attributes that make up the appearance of the text. To do so, you create what is called a **style by example**. First you select the text whose format you want to use, then you type a name in the Style text box on the Formatting toolbar. Creating a style by example makes the style available for use over and over again in the publication. This may sound similar to using the Format Painter, but there is an important difference. The Format Painter button reformats selected characters according to the formatting attributes of currently selected characters, but does not store or name the set of attributes, or update similarly formatted text automatically. You like the style of the story title and want to create a style from this format that you can use throughout the publication.

STEPS

1. **Click anywhere in the headline** Traveling America's Main Street **in the text box at** 3" H / 2¾" V

   The text box containing the headline is selected. The current style displays in the Styles and Formatting task pane, as well as in the Style box on the Formatting toolbar.

2. **Click** Heading 2 **in the Style box on the Formatting toolbar**

   The current style is selected.

3. **Type** 66 Heading, **then press** [Enter]

   The Create Style By Example dialog box opens, as shown in Figure E-7. You entered a new name in the Style box to create a style based on the formatting of the selected text in the lead story headline. The Sample box shows you the current style's font and size, as well as its alignment setting and new style name.

4. **Click** OK

   The Create Style By Example dialog box closes. Do you see that the new name, 66 Heading, appears in the Style box on the Formatting toolbar?

5. **Click anywhere in the text** Route 66 Traveler **in the text box at** 5" H / 1½" V, **click** Title 2 **in the** Style box **on the Formatting toolbar, type** 66 Masthead, **press** [Enter], **then click** OK **in the Create Style By Example dialog box**

   The new style is listed in the Pick formatting to apply list, and you can apply it to any text in the publication. Compare your publication to Figure E-8.

6. **Click the** Save button 🖫 **on the Standard toolbar**

Clues to Use

Using Styles in other publications

Suppose you've created styles in one publication that you want to use in other publications. Do you have to re-create them in the new publication? No, you only need to import them. You can import styles from any Publisher or Word document into the current, open publication. To do this, display the Styles and Formatting task pane, then click Import Styles. Select the publication (or Word document) that contains the styles you want to import, then click OK. All the styles from the selected publication or document will be imported.

FIGURE E-7: Create Style By Example dialog box

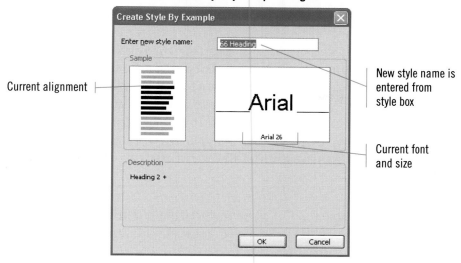

Current alignment ┤

New style name is entered from style box

Current font and size

FIGURE E-8: New style name appears in Style box and task pane

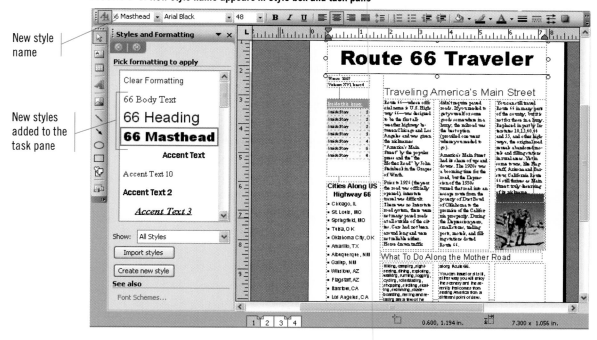

New style name

New styles added to the task pane

Design Matters

Horizontal text alignment

Text can be horizontally aligned in four ways: left-aligned so that text lines up at the left margin; right-aligned so that text lines up at the right margin; centered so that each line is equally spaced between the margins; and justified so that lines of text are balanced evenly between the right and left margins. Justified and left-aligned text are the most common settings for ordinary text. In most publications, text is left-aligned because the ragged right edge adds an element of white space, making it easier for the reader to move between lines. Some people are attracted to the neatness of text that lines up perfectly on the left and right when justified. While justified text may lend an air of formality to a publication, it requires extra attention to hyphenation and careful proofing to avoid awkward looking gaps of white space. It does offer the advantage of letting you pack more text in the same amount of space as left-aligned.

Publisher 2003

Creating Columns

Most newsletter stories are formatted in multiple columns to make them easier to scan and to improve their appearance. Two or more narrow columns on a page tend to be easier to scan than a single wide column of text that spans the whole page. When you create a publication using the Publication Gallery, a page may have a three-column layout, but you can use the Page Content task pane to change the layout to fewer columns, or a mixed number of columns, on the same page. These simple design techniques can add visual interest and help differentiate among stories. ▇▇▇▇ You want to see different ways the columns can be arranged on page three to evaluate how the arrangement of the columns affects the overall design of the publication.

STEPS

1. **Click the 2-3 page icon** ⌐2 ⌐3⌐ **on the horizontal status bar at the bottom of the screen, click the Zoom box** 51% ▾, **type 30, press [Enter], then use the scroll bars if necessary so that both pages are visible**

2. **If necessary, click the** Styles and Formatting task pane list arrow, **then click** Newsletter Options

3. **Click** Page Content, **click the** Select a page to modify list arrow, **then click** Right inside page
   Compare your screen to Figure E-9. The Page Content task pane lets you select the number of columns for specific pages.

4. **Click the** Mixed button **under Columns on Right Page**

5. **Position** � **over the** 2 button **under Columns on Right Page, click the** 2 list arrow, **then click** Apply to the Page
   The layout of page three, the right inside page, changes to two columns. This provides some visual interest, but is less attractive than the mixed columns, and is not consistent with the rest of the publication.

6. **Position** � **over the** 3 button **under Columns on Right Page, click the** 3 list arrow, **then click** Apply to the Page
   The layout changes to three columns, as shown in Figure E-10. The design is consistent with the rest of the publication and seems balanced.

7. **Close the task pane, then click the** Save button ▣ **on the Standard toolbar**

Clues to Use

Using Baseline guides to align columns

If you are working on a multi-column publication and want to align multiple columns of text so they are evenly spaced, you can use baseline guides. **Baseline guides** belong to the set of layout guides along with margin guides, column guides, and row guides. Text that is aligned to the baseline automatically adds equal line spacing so the text appears balanced along columns. You can adjust the baseline guides by clicking Arrange on the menu bar, then clicking Layout Guides. In the Layout Guides dialog box, click the Baseline Guides tab, adjust the settings, then click OK.

Select a page to modify list arrow

One column on Right Page box

Content options for Right Page

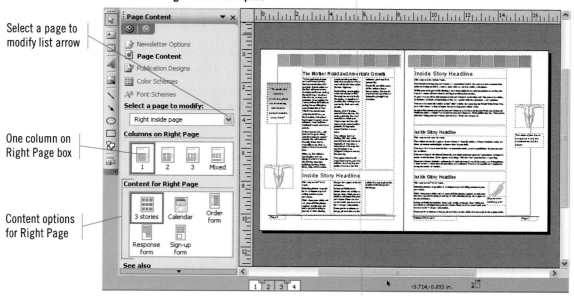

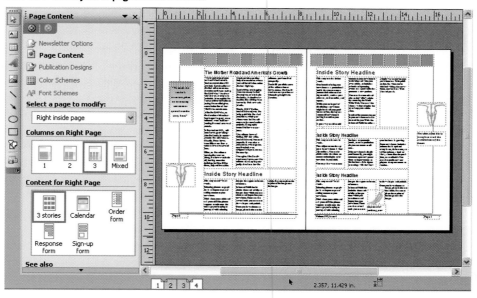

Clues to Use

Manually creating multiple columns

Using the Text Box button [📄] creates a text box with a single column. You can add multiple columns to a text box by clicking the Columns button [▦] on the Formatting toolbar and selecting the number of columns you want. The text box is then divided into multiple columns of equal width with equal space between them. The number of columns and the spacing between them can be changed using the Columns dialog box. In the Format Text Box dialog box (which you can open by right-clicking a text box, then clicking Format Text Box), select the Text Box tab, then click the Columns button. The Columns dialog box appears, as shown in Figure E-11.

FIGURE E-11: **Columns dialog box**

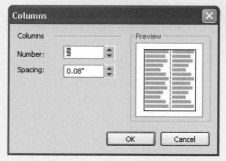

Publisher 2003

Adjusting Text Overflows

Text does not always fit neatly within a text box. Sometimes the text box is not large enough to contain it. Sometimes you don't want a story to fit in just one text box on a page, but instead you want it to continue on another page, or on several additional pages. Publisher makes it easy to take the overflow from one text box and flow it into another text box using the Connect button at the bottom of the text box. Text boxes that contain text flowed from another text box are linked to the previous text box, so it's easy to make editing and formatting changes to the entire story. You can use the **Autoflow** feature if you want text to flow automatically to another text box when necessary, or you can flow the text manually. Working manually gives you greater control over where the text is placed. ▓▓▓▓▓ You have a long story about Route 66 to insert in the newsletter. You want it to start on page two and continue on page three. First you need to import the text file into a text box on page two, then you can flow it into a text box on page three.

STEPS

1. **Click the** Zoom list arrow `51%  ▾`, **click** Whole Page, **click the** text box **on page 3 at** 10" H / 3" V, **right-click, then click** Delete Text

TROUBLE

If you get a warning saying that you need to install a converter, contact your instructor or technical support person.

2. **Right-click the** text box **on page 2 at** 5" H / 9" V, **point to** Change Text, **click** Text File, **select the file** PUB E-2.doc **from the drive and folder where your Data Files are located, click** OK, **then click** No **when asked if you want to use autoflow**
   The Text in Overflow button 🅰 ⚬⚬⚬ at the bottom of the text box indicates that there is overflow text. Text that does not fit in this text box can be continued in other text boxes, using 🥤 and ⚬⚬.

TROUBLE

If you do not see 🔗, click View on the menu bar, point to Toolbars, then click Connect Text Boxes.

3. **Click the** Create Text Box Link button 🔗 **on the** Connect Text Boxes **toolbar**
   The pointer changes to 🥤 when placed on objects on the page. When you place this pitcher over an empty text box, it changes to ⚬⚬, as shown in Figure E-12.

4. **Position** ⚬⚬ **at** 10" H / 3" V, **then click**
   The remaining text fills the text boxes. If additional overflow remained (indicated by the appearance of 🅰 ⚬⚬⚬), you would repeat this process until no overflow text remained. Compare your pages to Figure E-13.

QUICK TIP

To break a link between connected frames, click 🔗.

5. **Click the** Save button 💾 **on the Standard toolbar**

FIGURE E-12: Preparing to pour overflow text

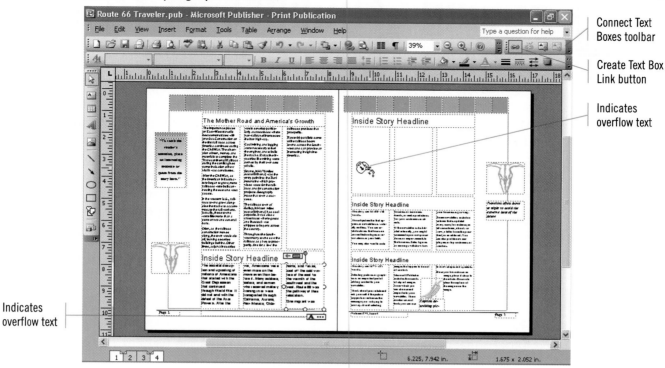

Connect Text Boxes toolbar

Create Text Box Link button

Indicates overflow text

Indicates overflow text

FIGURE E-13: Overflow text poured into text box

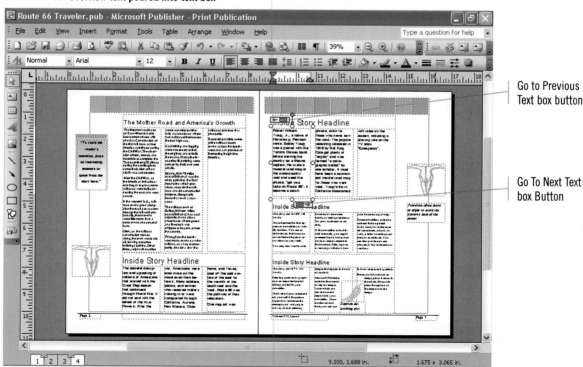

Go to Previous Text box button

Go To Next Text box Button

Adding Continued on/from Notices

To make it as easy as possible to find and read all segments of a story, you can create continued on and continued from notices. A **continued on** notice tells the reader where to find the next segment of the story. A **continued from** notice tells the reader where the story's previous segment can be found. These notices automatically insert text with the correct page reference, and they update automatically if you move the text box. Sometimes publications are specifically designed with stories spanning several pages to encourage readers to see all the pages in the publication. Be aware that continued on/from notices may add a few lines of length to a story. ░░░░ You insert Continued on and Continued from notices in the story that spans two pages.

STEPS

1. **Click the** text box at 7" H / 9" V, **then press** [F9]

   You want the first Continued on notice to appear at the bottom of this text box because the text continues on page three. You create a Continued on notice by modifying the text box's properties.

2. **Click** Format **on the menu bar, click** Text Box, **then click the** Text Box tab

   The Text Box options appear, as shown in Figure E-14.

TROUBLE
Continued on/from notices appear only if they refer to text on pages other than the current page.

3. **Click the** Include "Continued on page" check box, **then click** OK

   Compare your page to Figure E-15. You want to insert a Continued from notice in the text box on page three. If a single text box continues on another page, you can insert the Continued on and Continued from notices at the same time.

4. **Click the** Go To Next Text Box button [▭ →] **at the bottom of the text box**

   The insertion point is on page three at the continuation of the story. The story needs a Continued from notice on page three.

QUICK TIP
Continued on/from notices can be turned on or off for each text box. This can help you adjust the quantity of text in a text box to enhance its appearance.

5. **Press** [F9] **twice to center the selected text box on the screen, right-click the selected** text box, **click** Format Text Box, **click the** Text Box tab, **click the** Include "Continued from page" check box, **then click** OK

   The Continued from notice appears at the beginning of the text box, as shown in Figure E-16.

6. **Press** [Esc] **twice, then press** [F9]

7. **Click the** Save button [🖫] **on the Standard toolbar**

Design Matters

Changing the style of continued notices

If the appearance of a continued on or continued from notice does not appeal to you, you can change it. Each type of continued notice has a defined style—you can see the style name of a selected continued notice in the Style box on the Formatting toolbar. Change the style of a continued notice by selecting the notice you want to change, making formatting modifications, clicking the Style box, changing the name of the style, pressing [Enter], then clicking OK in the Create Style By Example dialog box.

FIGURE E-14: Format Text Box dialog box

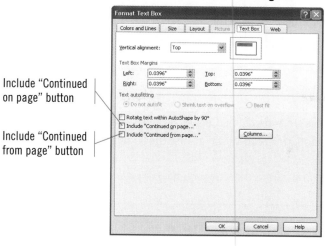

Include "Continued on page" button

Include "Continued from page" button

FIGURE E-15: Continued on notice

Notice automatically cites the correct page

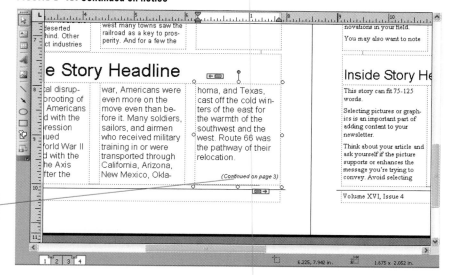

FIGURE E-16: Continued notices

Continued from notice

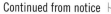

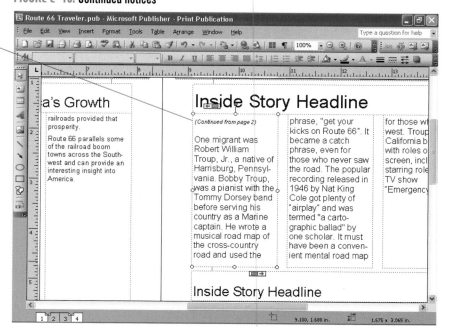

Adding Drop Caps

To draw attention to the beginning of a story, you can add a **drop cap**, a formatting attribute that enlarges the first character in a story or paragraph. Depending on your design goals, you can add just one drop cap to a publication, or you can add a drop cap to every story or even every paragraph in a publication. You can even apply drop cap formatting to the entire first word instead of just the first character, if you prefer. In Publisher, you can choose from predefined character types that use different fonts and line heights, or you can create your own custom drop cap style. Because the addition of a drop cap adds to the length of a story, this addition may cause a story to overflow. ░░░░ You want to dress up several stories using drop caps. You start by applying a drop cap to the story you have been working on.

STEPS

1. **Click the** text box **on page two at** 3" H / 9" V

2. **Click** Format **on the menu bar, then click** Drop Cap
   The Drop Cap dialog box opens, as shown in Figure E-17.

3. **Click the** Custom Drop Cap tab
   You can use this tab to change the default drop cap height, precisely position the drop cap, and adjust other aspects of the drop cap.

4. **Click** Dropped **if necessary, click the** Size of letters down arrow **twice, then compare your dialog box to Figure E-18**

5. **Click** OK, **then press** [F9]
   Compare your work to Figure E-19.

6. **Press** [Esc] **twice, then click the** Save button 🖫 **on the Standard toolbar**
   Your work is saved with the modifications.

Design Matters

Working with Font schemes

Using a font scheme ensures that the fonts in a publication work together to create a well-coordinated result. A font scheme is a defined set of two or more fonts associated with a publication. For example, a font scheme might be made up of one font for headings, one for body text, and another for captions. Font schemes facilitate changing all the fonts in a publication to give it a new look. Within each font scheme, both a major font and a minor font are specified. Generally, a major font is used for titles and headings, and a minor font is used for body text. To use a font scheme, click Format on the menu bar, then click Font Schemes.

FIGURE E-17: Drop Cap dialog box

Indicates plain text

Sample of selected style

List of choices may be different

Removes formatted drop cap style

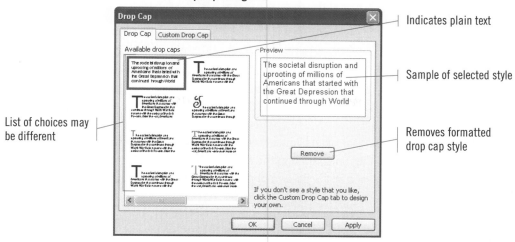

FIGURE E-18: Creating a Custom Drop Cap

Determines the letter's position

Controls the character's height

Sample of the current setting

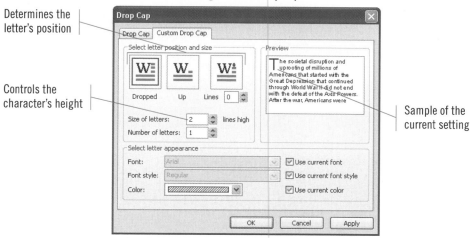

FIGURE E-19: Drop cap added

Drop cap added

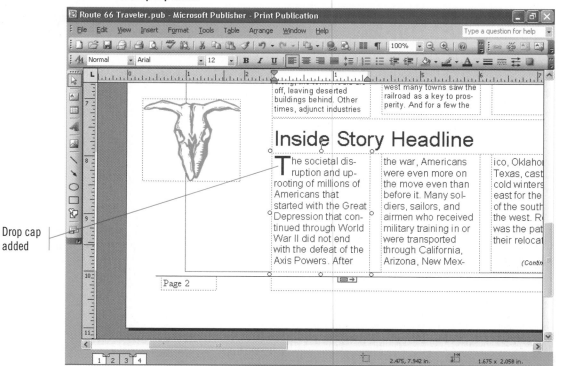

Publisher 2003

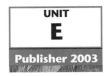

Creating Reversed Text

A great way to emphasize selected text on a page is to create reversed text. **Reversed text** is a formatting effect that changes text from the standard look of dark characters on a light background to the more dramatic look of light characters on a dark background. Although any color combination can be used, it is best to use contrasting colors to ensure readability. In print publications, reversed text is often used in titles and headings because it is eye catching and readable in larger text sizes. In smaller text sizes, reversed text can be more difficult to read, unless you are printing at high resolutions on good quality paper. To create this effect, you change the font color and the fill for the text you want to reverse. You want to format the inside story headline at the bottom of page two as reversed text.

STEPS

1. **Click the** Inside Story Headline text **at** 3" H / 7½" V

2. **Type** The Musical Map of Route 66

    The headline text is replaced.

3. **Press** [Ctrl][A], **click the** Font Color list arrow **on the Formatting toolbar, then click the** Accent 5 (White) option

    The text in the text box seems to disappear. When creating reverse text, the order in which you change the font color or fill color doesn't matter. Regardless of the order, when you create black and white reverse text, at some point, they will both be the same color.

4. **Click the** Fill Color list arrow **on the Formatting toolbar, then click the** Main (Black) option

    The background changes to black.

5. **Press** [Esc] **twice**

    You can see the reversed text effect. Compare your work to Figure E-20.

6. **Press** [F9], **click the** pull quote placeholder **at** 1" H / 3" V, **press** [F9], **then replace the existing text with the sample shown in Figure E-21, making sure Your Name displays**

    You've made good progress on the newsletter, applying many enhancements to the text.

7. **Click the** Save button **on the Standard toolbar, click** File **on the menu bar, click** Print, **then print page two of the newsletter**

8. **Click** File **on the menu bar, then click** Exit

FIGURE E-20: Reversed text

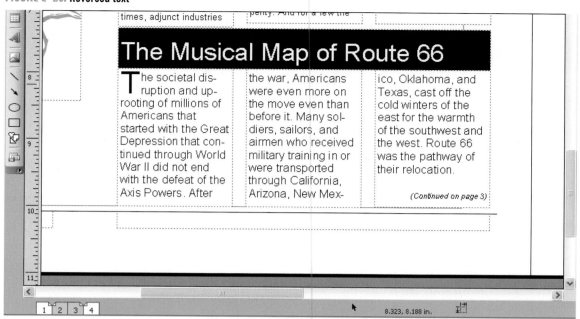

FIGURE E-21: Pull quote text

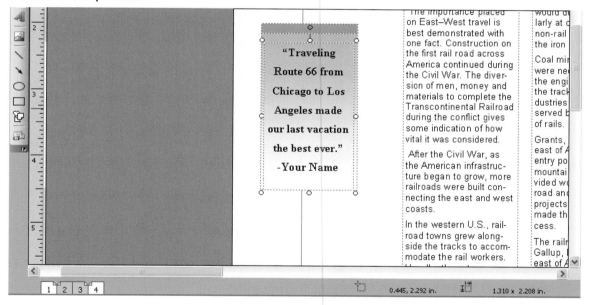

Design Matters

Attracting a reader's attention

Experts recommend that you never use more than three different fonts on a page, and usually suggest that two are enough. So, how do you make your publications attract a reader's attention? Instead of using more fonts, make full use of a limited palette. Use bold and italic versions of your fonts for prominence, and reverse text for a stylized headline. Never underline type, and don't use full capitalization in ordinary text. This was done on typewriters for emphasis when there were no alternatives, but is considered outdated now. With a desktop publishing program, you have the ability to attract readers with a wide variety of tools.

Capstone Project: Solar System Newsletter

You have learned the skills necessary to enhance a publication. You can modify and apply text styles, change a format into a style, create columns, and adjust text overflows. You know how to add continued on/from notices, add drop caps, and create reversed text. Now you will use these skills to add and manipulate text in a newsletter. ▓▓▓▓ You have been asked to produce a sample copy of a newsletter for a group of astronomers. You want to keep the client's objectives in mind: clarity, color, and elegance. You decide to use styles, continued on/from notices, drop caps, and reversed text to enhance the publication and make it easier to read.

STEPS

1. Start Publisher, open the file PUB E-3.pub from the drive and folder where your Data Files are located, then save it as Solar System Newsletter

2. Create a style based on the headline at 3" H / 3½" V, name it Space Headline, apply it to the headline at 3" H / 8½" V, then press [Esc]

3. Click the text box at 3" H / 9" V, insert the text file PUB E-4.doc, click No when asked if you want to use autoflow, then adjust the text overflow to fill the two empty columns on page two

4. Add Continued on and Continued from text to the inserted story

5. Add custom drop caps to the first paragraphs of both stories on page one with two-line high letters

6. Reverse the text in the headline at 3" H / 2" V using Accent 5 (White) for the text and Accent 1 (RGB(204, 102, 51)) for the fill

   You like the way the newsletter looks. You made it easy to read, consistent, and emphasized key text.

7. Replace the pull quote at 1" H / 4½" V on page one with Your Name, save your work, then print page one

   Compare your work to Figure E-22.

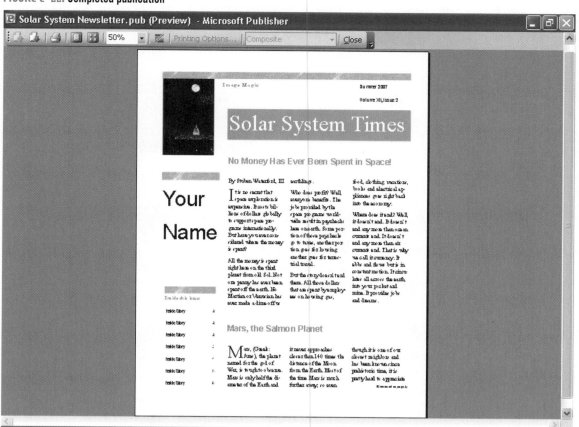

Practice

Label each of the elements in the Publisher window shown in Figure E-23.

FIGURE E-23

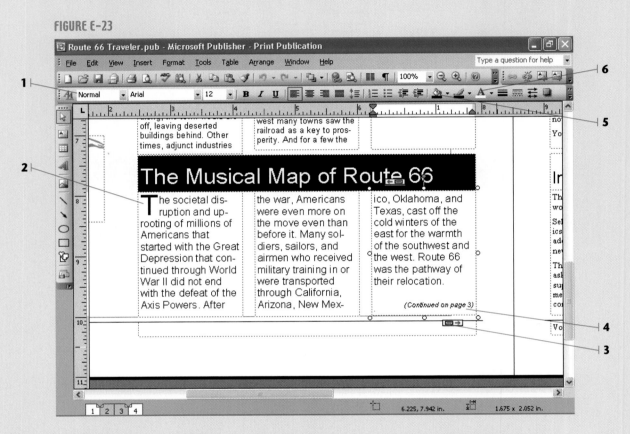

Match each of the buttons or pointers with the statement that describes its function.

7.

8.

9.

10.

11.

12.

a. Pouring pointer

b. Pitcher pointer

c. Go to Next Text Box button

d. Text in Overflow button

e. Go to Previous Text Box button

f. Create Text Box Link button

Select the best answer from the list of choices.

13. Changing a format into a style is called:
- **a.** Format stylization.
- **b.** Creating a style by example.
- **c.** Styling a format.
- **d.** Creating a format master.

14. Once you click the Connect Text Box button, the pointer looks like:
- **a.**
- **b.** ⌖
- **c.** 🔲
- **d.** A ···

15. Select the entire contents of a text box by pressing:
- **a.** [Shift][A]
- **b.** [Alt][A]
- **c.** [Ctrl][A]
- **d.** [Esc][A]

16. Which button indicates the existence of overflow text?
- **a.** A ···
- **b.** 🔗
- **c.** ↩
- **d.** ↻

17. Which dialog box is used to create Continued on/from notices?
- **a.** Continued Notices
- **b.** Notices
- **c.** Frame Formatting
- **d.** Format Text Box

18. Adjusting the spacing between a pair of characters is called:
- **a.** Spacing.
- **b.** Kerning.
- **c.** Fonting.
- **d.** Adjusting.

19. Which pointer do you use to flow overflow text into a different text box?
- **a.** ⌄
- **b.** ⌖
- **c.** 🔖
- **d.** ⌖

20. Which button takes you to the next text box?
- **a.** [text] →
- **b.** 🔗
- **c.** ← [text]
- **d.** 🔲

21. In which dialog box can you change the spacing of columns in a text box?
- **a.** Text Box Characteristics
- **b.** Columns in Text box
- **c.** Columns
- **d.** Text Box Formatting

22. In which dialog box can you add, modify, or remove a drop cap?
- **a.** Drop Cap
- **b.** Format Text Box
- **c.** Fancy First Letter
- **d.** Spacing Between Characters

▼ SKILLS REVIEW

1. Define styles.
- **a.** Start Publisher.
- **b.** Use the Publication Gallery to create a new newsletter. Select the Southwest Newsletter design, then use the Secondary Business Information set and the Sunset color scheme.
- **c.** Save the file as Guanajuato Newsletter to the drive and folder where your Data Files are located.
- **d.** Create a new text style that is 18 point Franklin Gothic Demi, left-aligned.
- **e.** Name the new style Southwest Headline.
- **f.** Save your work.

2. Apply and Modify a style.

   a. Click the 2-3 page icon, then apply the Southwest Headline style to the inside story headline at 3" H / 7¾" V.

   b. Return to page one of the newsletter.

   c. Change the font size of the Southwest Headline style to 20 point.

   d. Change the effect of the Southwest Headline style to Shadow.

   e. Apply the Southwest Headline style to the Secondary Story Headline on page one.

   f. Save your work.

3. Change a format into a style.

   a. Click the Lead Story Headline on page one. Use the Style box to create a style called **Amigos Headline** that uses the same formatting.

   b. Apply the Amigos Headline style to the Inside Story Headline on page three at 10" H / 7¾" V.

   c. Save your work.

4. Create columns.

   a. Open the Page Content task pane.

   b. Change the number of columns on the left inside page to a mixed-column layout, then close the task pane.

   c. Save the publication.

5. Adjust text overflows.

   a. Select the text box on page two at 3" H / 2" V, then delete the text.

   b. Above the empty text box, select the Inside Story Headline on page two and change it to **Guanajuato Rocks**.

   c. Select the text box on page three at 10" H / 6" V, then delete the text.

   d. Select the Inside Story Headline on page three at 10" H / 5" V, then change it to **Guanajuato Rocks**.

   e. Select the Lead Story Headline text on page one at 2½" H / 3" V, then change it to **Guanajuato Rocks**.

   f. Delete the text from the text box on page one at 3" H / 4" V and insert the text file PUB E-5.doc. Do not use autoflow.

   g. Click the Create Text Box Link button, then flow the text into the empty text box on page two.

   h. Click the Create Text Box Link button, then flow the remaining text into the empty text box on page three.

   i. Save the publication.

6. Add Continued on/from notices.

   a. Add a Continued on notice in the third column text box in the **Guanajuato Rocks** story on page one.

   b. Click the Go to Next Text Box button, then add a Continued from notice and a Continued on notice in the single column of the Guanajuato Rocks story on page two.

   c. Click the Go to Next Text Box button, then add a Continued from notice in the first column of the Guanajuato Rocks story on page three.

   d. Save the publication.

7. Add drop caps.

   a. Click anywhere in the first paragraph of the Guanajuato Rocks story on page one.

   b. Create a custom first letter drop cap three lines high, using the default font.

   c. Save your work.

8. Create reversed text.

   a. Select the contents of the Newsletter Title on page one at 1" H / 1½" V and replace it with the name **Guanajuato**.

   b. Change the font color to the color of your choosing.

   c. Change the fill color to the color of your choosing.

   d. Replace the text "Special Points of Interest" on page one at 1" H / 6¾" V with your name.

    e. Print pages one through three of the publication.

    f. Save your work.

    g. Exit Publisher.

▼ INDEPENDENT CHALLENGE 1

A local investment company, Finance Wizardry, wants to hold monthly seminars to make people feel more comfortable with financial instruments. They have hired you to create a brochure that announces these free seminars. You decide to use the Publication Gallery to create the brochure and start planning some of the brochure style elements.

    a. Start Publisher, if necessary, then create a new publication using the Slant Event Brochure from the Publication Gallery. Use the Personal Information set of your choosing to enter placeholder information.

    b. Change the color scheme to Parrot.

    c. Save the publication as **Finance Wizardry Brochure** to the drive and folder where your Data Files are located.

    d. Create a style called **Main Heading** that uses a 14 point Arial italic font and is center-aligned.

    e. Apply the Main Heading style to the Main Inside Heading at 1" H / ¾" V on page two.

    f. Select the story at 1" H / 4½" V and add a two-line custom drop cap.

    g. On page one, replace the text in the text box at 9" H / 4" V with the name **Finance Wizardry**.

    h. Create a reversed text effect in the text box at 9" H / 1¾" V. Change the text to the Accent 5 (white) color. Change the fill to the Main (black) color.

    i. Substitute your name for the business name at 5" H / 6½" V.

    j. Save and print both pages of the publication.

    k. Exit Publisher.

▼ INDEPENDENT CHALLENGE 2

To attract new homebuyers and businesses, the Chamber of Commerce hires you to create an informational Web site about your community. This Web site will be available to anyone seeking information about your community.

    a. Start Publisher, if necessary, then open the file PUB E-6.doc from the drive and folder where your Data Files are located.

    b. Change the color scheme to Meadow.

    c. Save the publication as **Community Promotion Web Site** to the drive and folder where your Data Files are located.

    d. Create a style by example called **Homepage Headline** based on the Our Home Town Home Page Headline.

    e. Apply the new style to the "A Great Place To Live" headline.

    f. Use your word processor to write a four- to six-paragraph story about what you like about your community. Save this story as **A Great Place**.

    g. Delete the text in the text boxes at 2" H / 5½" V and 2" H / 2" V.

    h. Insert the "A Great Place" text file into the text box at 2" H / 2" V. Do not use autoflow.

    i. Pour the overflow text from the first text box into the second text box at 2" H / 5½" V.

    j. Add a two-line-high drop cap to the first paragraph of your story.

    k. Substitute your name for the e-mail address at the bottom of the page.

    l. Replace the text in the text box at 2½" H / 1¼" V with your city and state.

    m. Save and print the publication.

    n. Exit Publisher.

▼ INDEPENDENT CHALLENGE 3

Your school wants to hold a fund-raiser for the local homeless shelter. You volunteered to create this flyer and choose the type of fund-raising activity.

    a. Start Publisher, if necessary, use the Mobile Fund-raiser Flyer from the Publisher Gallery to create a new publication. Use the Personal Information set of your choosing to enter placeholder information of your choosing.

    b. Change to the color scheme of your choice.

    c. Save the publication as **Homeless Shelter Flyer** to the drive and folder where your Data Files are located.

    d. Decide on a title for your fund-raiser, then enter it in the text box at 2" H / 2" V.

    e. Make up your own text describing the event for the text box at 5" H / 5" V.

    f. Create a new style called **Fundraiser Text** using 14 point Times New Roman, right-aligned.

    g. Apply this style to the text box at 5" H / 5" V.

    h. Substitute your name for the e-mail address at 1" H / 8½" V.

    i. Enter the time and date of the fundraiser in the text box at 1" H / 5½" V.

Advanced Challenge Exercises

    ■ Apply the Deckle font scheme.

    ■ Adjust the spacing between two letters in your flyer's title by 80%. Compare your publication to Figure E-24.

    j. Save and print the publication.

    k. Exit Publisher.

FIGURE E-24

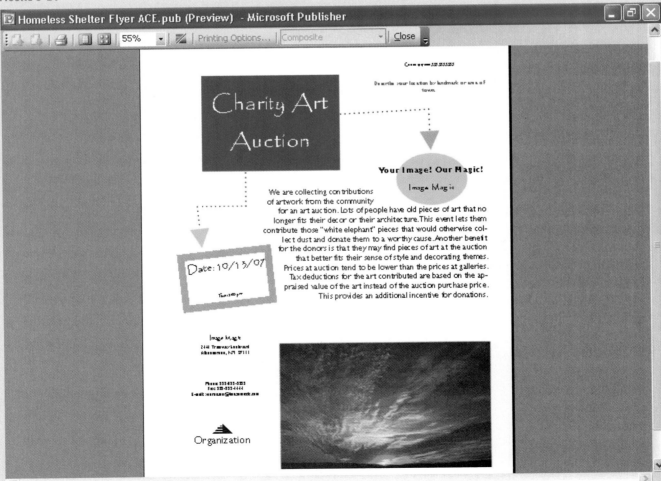

▼ INDEPENDENT CHALLENGE 4

BBB Road Club is organizing a bus trip to see the leaves change in New England during late September and October. They have asked you to design a promotional brochure for this event. Before you design this brochure, you want to use the Internet to find out more about the New England countryside and its foliage.

a. Connect to the Internet, then use your browser and favorite search engine to find information about the New England countryside and its foliage. Find out what towns and attractions might be of interest when the leaves are changing.

b. Start Publisher, if necessary, use the Profile Informational Brochure from the Publisher Gallery. Use the Personal Information set of your choice.

c. Change to the color scheme of your choice.

d. Save the publication as **New England Foliage Brochure** to the drive and folder where your Data Files are located.

e. Use the information you obtained from the Internet to write a four- to six-paragraph document about what to see and do in New England using a word processor program. Save this document to drive and folder where your Data files are located as **New England Attractions**.

f. Replace any default text with text about New England.

g. Choose two locations on different pages for the New England Attractions document. Create additional text boxes if necessary.

h. Delete any placeholder text from the text boxes, then flow the story into the text boxes.

i. Add drop caps to the beginning of each paragraph, and add to/from continued notices where appropriate.

j. Substitute your name for the e-mail address on page two of the publication.

Advanced Challenge Exercises

- Remove the drop caps from all but the initial paragraph on page 2.
- Change the style of the continued on/from notices using the style by example method. (Use a Bold Arial 7-point font. Name the new style "New Continued-On Text". You can also create a new continued from style called "New Continued-From Text".) Compare your publication to Figure E-25.

k. Print the publication.

l. Save the publication.

m. Exit Publisher.

FIGURE E-25

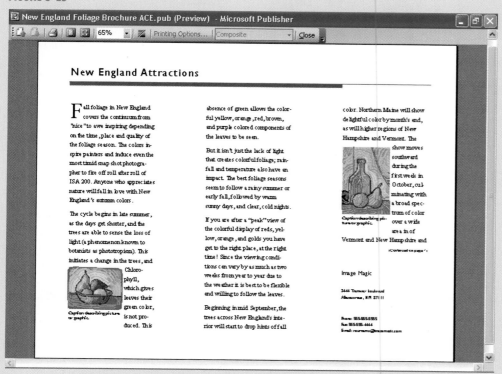

Open the file PUB E-7.pub from the drive and folder where your Data Files are located. Save this publication as **SW Brochure**. Using Figure E-26 as a guide, modify the styles and add additional formatting as necessary so your publication matches the one shown. Save the publication, then print it.

FIGURE E-26

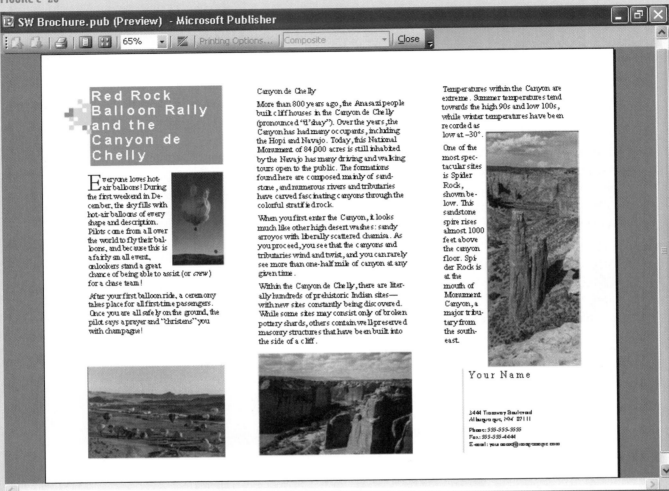

Improving a Design

OBJECTIVES

Critique a publication

Strengthen publication text

Rearrange elements

Modify objects

Refine a page

Experiment with design elements

Capstone Project: Flower Shop Flyer

You can be proficient at using features and tools in Publisher, but in order to create an attractive, professional publication you also need to focus on its design. **Design** involves the selection, formatting, and placement of elements on a page, as well as coordinating the elements throughout all pages within a publication. You can resize and reposition elements to make them more effective and better convey the message of your publication. The non-profit organization, Global Parenting, is an Image Magic client. You have been assigned the task of reviewing their in-house monthly newsletter and improving its design.

Critiquing a Publication

Casting a critical eye toward someone's work can be challenging for both the reviewer and the designer. Some of us feel uncomfortable criticizing someone else's work, and even more uncomfortable when that criticism is directed at our own work. But when done constructively, critiquing can be a positive learning experience for everyone involved. Many of us learn best by having our mistakes pointed out, and then making corrections. While design is a highly subjective process, there are some fundamental principles that can be applied to any critiquing process. Examining the strengths and weaknesses of another person's work can be a helpful method of refining a publication so that it looks professional and achieves its goals. It can also help you develop a more constructive eye toward your own designs. As you learn to critique designs, you may find that the most effective designs are the simplest. ▰▰▰▰ You are ready to review the client's in-house monthly newsletter, *Concerned Parent*. You open the publication shown in Figure F-1 and think about the critiquing process:

DETAILS

QUICK TIP

Remember that you can be critical of a person's work without being critical of that person. When evaluating someone else's work or listening to criticism of your own, keep this distinction in mind.

- **Take in all the elements**

  To get started, ask yourself a series of questions that determines the purpose of a particular page, and the arrangement of elements that helps you achieve that goal. These questions include: To what elements are your eyes drawn? Where is the text? Is the text legible? Are any/all of the elements on the page necessary? Are any elements distracting? In Figure F-1, your eyes may be drawn to the central graphic and the blue text box because they are colorful, and because of their size and position. Unfortunately, the text in the blue box is illegible, and the caption above and below the central graphic is broken up, which makes it difficult to read and comprehend the safety message. Also, the elongated table of contents distracts the eye from the image of the children and the crossing guard.

- **Decide what is important**

  Every publication has a goal, and each page should support that overall goal. While the goal of this issue of *Concerned Parent* is children and safety, the goal of a particular page may be getting readers to read the executive director's article on the topic. During the critiquing process, you should continually ask yourself whether the design achieves the goal—and if not, why not. What's getting in the way? What needs to be changed, removed, or strengthened to reach your audience and guide them toward important information?

- **Share the message with the reader**

  As the designer, your focus is on assembling various visual elements—graphic images, text, or tables—that share the message with the reader. Figure F-2 shows a preliminary rearrangement of the cover elements. In this design, the central element is the children and the crossing guard. This graphic has been cropped to eliminate unnecessary imagery. By rearranging the elements on the page, the message of children and safety is featured more prominently. The use of white space and elimination or refining of distracting elements, such as the blue text box and the table of contents, force the reader's eye to focus on the central image.

- **Keep it simple**

  Microsoft Publisher offers so many exciting and interesting design elements that it's often tempting to use as many graphics, Word Art, borders, etc., as possible. Such overindulgence can lead to a cluttered, ineffective design that will not help readers see the whole message, and they may miss the point entirely. It's usually best to choose a few key elements that convey the message, then feature those items prominently. In the redesigned cover, there is only one central design object. The reader is free to read the text beneath the image, but it is not necessary to understanding the safety message.

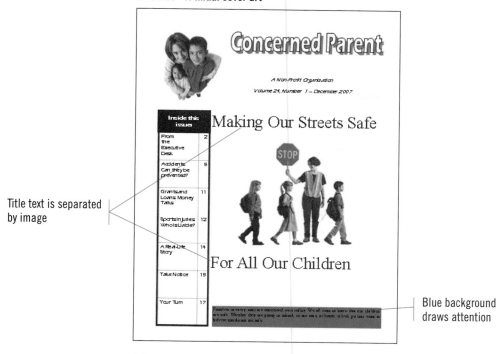

Title text is separated by image

Blue background draws attention

FIGURE F-2: Revised cover art

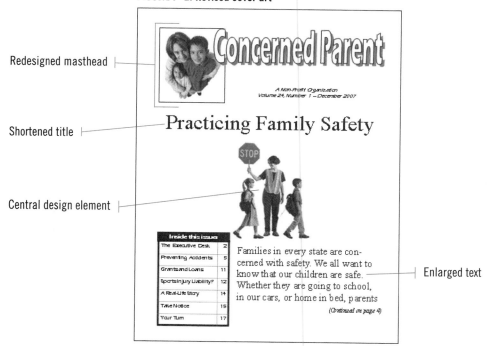

Redesigned masthead

Shortened title

Central design element

Enlarged text

Clues to Use

Using diplomacy

How do you tell people that their work could use some improvement? People's designs are a reflection of their own opinions about what makes an effective and attractive publication. Therefore, it isn't easy to tell people why and how their publications could be improved, and you must be sensitive to their feelings when delivering feedback. You may be able to minimize hurting someone's feelings by involving the person whose work you're critiquing in the solution phase. If you make the changes yourself, or instruct someone else to, not only will you create friction in the workplace, but the original author may be offended, and will have learned nothing in the process. By working with people to help them revise their work, they will benefit from maintaining control over it, and will learn some important design concepts in the process.

Strengthening Publication Text

Most newsletters feature a **masthead**, an arrangement of text and graphic elements that provide important information about the publication. A masthead contains important information that rarely changes, such as the newsletter's title. The only changing information in a masthead is the issue information, such as the publication month, or the number and volume. The masthead is generally featured prominently, and provides a first impression of the publication. When fine-tuning a design, you may find you need to use a mask. A **mask** is an object designed to hide a specific area so that the final result looks seamless. You've found several elements to improve in the newsletter. First, you want to modify the masthead so the graphic and text create a stronger, more unified impression. To achieve this, you want the title to be more prominent, and to overlap slightly with the graphic. You want to call more attention to the graphic with a border, and realize you'll need to mask part of the border to combine all the elements smoothly.

STEPS

1. **Start Publisher, open the file** PUB F-1.pub **from the drive and folder where your Data Files are located, then save it as** Concerned Parent Newsletter

QUICK TIP

Use the horizontal and vertical scroll bars to center the masthead on the screen if necessary.

2. **Click the** text box **at 4" H / 2½" V, press [F9], then close the task pane if necessary**

3. **Position** ⌖ **over the** upper-center handle, **click and drag** ↕ **to 2½" V, click the** blank line **above the first line of text, press [Delete], click the** blank line **beneath the text** A Non-Profit Organization, **press [Delete], then press [Esc] twice**

   The text box containing the issue information has been resized and is now in better proportion to the elements around it, as shown in Figure F-3.

TROUBLE

If the WordArt toolbar opens, close it by clicking the Close button.

4. **Click the** WordArt object **at 4" H / 1" V, position** ⌖ **over the** lower-center handle, **click and drag** ↕ **to 1¾" V, position** ⌖ **over the** left-center handle, **then click and drag** ↔ **to 2¼" H**

   The title is larger and partially obscured by the graphic image, as shown in Figure F-4.

5. **Click the** Bring to Front button 🔲 **on the Standard toolbar**

   The newsletter title appears to overlap part of the image.

6. **Right-click the** image **at 2" H / 2" V, click** Format Picture, **click the** Colors and Lines tab, **click the** Line Color list arrow, **click the** black color box (the first box), **then click** OK

   The masthead image is surrounded by a black outline. The black outline visible between the "C" and the "o" in the title can be hidden using a mask.

7. **Click the** Rectangle button 🔲 **on the Objects toolbar, drag** ✛ **from 2⁹⁄₁₆" H / ¹¹⁄₁₆" V to 2¾" H / 1¼" V (use the position coordinates 2.563" H / 0.688" V to start the mask)**

8. **Right-click the** rectangle, **click** Format AutoShape, **click the** Line Color list arrow, **click** No Line, **click the** Fill Color list arrow, **click the** white color box (the eighth box), **click** OK, **click the** Bring to Front list arrow 🔲▾, **then click** Send Backward

   The rectangle was formatted to blend into the background, and is positioned between the text and the graphic image.

9. **Press [Esc] to deselect the rectangle, then click the** Save button 🔲 **on the Standard toolbar**

   Compare your masthead to Figure F-5.

FIGURE F-3: Resized text box

Smaller text box reflects decreased importance

FIGURE F-4: Enlarged title

Masthead text partially hidden

FIGURE F-5: Redesigned masthead

Mask hides part of the border

Design Matters

Examine the components

As it can be overwhelming to critique an entire publication, you may find it helpful to examine its individual components. In the case of a newsletter cover, the components include the masthead, the artwork and text, and the table of contents. Within the masthead, you can consider the size, appearance, and placement of the newsletter title, and artwork, and the size and placement of other text boxes.

On inside pages, the elements can include the number of stories, related artwork, and the surrounding white space. When viewed in their entirety, it can be difficult to spot specific strengths and weaknesses. But looking at them individually can make it easier to locate and refine problem areas, so that the end result is a cohesive, powerful publication.

Rearranging Elements

The appearance of elements on a page is important, but of equal importance is the way in which the elements are arranged. The components of any page should form a cohesive unit so that the reader is unaware of all the different parts, yet influenced by the way they work together to emphasize a message or reveal information. For example, if a large image is used, it should be easy for the reader to connect the image with any descriptive text. There should be an easily understood connection between the text and the artwork, and the reader should be able to seamlessly connect them. ▰▰▱▱▱ You want to rearrange the elements so that the Table of Contents is smaller and the title for the story on page 1 is more concise and eye-catching.

STEPS

1. **Press [F9], click the** table **at** 1" H / 3½" V, **then drag the top-center sizing handle ↕ to** 7⅜" V
   The table is reduced in size, which opens up the left side of the page.

2. **Right-click the** text box **that reads "For All Our Children" at** 4" H / 8½" V, **then click Delete Object**
   Compare your screen to Figure F-6.

3. **Click the** text box **that reads "Making Our Streets Safe" at** 3" H / 3½" V, **then use ↔ to drag the** left-center handle **to** ½" H

4. **Click anywhere in the text box, press** [Ctrl][A], **click the** Font Size list arrow ▭ **on the Formatting toolbar, then click** 48
   The text is selected and enlarged. The location of this text is now at the optical center of the page. The **optical center** occurs approximately three-eighths from the top of the page and is the point around which objects on the page are balanced.

5. **Type** Practicing Family Safety, **click the** Center button ▤ **on the Formatting toolbar, then press** [Esc] **twice**
   The title is centered and better expresses the message of the cover. Compare your work to Figure F-7.

6. **Click the** Save button ▤ **on the Standard toolbar**

FIGURE F-6: **Text box deleted**

Text box
removed
from beneath
image

FIGURE F-7: **Title text completed**

Optical center
containing
centered text

Design Matters

Overcoming the fear of white space

What is the most important difference between the file open now and the one opened at the beginning of this unit? White space. The best example of the use of white space is margins surrounding a page. This white space acts as a visual barrier—a resting place for the eyes. Without white space, the words on a page would crowd into each other, and the effect would be a cluttered, ugly page. This technique makes it possible for you to guide the reader's eye from one location on the page to another. One of the first design hurdles that must be overcome is the irresistible urge to put too much *stuff* on a page. When you are new to design, you may want to fill each page completely. Remember, less is more. Think of white space as a beautiful frame setting off an equally beautiful image.

Modifying Objects

Once the optical center is located, objects can be positioned around it. A page can have a symmetrical or asymmetrical balance relative to an imaginary vertical line in the center of the page. In a **symmetrical balance**, objects are placed equally on either side of the vertical line. This type of layout tends toward a restful, formal design. In an asymmetrical balance, objects are placed unequally relative to the vertical line. **Asymmetrical balance** uses white space to balance the positioned objects, and is more dynamic and informal. A page with objects arranged asymmetrically tends to provide more visual interest because it is more surprising in appearance. ▰▰▰▱▱ You want to balance the few objects on the page using an asymmetrical layout. You want to crop the image and rearrange a few elements to make better use of the white space. You begin by zooming into the image on the page.

STEPS

1. **Click the object at** 5" H / 5" V, **then click the** Zoom In button 🔍 **on the Formatting toolbar until the Zoom factor is** 66%

   The image containing the crossing guard is selected, and the Picture toolbar appears.

2. **Click the** Crop button 🔲 **on the Picture toolbar, position** 🔧 **over the left-center handle, drag** ⊣ **to** 4⅛" H **as shown in Figure F-8, release the mouse button, then click** 🔲

   The little girl on the left is no longer visible. The object handles reappeared when the cropping tool was turned off.

3. **Position** ⬚ **over the selected object, press and hold** [Shift], **drag the** selected object **so its left edge is at** 3" H, **release** [Shift], **click the** Send Backward list arrow 🔲▾ **on the Standard toolbar, click** Send to Back, **then press** [Esc]

   The object is centered on the page, and the Picture toolbar is no longer visible. Holding [Shift] while you moved the object maintained the vertical measurement as you changed the horizontal position.

4. **Click the** Zoom Out button 🔍 **on the Formatting toolbar until the Zoom factor is** 50%, **click the** text box at 5" H / 10" V, **position** ⬚ **over the** upper-left handle, **then drag** ↖ **to** 3⅛" H / 7¾" V

5. **Press** [Ctrl][A], **click the** Format **on the menu bar, point to** AutoFit Text, **then click** Best Fit

   The text is readable.

6. **Click the** Fill Color list arrow 🔲▾ **on the Formatting toolbar, then click the** Accent 4 (RGB(204, 204, 204)) **color box**

   The background is now a light gray, making the text box easy to read.

7. **Click the** Zoom list arrow 51% ▾ **on the Formatting toolbar, click** Whole Page, **then click** [Esc] **twice**

   Compare your publication to Figure F-9.

8. **Click the** table at 1" H / 9" V, **use** ↔ **to drag the right-center handle to** 3" H, **then press** [Esc]

   The table width is increased, making it easier to read. Your screen should look like Figure F-10.

9. **Click the** Save button 💾 **on the Standard toolbar**

FIGURE F-8: Image cropped

Cropping pointer

FIGURE F-9: Text box improved

Text enlarged and blue background changed to gray

FIGURE F-10: Objects moved and resized

Title reworded and centered

Image cropped and moved

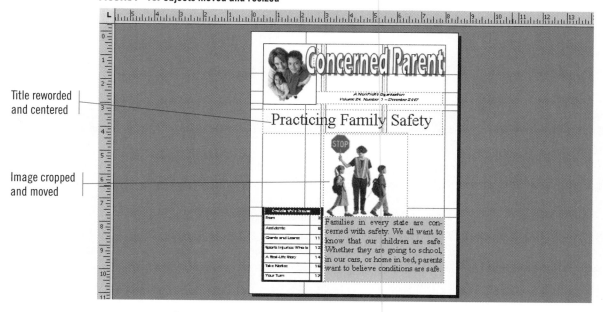

Refining a Page

The goal of page design is getting readers to read each story. Pages that contain nothing but text can overwhelm the reader, causing them to quit reading before the story is finished. To encourage readers to keep reading, you can break up the monotony of a large story with art and other elements. You can also split a story into multiple text boxes on two or more pages. ▰▰▰ The Executive Director of *Concerned Parent* wrote an important article that will be featured in this issue. The current layout has this story occupying the entire page. You decide to refine this page by adding vertical lines between the columns, splitting the story onto multiple pages, and formatting the story with a drop cap.

STEPS

1. **Click the** Page 2 icon, **click the** Line button ◥ **on the Objects toolbar, press and hold** [Shift], **drag** ✛ **from** 3" H / 1½" V **to** 3" H / 10" V, **then release** [Shift]

    Pressing [Shift] assures that the line is straight. The vertical line between the two columns provides a visual boundary that makes the column text easier to read.

TROUBLE

Before dragging a selected object, reposition the pointer until ⌖ appears, or the object will not be copied.

2. **Press and hold** [Ctrl] [Shift], **position** ⌖ **over the** selected object, **click the** left mouse button, **drag** ⌖ **to** 5½" H / 1½" V, **release the mouse button, then release** [Ctrl] [Shift]

    Compare your page to Figure F-11.

QUICK TIP

Distributing story text in columns and chunks across a page can open up the design and can provide visual relief from too much text.

3. **Click the** text box at 7" H / 9" V, **position** ⌖ **over the** bottom-center handle, **then drag** ↕ **to** 3" V

    The majority of column 3 is now available, as shown in Figure F-12. At a later date, you may want to include another story, an advertisement, or a graphic image in this space.

4. **Click the** text box at 2" H / 2" V, **click** Format **on the menu bar, then click** Drop Cap

    The Drop Cap dialog box opens.

5. **Click the** first choice **below the current selection, then click** OK

    The drop cap appears in the first paragraph of the story. The addition of this feature caused the text to be slightly rearranged, but because there are no other elements on this page, the effect on the current layout is not important.

6. **Press** [Esc] **twice to deselect the text box, then click the Save button** 🖫 **on the Standard toolbar**

    Compare your publication to Figure F-13.

Design Matters

Working with advertisements

Publications often depend on advertising dollars to defray costs and increase profits. So it's in a publisher's interest to display ads in a manner that will gain the greatest exposure. That's one reason stories usually are not laid out in one continuous text box, with ads lumped together in another section. If a reader turns through several pages to finish reading a story, he or she is more likely to see the ads that are interspersed with editorial content. This means that advertising artwork can become an integral part of page layout. Your advertisers and your readers want clever, attractive ads that potential clients will remember. In many cases, your advertisers will give you camera-ready artwork. This artwork is complete and only needs to be included in the layout. The good news is that you don't have to do the work of designing the ad. The bad news is that you often have no say in terms of the ad's appearance or design values. In most publications, the cost of running an advertisement is determined by size, color, and placement on the page.

FIGURE F-11: **Vertical lines between columns**

Lines provide visual boundary between columns

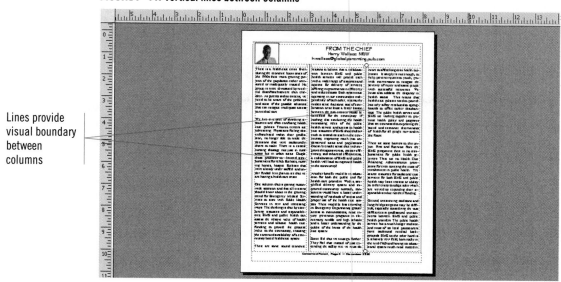

FIGURE F-12: **Text box shortened**

Additional elements can be placed here

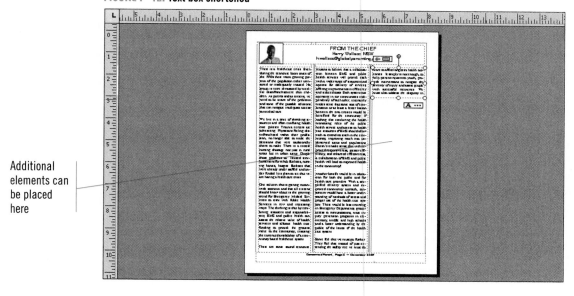

FIGURE F-13: **Drop cap added**

Experimenting with Design Elements

Solving layout problems often requires experimentation. Design elements should guide the reader from story to story, without providing unnecessary distractions. Some design elements, such as a relevant graphic image, or an interesting advertisement, can provide a nice mental break. Among the elements you can use to enhance the layout of a page are pictures, drop caps, and pull quotes. It's hard to say which element will best improve a particular page; sometimes you must experiment with a variety of elements and configurations until you find the layout that works. You want to experiment with several design elements to see which ones look most effective in the new space in column 3. In order to generate the reader's interest, you want to extract a compelling sentence from the story, modify it slightly, then use it as a pull quote. Also, this page seems to need some color so you want to include a health-related graphic image. The previous designer placed a piece of clip art on page 5 that you think will complement this article.

STEPS

1. **Click the** Design Gallery Object button 🖼 **on the Objects toolbar, click** Pull Quotes **in the categories list, click the** Bars Pull Quote, **then click** Insert Object
   The pull quote is inserted on the page.

2. **Using** ⬚, **move the selected** pull quote **until the upper-left corner of the object is at 2" H / 3" V, then press** [F9]

3. **Click the** center of the pull quote, **type** "No group is more devastated by the lack of medical attention than children.", **press** [F9], **then press** [Esc]
   Compare your page to Figure F-14. The text box is still selected, but you're not sure you like the effect of this element on the page because the page still looks busy.

4. **Use** ⬚ **to drag the pull quote to** 10" H / 3" V **on the scratch area**
   The object can be used later, if necessary.

5. **Click the** Page 5 icon, **click the image at** 7" H / 9" V, **click the** Copy button 📋 **on the Standard toolbar, then click the** page 2 icon
   The clip art is on the Clipboard, and can be placed on page two.

6. **Click the** Paste button 📋 **on the Standard toolbar, then use** ⬚ **to drag the image so that its** upper-left corner **is at** 2" H / 4" V
   The image is placed in a slightly lower location occupied by the pull quote, as shown in Figure F-15. You feel that the graphic image adds a splash of color to the page and looks more inviting than the pull quote. This page is far from finished, but you are done working on it for now.

7. **Click the text box at** 4" H / 1" V, **press** [F9], **replace Henry Wallace with** Your Name, **press** [Esc] **twice, then press** [F9]

TROUBLE
If prompted, do not save the items on the Clipboard.

8. **Click the** Save button 💾 **on the Standard toolbar, print pages one and two, then exit Publisher**

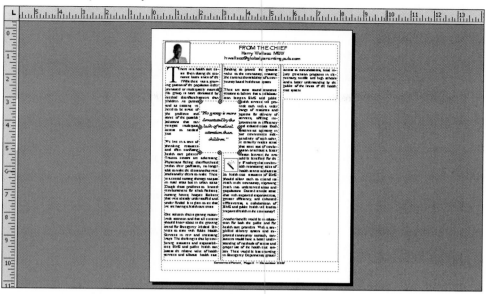

Artwork in story

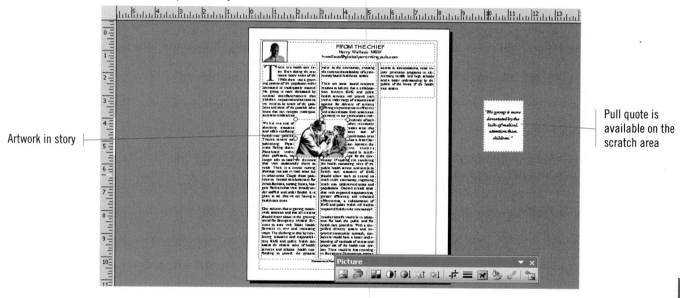

Pull quote is available on the scratch area

Design Matters

Using contrast to add emphasis

Contrast is an important design principle that provides variety in the physical layout of a page and publication. Just as you can use a font attribute to make some text stand out from the rest, you can use contrasting elements to make certain graphic objects stand out. You can create contrast in many ways: by changing the sizes of objects; by varying object weights, such as making a line heavier surrounding an image; by altering the position of an object, such as changing the location on the page, or rotating the image so it is positioned on an angle; by drawing attention-getting shapes or a colorful box behind an object that makes it stand out (called a **matte**); or by adding carefully selected colors that emphasize an object.

Capstone Project: Flower Shop Flyer

You have learned how to critique a publication, strengthen publication text to grab your reader's attention, rearrange elements so they work together effectively, and work with objects and page layouts to create a professional publication. ▰▰▰ You are asked by the owner of a flower shop to critique a problematic flyer. The flyer is for a newly opened flower shop, and the owner wants to offer a 40% discount on perennials during the grand opening celebration. The initial publication is colorful, but it is disorganized and fails to promote the discount. In critiquing the flyer, you find that the border of roses distracts from the text and central object in the flyer. Instead of having many images of flowers, you think it might be more dramatic to make one image the focal point of the flyer. You also think that the text at the top of the flyer is too long and poorly aligned. The name of the shop should stand out more, and you think using WordArt could help achieve this. You start improving this design by removing the border of roses.

STEPS

1. **Start Publisher, open the file** PUB F-2.pub **from the drive and folder where your Data Files are located, then save it as** Flower Shop Flyer

   Compare your screen to Figure F-16.

2. **Click the** graphic object **at** 7" H / 4" V, **then press** [Delete]

3. **Click the** tulips **at** 5" H / 5" V, **press and hold** [Ctrl], **then use** ↖ **to drag the upper-left sizing handle up and to the left until the sizing handle snaps to the ruler guides at** 1½" H / 2½" V

4. **Click the** text box **at** 4" H / 7" V, **use** ↖ **to drag the object so that its upper-left corner is at the guides at** 1" H / 8" V, **select the** date and time text, **click the** Bold button **B** **on the Formatting toolbar, change the font size of the selected text to** 20, **then press** [Esc]

   The repositioned text box and the contrasting text are more attractive.

5. **Click the** text box **at** 2" H / 2" V, **press** [Ctrl][A] **to select the text, type** Your Name's Flowers, **press** [Enter], **then type** Grand Opening and Sale

6. **Press** [Ctrl][A], **click the** Center button ≣ **on the Formatting toolbar, select the text** Your Name's Flowers, **click the** Font Size list arrow ⬚ ▾ **on the Formatting toolbar, then click** 48

   The text now looks balanced, and the name of the shop is more prominent.

7. **Click the** Rectangle button ▭ **on the Objects toolbar, create a shape from** 1" H / 1" V **to** 7½" H / 8" V, **click the** Dash Style button ▦ **on the Formatting toolbar, click** No Line, **click the** Fill Color list arrow ⬚ ▾ **on the Formatting toolbar, click the** third color box from the left, **click the** Send to Back button ⬚ **on the Standard toolbar, then press** [Esc]

8. **Click the** Design Gallery Object button ⬚ **on the Objects toolbar, click** Coupons, **click** Open Background Coupon **if necessary, click** Insert Object, **modify the text to advertise** Featured Perennials **at** 40% OFF, **with the flower shop name and address shown in the flyer, then modify the size and placement of the object as shown in Figure F-17**

   Your design changes have resulted in a stronger flyer that is sure to capture the attention of potential customers.

9. **Save your work, print the publication, then exit Publisher**

FIGURE F-16: **Existing flyer**

FIGURE F-17: **Modified flyer**

Practice

Identify the design flaw in each element in Figure F-18.

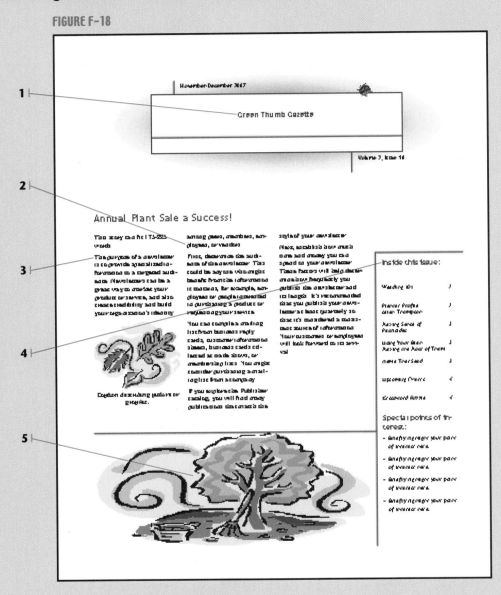

FIGURE F-18

Match each of the design flaws noted below with a solution.

6. Stories that span several pages have no reference to where the next part of the story is located

7. Too many design elements on the page

8. Columns of text run together

9. The publication looks monotonous and boring

a. Add contrast, such as a matte, to the publication

b. Increase the amount of white space

c. Insert continued on/continued from notices

d. Add a visual boundary

Select the best answer from the list of choices.

10. Objects placed equally on either side of an imaginary vertical line in the center of the page is called:
    a. Asymmetrical objectivity.
    b. Asymmetrical balance.
    c. Symmetrical balance.
    d. Symmetrical positioning.

11. A consistent arrangement of text and graphic elements that appears at the top of each issue of a publication is called a:
    a. Mask.
    b. Matte.
    c. Masthead.
    d. Mark.

12. The optical center occurs where on the page?
    a. three-eighths from the top
    b. In the center of the publication
    c. three-eighths from the bottom
    d. Upper-right corner

13. Which of the following is NOT an example of white space?
    a. Margins
    b. Space between lines of text
    c. Space around a graphic
    d. Lines separating columns of text

14. In asymmetrical balance, the elements on a page are _____.
    a. Placed equally on either side of the vertical line
    b. Grouped near the center of the page
    c. Placed unequally on either side of the vertical line
    d. Placed in the white space

15. Which of the following is NOT true about working with advertisers?
    a. They may give you camera-ready artwork to place.
    b. They help support your publication financially.
    c. The cost of running an advertisement is determined by its size, amount of colors, and placement in the publication.
    d. Ads are most likely to be read when grouped together on a single page.

16. _____ is an important design principle that provides variety in a physical layout.
    a. Contrast
    b. Symmetrical balance
    c. White space
    d. Diplomacy

Publisher 2003

▼ SKILLS REVIEW

1. **Critique a publication.**
   a. Start Publisher, open the file PUB F-3.pub from the drive and folder where your Data Files are located, then save it as **Daily Specials Menu**. Throughout this exercise, zoom in and out as necessary.
   b. Take a look at each visual element on the page, and determine where the focal points are, and whether there are any unnecessary or distracting elements on the page. Find three things you would change to improve the publication.
   c. Create a text box on page 2 that includes your thoughts on what the goals of the publication are, and how well you think the publication meets the goals.
   d. Create a second text box on page 2, type **Critiquing the publication**, then write your three improvements and how you would implement them.

2. **Strengthen publication text.**
   a. Think about how you can use what you've learned about effective design to strengthen text in the menu.
   b. Move the text boxes for the name of the restaurant, the text **Daily Specials**, and the text box that includes the date (in this order) up near the top of the page. Leave a 2" margin between the top of the page and the restaurant name text box. Leave a 3½" margin between the left edge of the page and the three text boxes.
   c. Delete the graphic in the upper-right corner of page one, then increase the size of the graphic in the upper-left corner of the page to 2¾" H x 2¾" V.
   d. AutoFit the text containing the restaurant name, left-align the text in the text box, then change the font color from black to something more colorful. Adjust the size of the text box as necessary.
   e. Increase the font size of the **Daily Specials** text to 14 point, left-align the text in the text box, then make it the same font and font color as the restaurant name.
   f. Increase the font size of the date text to 12 point, and make it the same font but a different font color than the restaurant name. Adjust the size of the text box if necessary.
   g. Save your work.

3. **Rearrange elements.**
   a. Move the table so that its upper-left corner is 1" H / 4¼" V.
   b. Delete the graphics in the lower-left and right corners.
   c. Move the text box containing the payment information to the bottom of the page at ¾" H / 8¼" V.
   d. Move the text box containing the address, phone number, and Web site so that its upper-left corner is ¾" H / 9½" V.
   e. Save your work.

4. Modify objects.

a. Click the table.

b. Press [Ctrl][A] twice, then increase the font size by pressing [Ctrl] []] (right bracket) five times.

c. Resize the table so that its dimensions are 6½" H x 3½" V. Adjust any rows as necessary so that the text fits.

d. Use the fill color of your choice on the table to provide contrast between the background and the table. Make sure that the fill color complements the font colors you used in the masthead.

e. Save your work.

5. Refine a page.

a. Select all the cells in the table on page 1.

b. Format the table so that black lines surround each cell. (*Hint*: Use the Colors and Lines tab in the Format Table dialog box.)

c. Save your work.

6. Experiment with design elements.

a. Click the Design Gallery Object button on the Objects toolbar, click Coupons, click Top Oval Coupon, then click Insert Object.

b. Drag the coupon to the scratch area.

c. Click the 2 for 1 text box, then type Dessert Special.

d. Click the Name of Item or Service text box, then type Free dessert with lunch entrée.

e. Click the Describe your location by landmark or area of town text box, then type 12 Kimball Street.

f. Enter an expiration date of September 1, 2007 in the remaining text box, and replace all the instances of 'Carole' with Your Name.

g. Move the coupon to 4¼" H / 8¼" V, then compare your publication to figure F-19.

h. Save the publication, print it, then exit Publisher.

FIGURE F-19

▼ INDEPENDENT CHALLENGE 1

Pastiche Martinez is an attorney who has hired you to redesign his business card. He is concerned that the layout of his current card makes it too hard to read and does not convey an elegant, organized image. Start Publisher, open the file PUB F-4.pub from the drive and folder where your Data Files are located, then save it as **Corporate Business Card**. Use your design knowledge to make corrections, then replace the existing name in the business card with your name. Save the changes, print the publication, then exit Publisher.

▼ INDEPENDENT CHALLENGE 2

Your design services consulting firm is really taking off. A local business has asked you to redesign a certificate they use to recognize excellence among their staff. The firm wants to convey a professional, cutting-edge image, although they are not averse to having fun.

a. Start Publisher, open the file PUB F-5.pub, then save it as **Certificate of Appreciation** to the drive and folder where your Data Files are located.

b. Change the name in the existing publication to Your Name.

c. Print the publication before any other changes are made, then mark at least five areas that need improvement.

d. Make the changes you noted in the previous step.

Advanced Challenge Exercises

■ Change the color of the green matte to red, to add contrast.

■ Find and insert appropriate clip art.

e. Save and print the publication.

f. Exit Publisher.

FIGURE F-20

Certificate of Appreciation

This certificate is awarded to

YOUR NAME

In recognition of the many contributions to our clients, our staff and our work
With our best wishes and fondest regards

Bascom Bryant, Director   Date

Mae Bryant, Office Manager   Date

▼ INDEPENDENT CHALLENGE 3

As the Design Coordinator at Super Design and Layout, you want to find convincing examples of good and bad design in print and on Web sites. Seeing both types of examples will be helpful to your students. You can use the Web to find examples of good and bad design.

a. Connect to the Internet, then open your browser and favorite search engine.

b. Find one site that offers design tips, then print out the home page.

c. Find one example of a site you consider to have bad design, then print the home page. Mark on the printed page the elements you think exhibit bad design, and note how you would fix these elements.

d. Create a document describing your findings using your favorite word processor and save it as **Good and Bad Design Critique** in the folder where your Data Files are located. (Make sure your name appears somewhere on each printed page.) If you wish, you can illustrate the document with examples of the Web pages by navigating to the page in your browser, pressing [Print Scrn] or [PrtSc], then switching to the document and pressing [Ctrl] [V].

▼ INDEPENDENT CHALLENGE 4

You are asked to be the guest speaker at an upcoming class on Microsoft Publisher, and the topic is design techniques. As part of the class, you want to be able show a publication that has elements of poor design. During the class, you plan an active discussion to address the flaws in this problematic publication.

a. Start Publisher, create a newsletter using your choice of design, then save it as **Design Techniques** to the drive and folder where your Data Files are located.

b. Using the first page in the publication, incorporate improper techniques, such as a page that has too little white space, text that is too small, or a story that has no visual boundaries. Use as many incorrect elements as possible. (*Hint:* You can use any graphic elements and text stories available on your computer.)

c. Add your name to the masthead at the top of the first page.

Advanced Challenge Exercises

■ Save this publication as **Design Techniques-Good ACE** to the drive and folder where your Data Files are located. See Figure F-21.

■ Fix all the areas you consciously created using poor design techniques.

d. Save the publication, then print the first page.

e. Exit Publisher.

FIGURE F-21

Open the file PUB F-6.pub and save it as **Tour Guide Flyer** to the drive and folder where your Data Files are located. Use your knowledge of design techniques and your Publisher skills to make the Data File look like the flyer in Figure F-22. Print the publication.

FIGURE F-22

Your Name's Vacation Nation
Hospitality Enterprises – Invites YOU

Apply for Tour Guide Training. The hospitality industry is booming and you can capitalize on its growth. You can become a Certified Tour Guide.

- Retirement benefits
- 401 K plans
- Interesting people
- Exotic locales
- Unlimited growth
- Subsidized shelter
- Good pay
- Rapid promotions

Call 555 555-5555 today for an application packet and complete information

Working with Multiple Pages

OBJECTIVES

Add pages	
Delete pages	
Work with a master page	
Create a header and footer	
Add page numbers	
Edit a story	
Modify a table of contents	
Create labels	
Capstone Project: Jewelry Tools Catalog	

Many publications, such as flyers, business cards, and signs, consist of a single page. However, other publications, such as catalogs and newsletters, require multiple pages. You can easily add, copy, and delete pages in Publisher; the bigger challenge is planning a multi-page document that is easy to understand and reference. For a more professional and compelling design, you'll want to repeat informative text, such as the page number, the date, or a company tagline, at the top or bottom of each page. You can also add a table of contents so readers can find specific stories. You have been asked to design a catalog of Navajo rugs for a Native American trading company. The client wants a tasteful catalog that educates potential customers, but lets the colorful rug designs speak for themselves. When finished, this catalog will be approximately 65 pages long. For now, you'll focus on getting the major design elements in place.

Adding Pages

You can add pages to a publication one at a time or in batches. Depending on the type of publication you are creating and how it is laid out for printing, you may want to add pages in multiples of two or four. A catalog, for example, prints pages in sets of four, so adding pages in multiples other than four can make printing difficult. You can add background items (such as layout guides) and objects (such as headers and footers) to new pages using the Master Page feature. A **master page** is the background of a publication page, where repeated information such as a pattern, header, or footer, can be viewed and edited. You also have the option to copy text or graphic objects from any page to a newly inserted page. You have created a new publication for the catalog, and are ready to add pages to it.

STEPS

1. **Start Publisher, open the file** PUB G-1.pub **from the drive and folder where your Data Files are located, then save it as** Rug Catalog

   The catalog appears on the screen, and the Catalog Options task pane opens. You can use this task pane to make changes in the design and layout of a catalog.

2. **Click the** Close button **on the Catalog Options task pane**

   This catalog has eight pages. You can add pages either before or after the current page. To retain a consistent design, you can insert whole pages with objects, such as text boxes or picture frames, on any page.

3. **Click the** page 2–3 icon ⌈2│3⌉ **on the status bar, click** Insert **on the menu bar, then click** Page

   The Insert Catalog Pages dialog box opens, where you can choose from 19 catalog-style layouts for the new page or pages.

4. **Click the** Left-hand page list arrow, **click** 4 items, offset pictures, **click the** Right-hand page list arrow, **then click** 4 items, squared pictures

   Compare your Insert Catalog Pages dialog box to Figure G-1.

QUICK TIP

To move a page, insert a new page, duplicate the objects from the page you want moved, then delete the original page.

5. **Click** More

   The Insert Page dialog box opens, as shown in Figure G-2. You can use this dialog box to control the number of new pages to add, as well as options, such as inserting blank pages, duplicating all of the objects on a specific page, or adding a hyperlink to a Web navigation bar.

6. **Click** Cancel **in the Insert Page dialog box, click** OK **in the Insert Catalog Pages dialog box, then click** Yes **to automatically insert four pages**

   Compare your work to Figure G-3. The page 4–5 icon button is selected on the status bar, and the additional icon buttons indicates that the publication now has 12 pages. The newly inserted pages (4–7) have the same layout on both pairs of pages.

7. **Click the** Save button 🖫 **on the Standard toolbar**

Clues to Use

Using multiple master pages

A master page gives you the freedom to create a consistent background for pages. In Publisher, you can also create multiple master pages. This means, for example, that in a newsletter publication you can have a specific master page for Classified Ads, and another master page for daily news stories. When the Edit Master Pages task pane is visible, click the New Master Page button at the bottom of the task pane to create a new master page. You can also create a new master page by clicking the New Master Page button ⬜ on the Edit Master Pages toolbar.

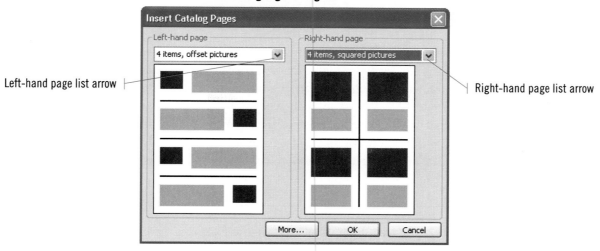

Left-hand page list arrow

Right-hand page list arrow

FIGURE G-2: Insert Page dialog box

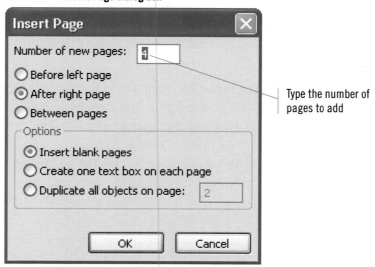

Type the number of pages to add

FIGURE G-3: Publication with added pages

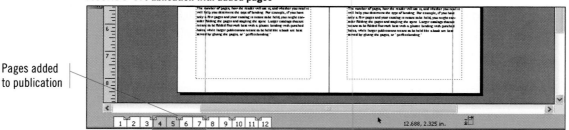

Pages added to publication

Design Matters

Printing multi-page documents

When you think of a page, you probably think of one 8½" × 11" sheet of paper; but from a printer's point of view, several pages may actually fit on one sheet of paper. A four-page brochure can be printed front and back on one sheet of paper and folded in half so that there are four pages. Commercial printing of publications larger than four pages prints pages this way, then the folded pages are bound together. This is why catalogs print in multiples of four, because they are printed on the front and back of a single piece of paper. When printing books or other large publications, paper is printed in multiples of eight, called **signatures**. Blank pages at the end of a book indicate there was not enough text to fill the last signature.

Deleting Pages

You should delete unnecessary pages to streamline your publication and keep file sizes down. Always view the pages that you are deleting to ensure that you are deleting the correct pages, and that there aren't any elements you want saved, such as clip art or a pull quote. You can store any elements that you want to retain on the scratch area. When you delete a page, any objects on that page are deleted from the publication, continued on/continued from notices are automatically recalculated, and text in a connected text box is moved to the closest available text box on the next page. You need to eliminate some unnecessary pages in the catalog. You want to delete a total of eight pages: the four new pages as well as four additional pages.

STEPS

1. **Click Edit on the menu bar, then click Delete Page**

   The Delete Page dialog box opens, as shown in Figure G-4. The Both pages option button is selected, although you could just delete the left or right page.

2. **Click the Left page only option button, then click OK**

   The warning dialog box shown in Figure G-5 opens. This tells you that you can delete a single page, but your layout may be negatively affected, or you can cancel the single page deletion.

QUICK TIP

If you delete a page in error, immediately click the Undo button 🔄 on the Standard toolbar.

3. **Click Cancel**

4. **Click Edit on the menu bar, click Delete Page, verify that the Both pages option button is selected, click OK, then click OK in the Multiple page spread warning box**

   The Multiple page spread warning box appeared because you were deleting only two pages, not a multiple of four. Your publication now has 10 pages.

5. **With pages 4–5 still active, click Edit on the menu bar, click Delete Page, verify that the Both pages option button is selected, then click OK**

   The Multiple-page spread warning box does not appear because the total number of remaining pages is a multiple of four. There are now eight pages in the publication.

6. **With pages 4–5 still active, click Edit on the menu bar, click Delete Page, verify that the Both pages option button is selected, click OK, then click OK in the Multiple page spread warning box**

   The catalog now contains six pages.

7. **With pages 4–5 still active, click Edit on the menu bar, click Delete Page, verify that the Both pages option button is selected, click OK, then click the page 2–3 icon** [2 | 3]

   Compare your catalog to Figure G-6. There are now four pages in the publication.

8. **Click the Save button 💾 on the Standard toolbar**

FIGURE G-4: Delete Page dialog box

FIGURE G-5: Multiple pages warning dialog box

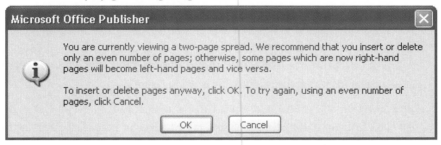

FIGURE G-6: Two-page spread

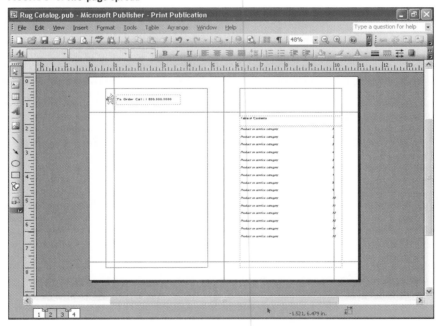

Design Matters

Saving objects on a page

When a page is deleted, all the objects on that page are also deleted. But what if you want to save some of those objects for later use? Simply drag the object onto the scratch area. Objects in the scratch area are saved along with the publication, and can be viewed and accessed from all pages in the publication. When you decide where you want an object from the scratch area to be used, move it to its new location using any copying or pasting technique. Alternately, you can cut an object before deleting the page so it will automatically be stored on the Clipboard, where you can easily retrieve it until you close the publication.

Working with a Master Page

Every publication has at least one master page that can be used to add text or objects that you want on every page. A publication with **mirrored guides** has both left and right master pages, a publication without mirrored guides has a single Master Page. You can use a master page to add an object, such as a logo, to each page. A **washout**, also known as a **watermark**, is another element you can add to the Master Page. It's a faded or washed-out looking image that appears behind text and objects on a page. You have prepared descriptive text about Navajo rugs which you want to insert in a text box on page 2. Once you insert this text, you will add a muted image of a rug to the background page.

STEPS

1. **Click the** Text Box button 🔠 **on the Objects toolbar, then drag** + **from** 1" H / 1½" V **to** 4⅞" H / 7¾" V

   The text box appears on the page.

2. **Right-click the** text box, **point to** Change Text, **click** Text File, **locate and select the file** PUB G-2.doc **from the drive and folder where your Data Files are located, then click** OK

   All of the text fits within the text box, as shown in Figure G-7.

QUICK TIP

You can modify an existing Master Page by switching to the Master Page view and editing objects.

3. **Click** View **on the menu bar, then click** Master Page

   The Master pages appear, with guides and placeholders for headers and footers. Because this is a mirrored page publication, the Master Pages are mirrored pages as well. You can easily tell that master pages are being displayed when you see the yellow background. Regular pages display against a gray background. The Edit Master Pages toolbar and Edit Master Pages task pane open for working with all elements of the master pages. Master Pages can accommodate both text and graphics.

4. **Click the** Rename Master Page button 🔃 **on the Edit Master Pages toolbar, type** Intro Master **in the Description text box, then click** OK

5. **Click** Insert **on the menu bar, point to** Picture, **click** From File, **navigate to the drive and folder where your Data Files are located, click** PUB G-3.tif, **then click** Insert

   The picture is across the two master pages.

6. **Close the** Edit Master Pages task pane, **then position the picture so that its top-left corner is at** 0" H / 0" V

   The picture is inserted into the picture frame.

7. **Right-click the picture, click** Format Picture, **click the** Picture tab **if necessary, click the** Color list arrow, **click** Washout, **then click** OK

   Compare your screen to Figure G-8.

8. **Position the mouse pointer over the** top-left sizing handle **of the image until the pointer changes to** ⬉, **press and hold** [Shift], **drag** ⬉ **to** 1" H /1⅜" V, **release** [Shift], **then press** ⬆

QUICK TIP

You can toggle between the regular and Master Page views by pressing [Ctrl][M].

9. **Click** Close Master View **on the Edit Master Pages toolbar, then click the** Save button 💾 **on the Standard toolbar**

   The washout image appears behind the text in the frame. Compare your publication to Figure G-9.

FIGURE G-7: Text file added to publication

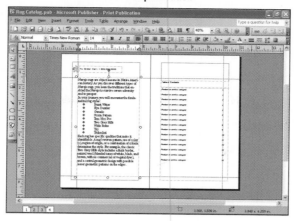

FIGURE G-8: "Washout" image added to master page

Image on left
master page

Left master pages will be
even numbered pages

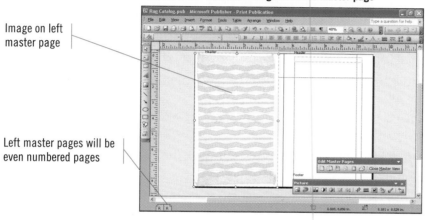

FIGURE G-9: Text in foreground, image on master page background

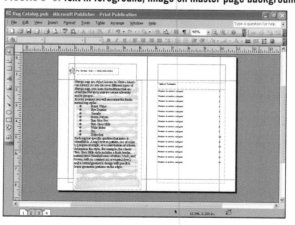

Design Matters

Using left and right master pages

If you have mirrored layout guides, you also have left and right master pages. Having both a left and right master page increases your design options. For example, you might want to have an image appear in the bottom-left corner on the left master page, and the bottom-right corner on the right master page. To change from double to single master pages, click Arrange on the menu bar, click Layout Guides, then deselect the Two-page master check box in the Layout Guides dialog box. When this check box is not selected, you have only one master page. What was previously the right master page is now used as the publication's background page and is applied to all the pages.

Creating a Header and Footer

Text you commonly see in a header or footer can include the document title, page number, or date. Text that appears on the top of each page is called a **header**, and text that appears on the bottom of each page is a **footer**. Special text boxes for the header or footer text are located on the right and left master pages. Images can also be included in headers or footers to enhance the publication. Usually, the headers and footers are not shown on the first page of a publication, although you can choose to display them. Table G-1 describes the buttons on the Header and Footer toolbar. ▰▰▰▰ You want to give the catalog a more professional look and feel, so you decide to add descriptive headers. In this case, the name of the trading company is Navajo Rugs: Cultural Expressions, and the theme for this catalog is Navajo Rugs: Strong Visual Statements.

STEPS

1. **Click** View **on the menu bar, then click Header and Footer**

   The view changes to the Master Page. The Header and Footer toolbar is open, and the background page header text box at the top of the left page is selected.

2. **Type** Navajo Rugs: Cultural Expressions **in the header text box on the left master page**

   Because you typed this in the header text box, this text will appear in the publication on all left-hand pages.

3. **Click the** header text box at 6¼" H / ¼" V, **type** Navajo Rugs: Strong Visual Statements, **then click the** Align Right button ▤

   When you clicked the right-page text box, the display changed so that the left-page text box was no longer visible. Compare your page to Figure G-10.

4. **Click** Close **on the Header and Footer toolbar, click the** Zoom list arrow 51% ▾, **then click** Whole Page

   The page background is gray, indicating that the publication pages, rather than the background pages, are visible. The headers appear on pages 2 and 3, as shown in Figure G-11.

5. **Click the** page 1 icon **on the status bar**

   The header is visible on page 1. Catalogs, like other multi-page publications, typically don't display headers on the first page.

6. **Click** View **on the menu bar, then click** Ignore Master Page

   Because you chose to ignore the background on this first page, any objects on the right master page are not visible on this page.

7. **Click the** Save button ▤ **on the Standard toolbar**

TABLE G-1: Header and footer toolbar buttons

button	name	description
▣	**Insert Page Number**	Inserts a page number automatically into a header or footer
▣	**Insert Date**	Inserts current date into a header or footer
◉	**Insert Time**	Inserts current time into a header or footer
▣	**Show Header/Footer**	Used to toggle between the header and footer

FIGURE G-10: Header on right master page

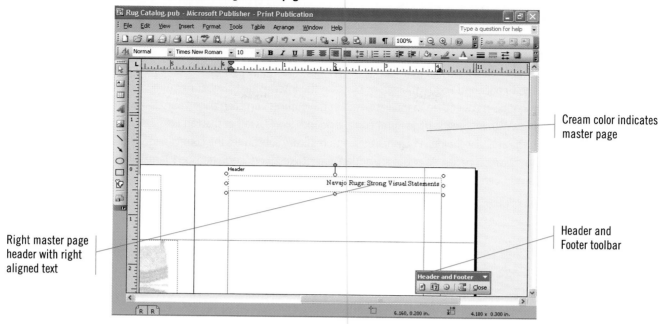

Cream color indicates master page

Right master page header with right aligned text

Header and Footer toolbar

FIGURE G-11: Headers visible on left and right pages

Header text boxes

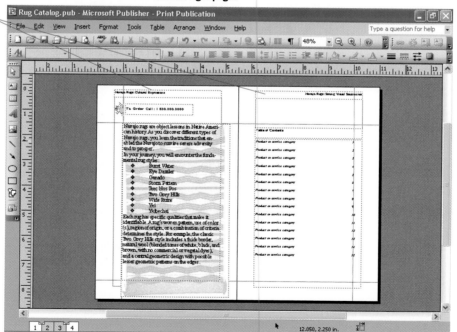

Adding Page Numbers

Page numbers help readers find specific stories, and find the continued parts of stories that appear in multiple text boxes on different pages. You can insert automatic page numbers either by using the Page Number button on the Header and Footer toolbar, or by using the Insert Page Number dialog box. Using Publisher's page numbering tools is easier than manually typing in the numbers on each page yourself—and ensures the numbers stay correct. With automatic page numbering, a pound sign (#), rather than an actual number, is inserted on the master page as a placeholder. Publisher then automatically substitutes the correct page number for the placeholder in the publication pages. As pages are added and deleted, your page numbers remain accurate. ███████ You want page numbers to appear in the footers at the bottom of each page, except the first page. You want the page numbers to appear in the bottom-left corner of the left pages and the bottom-right corner of the right pages.

1. **Click the** page 2–3 icon ⌐2 ┌3⌐ **on the status bar, click** Insert **on the menu bar, then click** Page Numbers

   The Page Numbers dialog box opens, as shown in Figure G-12.

2. **Click the** Position list arrow, **then click** Bottom of page (Footer)

3. **Click the** Alignment list arrow, **then click** Outside

4. **Deselect the** Show page number on first page check box

   The page numbering feature will count the first page, but the number will not appear. In most cases, it's not necessary to display the page number on the first page of a publication.

5. **Click** OK

   Compare the placement of your page numbers with Figure G-13.

6. **Press** [Ctrl][M], **click the** footer **at 7" H / 8" V, then press** [F9]

   The master page shows the page number feature as "#" inside the footer.

7. **Press** [F9], **close the** Edit Master Pages task pane, **then press** [Ctrl][M]

   The publication is displayed in Two Page Spread view. You like the balanced look of the headers and footers aligned at the outer margins of both pages.

8. **Click the** Save button 🔲 **on the Standard toolbar**

> **QUICK TIP**
>
> Clicking Close Master View on the toolbar has the same effect on master pages as pressing [Ctrl][M].

FIGURE G-12: **Page Numbers dialog box**

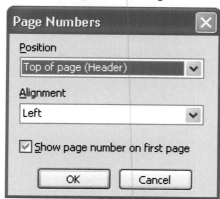

FIGURE G-13: **Page numbers on both pages**

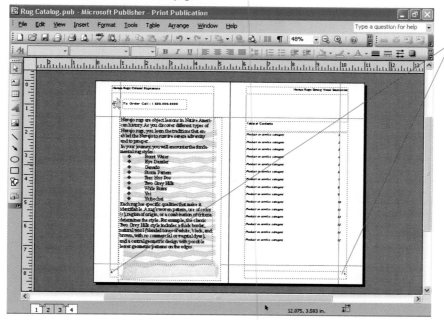

Page numbers displayed in footers

Publisher 2003

Clues to Use

Renaming a master page

You can rename a master page to give it a more meaningful name. To rename a master page, position the pointer over the master page in the Edit Master Pages task pane, click the list arrow that displays to the right of the current name, then click Rename. You can also rename a master page by clicking the Rename Master Page button 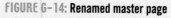 on the Edit Master Pages toolbar. Figure G-14 shows the Edit Master Pages task pane containing a master page that has been renamed.

FIGURE G-14: **Renamed master page**

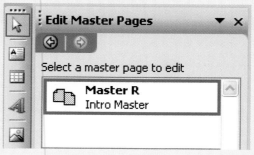

Editing a Story

As you have learned, you can type a story directly into a text box, or prepare it in another program and insert it as a text file. Once you have placed a story in publication, you have a choice when editing it: You can edit in Microsoft Word (if you have Microsoft Word 6.0 or later installed) or in Publisher. Editing in Word gives you access to the features of a powerful word processor from within Publisher. If you don't require those features, you might find it simpler to edit the story using Publisher's editing features. If you edit the story in Word, you can choose to save the changes to the original Word file as well as to the Publisher document. If you edit in Publisher, your changes are saved only to the publication, not to the original text file. ▇▇▇▇ After reading the publication, you realize you need to edit the descriptive text on page 2, to tighten up some of the wording.

STEPS

TROUBLE

If Word isn't installed on your computer or you receive a low memory error message, edit the story directly in Publisher.

1. **Right-click the** text box **at** 3" H / 3" V, **point to** Change Text, **click** Edit Story in Microsoft Word, **then click the** Maximize button **in the upper-right corner of the Document in Rug Catalog window if necessary**

   Microsoft Word opens, displaying the story's text, as shown in Figure G-15. Any edits you make to this text in Word will be applied to the selected story in the Publisher text box.

QUICK TIP

When working in Microsoft Word, you can save your changes to the Word document by clicking the **Save button** 🖫 on the Standard toolbar.

2. **Select the text** discover different types of, **then type** explore

   You changed the phrase "discover different types of" to "explore" in the first paragraph to make it more succinct.

3. **Click to the right of** Yei (the eighth bullet text), **press** [Spacebar], **type** and, **press** [Spacebar], **then press** [Delete] **twice**

   You combined the two related bulleted items into one bullet. Your edits are complete.

4. **Click** File **on the menu bar, then click** Close & Return to Rug Catalog

   (If you are editing directly in Publisher, skip this step.) Word closes and you see your edits applied to the text in the Publisher story.

QUICK TIP

Some text formatting, such as drop caps, are lost when moving from Word to Publisher.

5. **Click anywhere within the** first paragraph, **click** Format **on the menu bar, click** Drop Cap, **click the** drop cap style **directly under the current selection, then click** OK

   The drop cap is added to make the story stand out. Compare your work to Figure G-16.

6. **Click the** Save button 🖫 **on the Standard toolbar**

Design Matters

Copyfitting text

As you create a publication, you may find that you have either too much or too little text to fit comfortably in a column or page. **Copyfitting** is a term used to describe the process of making the text fit the available space within a publication. If you have too much text, you can narrow the margins, decrease the point size of the font, enlarge the text box, flow text into a text box on another page, or delete some text by editing. You can solve the problem of too little text by inserting a graphic image or pull quote, making margins wider, increasing the point size of the font, or adding some text. The AutoFit Text command found on the Format menu works by increasing or decreasing the point size of the fonts.

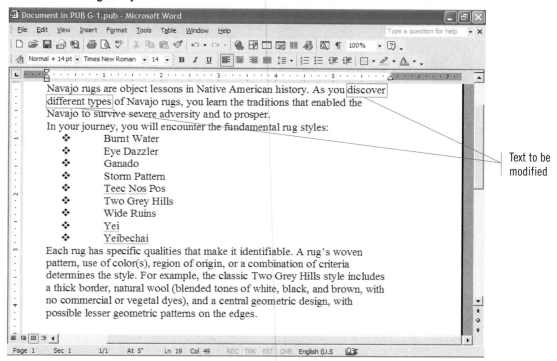

FIGURE G-16: Edited story

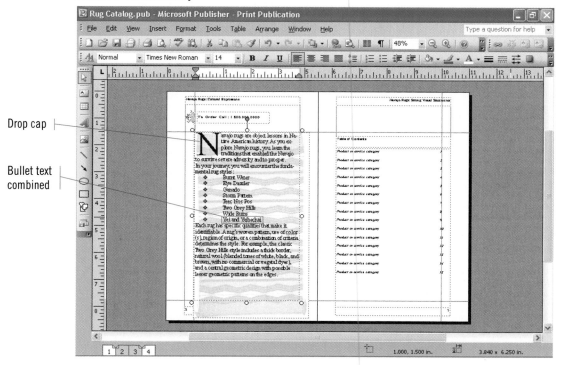

Publisher 2003

Modifying a Table of Contents

A **table of contents** helps readers locate specific information in a multi-page publication. A table of contents in Publisher uses tabs to align columns of information concerning content and the page numbers of the content. To create a table of contents, type text into a text box, then add tabs and leaders to connect the text and page numbers. A **tab**, or tab stop, is a defined location to which the insertion point advances when you press [Tab]. **Leaders** are a series of dots, dashes, or lines that lead up to a tab, and automatically adjust to fit the space between the columns.  You want to modify the table of contents in the catalog by adding dot leaders to make reading easier. Although you still have several pages of content to add to this publication, you'll also make entries to approximate where information will be located.

STEPS

1. **Click the text box at 7" H / 2½" V, then press [F9]**

   The first item in the table of contents is for page 1. The reference to this page is not necessary, as the reader can easily see everything that's on page 1.

2. **Select the first line of text, then press [Delete]**

   The first line is deleted, and the second line begins with page 2.

3. **Press [Ctrl][A], right-click the text, point to Change Text, then click Tabs**

   The Tabs dialog box opens, as shown in Figure G-17.

4. **In the Leader section of the Tabs dialog box, click the Dot option button, click OK, then click outside of the text box to deselect the text**

   Each of the entries in the text box now has a dot leader preceding the page number.

5. **Select the text Product or service category in the first line, then type Introduction to Navajo Rugs**

   The first entry in the table of contents is complete.

6. **Delete the entry for page 3, then delete the entries for pages 13–15**

7. **Type the table of contents information as shown in Figure G-18 using the techniques described in Step 5, then substitute Your Name as a final entry to the table of contents**

   The table of contents looks good and is a tool that will help clients locate information about the rugs when the catalog is complete.

8. **Press [F9], click the Save button 🖫 on the Standard toolbar, then click the Print button 🖨 on the Standard toolbar**

   Review the four printed pages of the catalog.

9. **Click File on the menu bar, then click Close**

   The publication closes. Publisher remains open and available for additional work.

FIGURE G-17: Tabs dialog box

Alignment options

Defined tabs appear here

Leader options

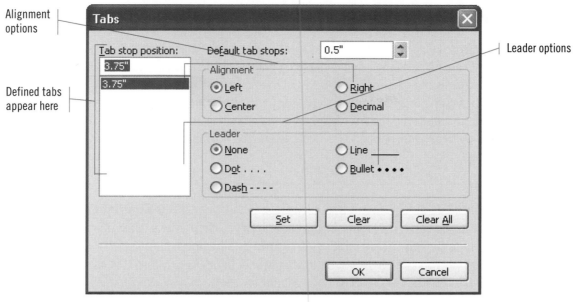

FIGURE G-18: Completed table of contents

Dot leaders inserted

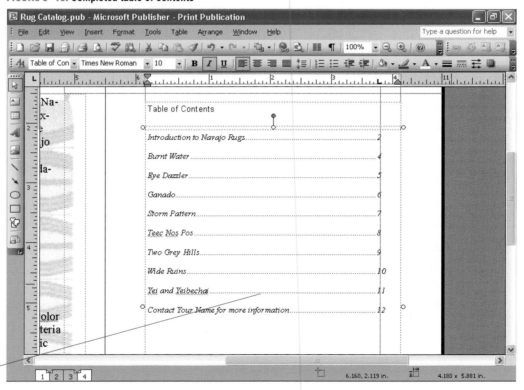

Publisher 2003

Creating Labels

You can use Publisher to create professional-looking labels for a variety of items, such as retail products, CDs, or notebooks. These labels are designed to print directly on a page of commercially available labels in a wide range of sizes and styles. ▄▄▄▄▄ As part of a temporary promotion, the client is planning to offer a 15% discount on online orders. Because this is a sort-term offer, it won't be printed directly on the catalog. You plan to include a sticker on the first mailing of the catalogs that indicates the amount of the discount. You use the New Publication task pane and the Publication Gallery to create a sheet of labels that can be attached to the catalogs.

STEPS

QUICK TIP

The label brand and model number required for printing varies based on the label design you use. You may need your Microsoft Publisher Installation CD to complete this step.

1. **Click File on the menu bar, click New, click Publications for Print in the New from a design category on the New Publication task pane, click Labels, click Identification, then click the Made By Tag (Avery label 5160) in the Publication Gallery**

   The label appears on the screen. It is ready to print on Avery Label #5160, as indicated on the screen; this information will not show up when printing the labels.

2. **Click Color Schemes on the Publication Designs task pane, click Desert, then save the publication as Rug Label to the drive and folder where your Data Files are located**

3. **Click the Close button on the Color Schemes task pane, press [Ctrl][M], click Insert on the menu bar, point to Picture, click From File, click the file PUB G-4.tif from the drive and folder where your Data Files are located, then click Insert**

   Compare your label to Figure G-19.

4. **Use ✛ to drag the picture so that the left edge is at ½" H and it is centered between the vertical margin guides, right-click the object, click Format Picture, select the contents of the Brightness control box, type 75%, select the contents of the Contrast control box, type 25%, then click OK**

   The image is now a much lighter shade than before.

5. **Click the Close Master View button on the Edit master Pages toolbar, close the task pane, select the text Made especially for you by:, type Authentic Navajo Rug, then press [Ctrl][T]**

   Pressing [Ctrl][T] changed the text box fill from white to clear. You can now see the image of the rug very clearly behind the text.

6. **Click the text box at 1" H / ¾" V, type 15% online discount, press [Ctrl][A], then click the Bold button 𝐁 on the Formatting toolbar**

7. **Click Format on the menu bar, point to AutoFit Text, click Best Fit, press [Ctrl][T], then press [Esc] twice**

   Compare your label to Figure G-20.

8. **Click the Save button 🔳 on the Standard toolbar, click File on the menu bar, click Print, then exit Publisher**

FIGURE G-19: Label master page with image inserted

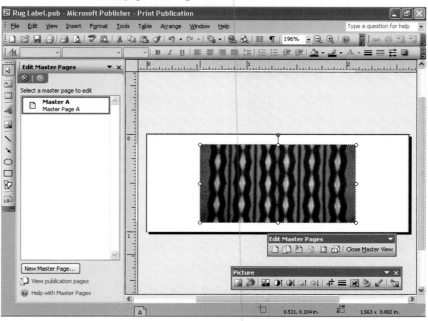

FIGURE G-20: Completed label with recolored image

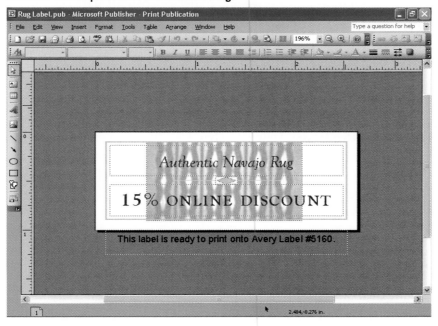

Clues to Use

Creating CD/DVD labels

If you like creating CDs of your original music and photographs, or DVDs of converted VCR tapes, you may want to create jewel case labels for them. To do so, open the New Publication task pane, click the Labels category in the New from a design Publications for Print section. When you click CD/DVD Labels, you'll see a variety of case inserts and jewel case labels you can use.

Capstone Project: Jewelry Tools Catalog

You have inserted and deleted pages, worked with Master Pages, created headers and footers, added page numbers, modified a table of contents, and edited a story in Word. You will use these skills to work on a new catalog. You are designing a metal workers' catalog. The target customers for this catalog are jewelers. You think they will appreciate a simple, uncluttered design that conveys the elegance of their craft. The client will add pictures and text later.

STEPS

1. **Start Publisher, open the file** PUB G-5.pub **from the drive and folder where your Data Files are located, save it as** Jewelry Tools Catalog, **then change the color scheme to Sunset**
   Most of the elements of design in the first three pages will be carried throughout the catalog.

2. **Close the Catalog Options task pane, click the** page 4-5 icon **on the status bar, click** Edit **on the menu bar, click** Delete Page **to delete pages 4-5, click** OK **at each warning or dialog box, then repeat the process to delete the next two pages, which are now pages 4 and 5**
   The publication now has four pages.

3. **Click the** page 2-3 icon ⌐2│3⌐ **on the status bar, click** View **on the menu bar, click** Master Page, **click** Insert **on the menu bar, point to** Picture, **click** From File, **then double-click the file** PUB G-6.tif **from the drive and folder where your Data Files are located**

4. **Position the image so that its top-left corner is at 1¼" H / 3" V, resize it so the bottom-right corner is at 4½" H/6" V, right-click the image, click Format Picture, click the Picture tab if necessary, click the Color list arrow, click Washout, then click OK**
   The image is now centered and washed-out, and will look elegant with black text imposed over the gold color.

5. **Click** View **on the menu bar, click** Header and Footer, **type** Matisse Tools for the Jewelry Arts **in the header text box on the left master page, click the** Show Header/Footer button 🔳 **on the Header and Footer toolbar, type** Page, **press** [Spacebar], **click the** Insert Page Number button 🔳, **copy the entries in the left footer to the right footer, click the** Align Right button 🔳 **to right-align the right footer, then click** Close Master View **on the Edit Master Pages toolbar**
   Page numbers will help customers navigate to specific items.

6. **Press** [F9], **click the** text box at 6½" H / 2" V, **click** Format **on the menu bar, click** Tabs, **click the** Line option button, **then click** OK
   There is still an entry for page 1 that must be deleted.

7. **Right-click the** text box, **point to** Change Text, **click** Edit Story in Microsoft Word, **delete the entry for page 1, click** File **on the menu bar, then click** Close & Return to Jewelry Tools Catalog

8. **Click the** text box at 2" H / ¾" V **on page 2, substitute your name for the phone number, press** [Esc] **twice, then compare your work to Figure G-21**

9. **Click the** Save button 🔳 **on the Standard toolbar, print pages 2 and 3, then exit Publisher**

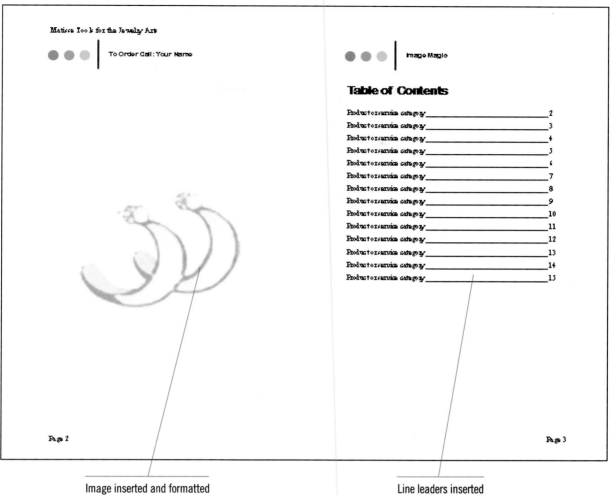

Image inserted and formatted

Line leaders inserted

Publisher 2003

Practice

▼ CONCEPTS REVIEW

Label each of the elements in the Publisher window shown in Figure G-22.

FIGURE G-22

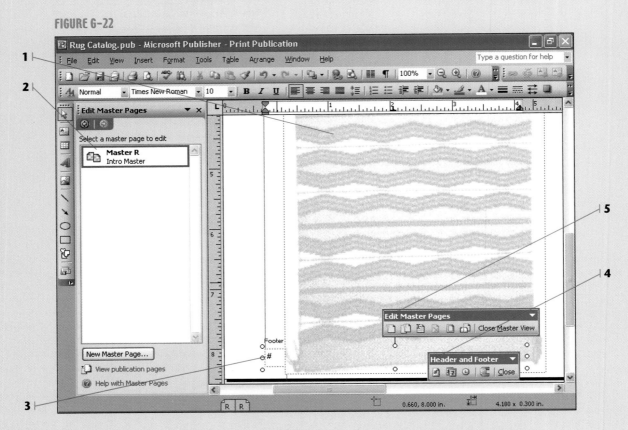

Match each of the features with the correct term, menu, dialog box, or command.

6. **Footer**

7. **Format menu**

8. **Header**

9. **[Ctrl][M]**

10. **Tabs dialog box**

11. **Edit menu**

a. Switches in and out of Master Page view

b. Text that repeats on the bottom of each page

c. Text that repeats at the top of each page

d. Contains the command that deletes a page

e. Contains the command that adds dot leaders

f. Contains the command that adds a drop cap

Select the best answer from the list of choices.

12. **Each of the following is true about adding a page, except:**

a. Pages can be added before or after the current page.

b. You can only add one page at a time.

c. Existing layout guides are added to the new page(s).

d. You can duplicate objects found on other pages in the publication.

13. Which command is used to change the text box fill from white to clear?

   a. [Ctrl][M]   **c.** [Ctrl][N]

   b. [Ctrl][T]   **d.** [Ctrl][B]

14. Where in a publication are headers and footers usually placed?

   a. AutoShapes   **c.** On the Clipboard

   b. Picture frame   **d.** On the Master Page(s)

15. Which character symbolizes automatic page numbers?

   a. @   **c.** !

   b. #   **d.** &

▼ SKILLS REVIEW

1. Add pages.

   a. Start Publisher, then use the New from a design list to create a catalog for a video store. Use the Marquee Catalog design. Use the Secondary Personal Information set and the Tropics color scheme. Close the task pane.

   b. Save the file as **Video Store Catalog** to the drive and folder where your Data Files are located.

   c. Display pages 2-3 in foreground view.

   d. Insert four pages after page 3 (each with two columns, text and picture layout). You now have 12 pages.

   e. Save your work.

2. Delete pages.

   a. Display pages 8 and 9, delete them, then display and delete the new pages 8 and 9.

   b. Display pages 6 and 7, delete them, then delete pages 4 and 5. You now have four pages.

   c. Display pages 2 and 3, then save your work.

3. Work with a master page.

   a. Change to Master Page view.

   b. Open the Insert Clip Art task pane, search My Collections and Office Collections using the text **TVs.**, select the image with the filename j0229385.WMF, then close the Insert Clip Art task pane.

   c. Position the image so that its top-left corner is at ¾" H / 3" V.

   d. Press and hold [Shift], then drag the lower-right sizing handle until the image is approximately 4" wide and 2¾" high.

   e. Save your work.

4. Create a header and footer.

   a. Open the header on the left master page, type **Classic Videos**, then make the text bold.

   b. Type **Classic Videos** in the header on the right master page.

   c. Right-align the text in the right header text box, make the text bold, then save the publication.

5. Add page numbers.

   a. View the footer on the right page, then add page numbers to the footers on both pages aligned at the outer margins.

   b. Close the Header and Footer toolbar, then return to foreground view.

   c. Delete the Page Number text boxes at the bottom of the left and right foreground pages (at 1" H / 7¾" V, and 9½" H / 7¾" V), then go to page 1.

   d. Prevent the page number from appearing on the first page, then save the publication.

6. Edit a story.

   a. Use the page icon button on the status bar to return to page 2.

   b. Draw a text box at 1¼" H / 2½" V to 4¼" H / 6½" V.

   c. Insert the text file PUB G-7.doc into the text box, then open Word to edit the story.

   d. Add the following text in a matching font and text size as a new paragraph at the end of the story: **If we don't have what you're looking for, we can get it for you**. Close Word and return to the catalog, then verify that the text was added to the story.

   e. Add a three-line custom drop cap character to the first paragraph, then save the publication.

7. Modify a table of contents.

   a. Select the text box at 6½" H / 2" V on page 3 (the table of contents text), then open it in Word.

   b. Delete the entries for pages 1-3, then close Word and return to the catalog.

   c. Select the table of contents text, then change the tabs for the remaining entries to dot leaders.

   d. Change the remaining entries, using Table G-2 below. Delete any unnecessary text.

   e. Add a final entry to the Table of Contents that contains your name.

   f. Save your work, then print pages 2 and 3. Close the publication, but do not exit Publisher.

8. Create a label.

   a. Use the Publications for Print category in the New from a design list to create a label using the Video Face Label design and the Bluebird color scheme.

   b. Save the label as **Video Store Label** to the drive and folder where your Data Files are located.

   c. Change the Video Title text to **Citizen Kane**.

   d. Change the date text to the current date.

   e. Change the company name text to your name.

   f. Save your work, print the publication, then exit Publisher.

TABLE G-2

page headings	page #
1930s	4
1940s	6
1950s	8
1960s	10
Award Winners	12
Independent Films	14

▼ INDEPENDENT CHALLENGE 1

You are a member of a small theater group. You are asked to create the program for the next production.

   a. Start Publisher, then use the New Publication task pane and the Programs category in the Print Publications category of the New from a design list to select the Theater Program design.

   b. Use the Personal Information set of your choice to enter appropriate information, then close the Publication Designs task pane.

   c. Save the publication as **Play Program** to the drive and folder where your Data Files are located.

   d. Use the Master Page view to add a header displaying the name of the play. Choose any play with which you are familiar, such as Rent, A Chorus Line, or Man of La Mancha. Right-align the header on the right page.

   e. Insert page numbers at the bottoms of the pages. If necessary, move any information so that your header and footer fit correctly and are visible.

   f. Add any appropriate clip art to the master page, recoloring the clip art if necessary.

   g. Return to the foreground view, then make sure the page number, header, and footer do not appear on the first page.

   h. Replace the text in the table containing the cast with the names of characters and cast members. Use the names of friends and family members or make up fictitious names.

   i. Use Word to create and edit a paragraph describing the play in the existing text box on page 3.

   j. Replace any placeholders so that all of the text in the program pertains to the play you chose.

   k. Add your name as the director on page 1.

   l. Rearrange and format any objects to create an attractive, effective design.

   m. Check the spelling in the publication, save and print the publication, then exit Publisher.

▼ INDEPENDENT CHALLENGE 2

You have recorded several original songs and want to get feedback on your work from a friend who works in the music business. You decide to use the Label Wizard in Publisher to create a shipping label you can use to send the CD to your friend.

a. Start Publisher, then create a new label based on the Borders Shipping Label (Avery 5164).
b. Use any Personal Information set to enter appropriate information, including your name, change to any color scheme you choose, then close the Publication Designs task pane.
c. Save the publication as **Personal Shipping Label** to the drive and folder where your Data Files are located.
d. Edit the mailing address information at 2" H / 2" V, using a fictitious name and address.

Advanced Challenge Exercise

- Create a DVD Label using the Mosaic CD/DVD Label (Avery 8931).
- Save the publication as CD-DVD Label ACE.
- Add actual or fictitious information to the label placeholders, but use Your Name as the Performer's Name.
- Compare your work to Figure G-23.

e. Save and print the publication, then exit Publisher.

FIGURE G-23

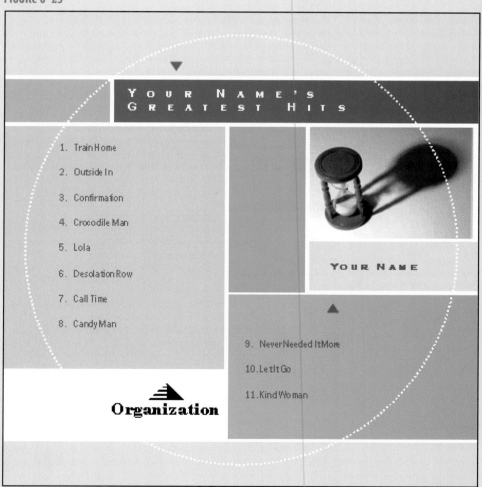

▼ INDEPENDENT CHALLENGE 3

A local elementary school asks you to design a newsletter for its staff and students. The staff and students will provide all of the stories except for one that you will write.

a. Start Publisher, use the New Publication task pane to create a new newsletter based on the Kid Stuff Newsletter design.

b. Use any Personal Information set to enter appropriate information.

c. Change the color scheme to a scheme of your choice, then close the Color Schemes task pane.

d. Save the publication as **School Newsletter** to the drive and folder where your Data Files are located.

e. Delete pages 2 and 3. Open the Insert Pages dialog box. Click the Left-hand page list arrow, then click Calendar. Click the Right-hand page list arrow, click Response Form, then click OK.

f. Replace the newsletter title with your elementary school's name, followed by the word **News**.

g. Make up your own headings and replace at least one story with your own original story on the topic of your choice.

h. Edit the story in Word (if you have this program installed), then check the spelling in the publication.

i. Add your name in the Table of Contents on the first page of the newsletter.

Advanced Challenge Exercise

■ Change the single master page to left-right master pages.

■ Add a footer to the master pages, then compare your work to the sample shown in Figure G-24.

j. Save and print the publication, then exit Publisher.

FIGURE G-24

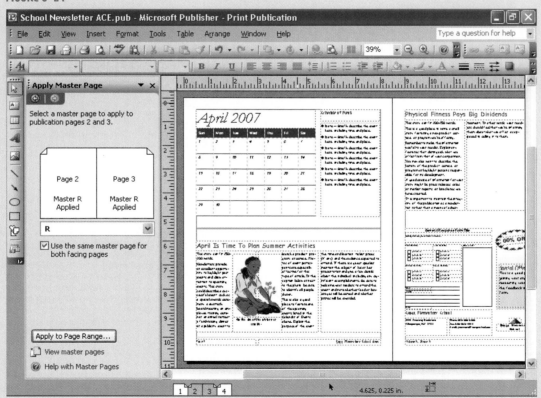

▼ INDEPENDENT CHALLENGE 4

Your employer asks you to teach a one-day course on how to use Publisher. You decide to create a newsletter to inform the students about the features of Publisher, and show them an example of a great publication.

a. Connect to the Internet and use your browser to go to www.microsoft.com. Find the home page for Publisher 2003.

b. Find information about Publisher's highlights and capabilities, then print out information pertaining to two topics of interest to you.

c. Start Publisher if necessary, then select the newsletter of your choice.

d. Save the publication as **Publisher Newsletter** to the drive and folder where your Data Files are located.

e. Use the Personal Information set of your choice to enter appropriate information, then delete pages so that only two pages remain.

f. Create a title for the newsletter. Use the information you found on the Microsoft Web site to compose two stories for the newsletter, a lead and secondary story. You can copy and paste information from the Web site, or write your own stories from scratch.

g. Add any clip art you feel is appropriate, then check the spelling in the publication.

h. Type your name in a text box on page 1, type your name, then compare your work to Figure G-25. Save and print the publication, then exit Publisher.

FIGURE G-25

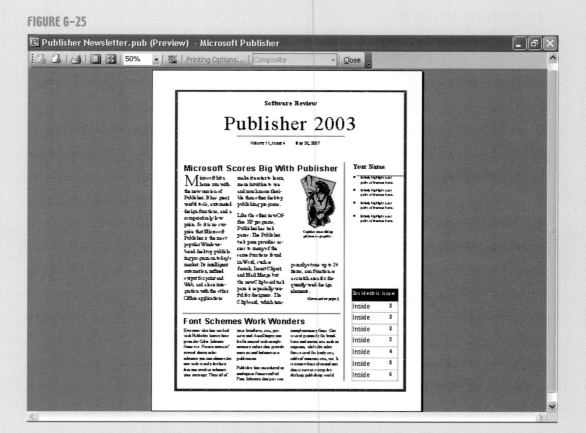

Open the file PUB G-8.pub from the drive and folder where your Data Files are located. Save the publication as **Rug Collection Binder**. Modify the publication so that it looks like Figure G-26 (*Hint*: You'll find the image, PUB G-9.tif, which you need to add to the master page, in the drive and folder where your Data Files are located.) Be sure to include your name where indicated. Save and print the pages.

FIGURE G-26

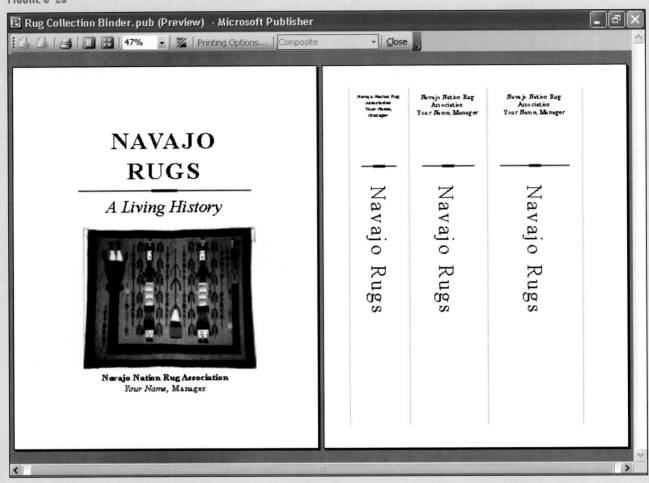

UNIT H
Publisher 2003

Using Advanced Features

OBJECTIVES

Add BorderArt

Design WordArt

Wrap text around an object

Rotate a text box

Understand mail merge

Create a mail merge

Prepare for commercial printing

Use the Pack and Go Wizard

Capstone Project: Automotive Gift Certificate

Now that you have a grasp of Publisher basics, you are ready to add sophisticated design elements to your work, and get your message in the mail. Publisher makes it easy to add fancy borders to text boxes, create curved text designs, wrap text around a frame, rotate text boxes, make your work portable, and get it into the hands of your audience. ▰▰▰ Image Magic has been hired to create a brochure for Piano Forte, a company that sells and services pianos. You have created a draft of the brochure and are making final enhancements to it. In addition to your design work, the client also wants you to send the brochure to their customers. Your contact at Piano Forte, Emma Rose, has given you a customer database you can use to address each brochure.

Adding BorderArt

Attractive borders can add pizzazz to a publication. You can add borders to any frame or text box. As with any design element, judicious use creates a smart, professional look; overuse distracts from the message. **BorderArt** lets you choose from a wide variety of decorative borders that come with Publisher. You can add a border to a text box using the BorderArt dialog box. In this dialog box, you can choose a border style and modify the border's appearance. ██████ You want to add an eye-catching, imaginative border design to the first page of the brochure.

STEPS

1. **Start Publisher, open the file** Pub H-1.PUB **from the drive and folder where your Data Files are located, then save it as** Piano Brochure

2. **Click the** text box **containing the text "Piano Forte" at** 8" H / 1" V
   In order to modify a frame or object, you must first select it. Compare your screen to Figure H-1.

3. **Press** [F9], **right-click the** text box, **click** Format Text Box, **click the** Colors and Lines **tab if necessary, then click** BorderArt
   The BorderArt dialog box opens. Borders can be simple lines of varying thickness or color, or they can be more elaborate designs that will help reinforce the theme of your document.

4. **Scroll through the** Available Borders list, **then click** Music Notes
   Figure H-2 shows the BorderArt dialog box with the Music Notes border selected. Available borders are listed in alphabetical order. When you click a border, the sample appears in the Preview box.

QUICK TIP
To remove existing BorderArt from a selected text box, open the Format Text Box dialog box, select the Color and Lines tab, click the Preset that represents the configuration you want, then click OK.

5. **Click the** Always apply at default size check box **to deselect it, then click** OK

6. **Select the contents of the** Weight text box, **type** 14, **then click** OK
   The BorderArt pattern appears on the edge of the text box, as shown in Figure H-3.

7. **Press** [F9], **then click the** Save button 🖫 **on the Standard toolbar**

Clues to Use

Creating custom BorderArt

In addition to choosing a border style in the BorderArt dialog box, you can create your own custom borders using almost any simple clip art or graphic image. To do so, open the BorderArt dialog box, then click the Create Custom button. You can choose from images in the Clip Gallery, or elsewhere on your computer. You can even create BorderArt from images you created. Click the Choose Picture button, locate the image, click the image, click OK, choose a name for your border, then click OK.

FIGURE H-1: **Text box selected**

BorderArt will be
applied to text box

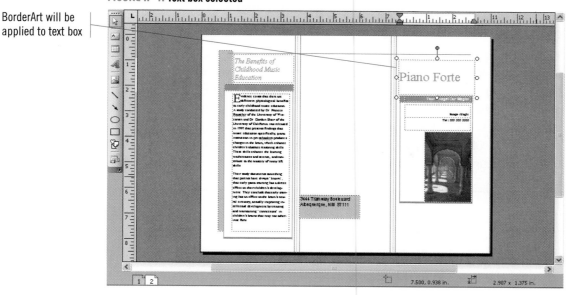

FIGURE H-2: **BorderArt dialog box**

Available borders
appear here

Deselect checkbox to
change the size of
the border

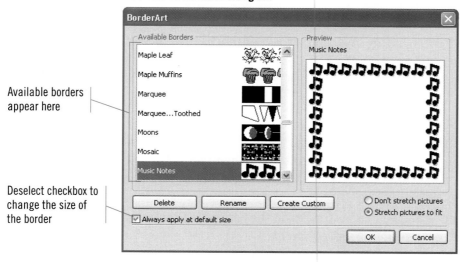

FIGURE H-3: **BorderArt added to text box**

BorderArt added

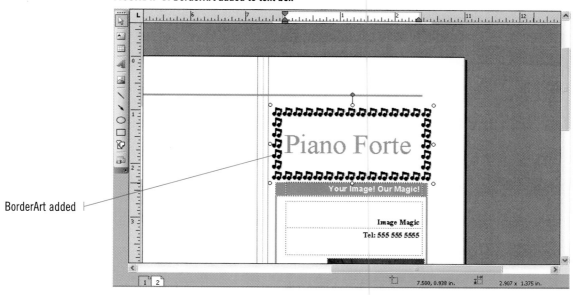

Designing WordArt

You have probably seen text that is curved, or in a specific shape, such as a circle or semi-circle. You can create this effect in Publisher by using **WordArt**. WordArt gives you a wide variety of text styles and effects from which to choose. You can transform text into all kinds of shapes, you can add shadows and patterns, and you can change text color. ░░░░░ You want to add WordArt to the right panel of page 2 to identify the store on what will be the back cover of the flyer. You want to emphasize the curve of the piano in the image at the bottom of the panel, so you decide to change the shape of the WordArt once you've inserted it, so that the text curves in a way to complement the piano's shape.

STEPS

1. **Click the page 2 icon on the status bar, then click the Insert WordArt button ▟ on the Objects toolbar**
   The WordArt Gallery displays 30 WordArt styles.

2. **Click the first box in the second row of the WordArt Gallery, as shown in Figure H-4**

3. **Click OK, type Piano Forte in the Edit WordArt Text dialog box, click the Size list arrow, click 28, then click OK**
   The Piano Forte WordArt object and the WordArt toolbar appear on the screen.

4. **Point to the WordArt object until the pointer changes to ⁺ᐟₖ, then drag the object so that its upper-left corner is at 8¼" H / ½" V**

5. **Click the WordArt Shape button ▲ on the WordArt toolbar, then click Wave 1 (the fifth shape in the third row)**
   The text takes on a "wavy" shape.

6. **Click the Format WordArt button ▧ on the WordArt toolbar, click the Fill Color list arrow, click the Accent 1 (Red) color box, then click OK**
   The color of the WordArt has been changed to match the color scheme in use. It creates a focal point that draws the reader's eye across the page.

7. **Click the Shadow Style button ▣ on the Formatting toolbar, then click Shadow Style 6 (the second style in the second row)**
   The shadows appear in the text design. This addition improves the design by adding an illusion of depth.

8. **Click anywhere on the scratch area**
   The WordArt is deselected and the WordArt toolbar closes. Compare your page to Figure H-5.

9. **Click the Save button ▣ on the Standard toolbar**

FIGURE H-4: WordArt Gallery

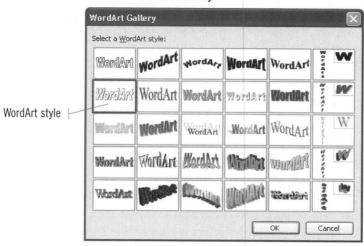

WordArt style

FIGURE H-5: WordArt design in publication

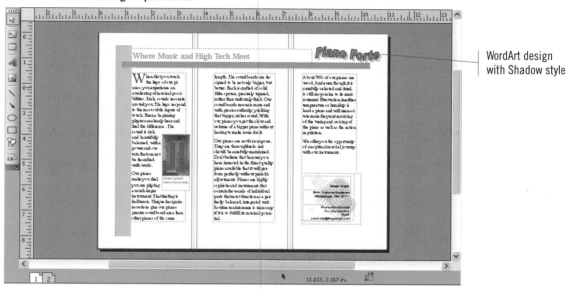

WordArt design with Shadow style

TABLE H-1: WordArt toolbar buttons

button	name	description
	Insert WordArt	Opens WordArt Gallery
Edit Text...	**Edit Text**	Opens Edit WordArt Text dialog box for modifying text in the current WordArt object
	WordArt Gallery	Displays available WordArt styles
	Format WordArt	Opens the Format WordArt dialog box for modifying the current WordArt object
	WordArt Shape	Opens a palette of available WordArt shapes for changing the current WordArt object
	Text Wrapping	Opens a list of text wrapping options for the current WordArt object
	WordArt Same Letter Heights	Makes all letter heights equal
	WordArt Vertical Text	Places text on the vertical axis
	WordArt Alignment	Opens a list of options for modifying text alignment in the current WordArt object
	WordArt Character Spacing	Allows you to change the character spacing within the current WordArt object

Wrapping Text Around an Object

The careful integration of an image with text creates a polished look, and can contribute to your overall design. One way to integrate text and images is to wrap text around an object. **Wrapping** text reshapes a text box (or just the flow of text in a text box) so it conforms to the shape of a nearby image or other object. Depending on an object's width, wrapped text can appear at the top and bottom, or along the sides, of the frame surrounding the object. You like what you have done so far, but you want to experiment with adding another image of a piano to page 2. You think that adding an object to the lower-left of the publication would create a new focal point, and wrapping text around an image could guide the reader's eyes across the page. The image of a piano will reinforce the subject matter of the brochure and direct the reader's eyes up and to the right.

STEPS

1. **Press [F9] if necessary, right-click the** photograph **at 3" H / 4½" V, then click** Delete Object
   The image disappears, and the text fills that space.

2. **Click** Insert **on the menu bar, point to** Picture, **click** From File, **click** Pub H-2.tif **from the drive and folder where your Data Files are located, then click** Insert
   The piano image is attractive.

3. **Right-click the** picture, **click** Format Picture, **then click the** Layout tab

4. **Select the contents of the** Horizontal text box **in the Position on page section, type** 1.25, **select the contents of the** Vertical text box **in the Position on page section, type** 5.5, **then click** OK
   The picture frame is inserted into the text box and Publisher's default text wrapping style, square, has been applied, as shown in Figure H-7. The image takes up so much space inside the connected text boxes that some text in the third text box doesn't fit.

QUICK TIP
Review text carefully after wrapping it to remove any awkward-looking hyphenation or isolated gaps of white space.

5. **Right-click the** picture, **click** Format Picture, **click the** Layout tab, **click the** Tight Wrapping Style button, **then click** OK
   Text is tightly wrapped around the image and slants upward along the lines of the image, as shown in Figure H-8. You don't see any problems with hyphenation, and the text that was in overflow is now inside the text box.

6. **Click the** Save button **on the Standard toolbar**

Design Matters

Editing wrap points

You can fine-tune the way text wraps around a detailed object by editing the **wrap points**, the sizing handles that surround the object. To edit these points, select the image, click Arrange on the menu bar, point to Text Wrapping, then click Edit Wrap Points. The handles appear around the image. You can add or delete handles by pressing and holding [Ctrl] as you click (to delete) or drag (to add). Figure H-6 shows the handles on an irregularly shaped picture with some of the handles moved to illustrate how that affects text wrapping. You can click and drag any handle to create interesting effects.

FIGURE H-6: Text wraps around points edited wrap

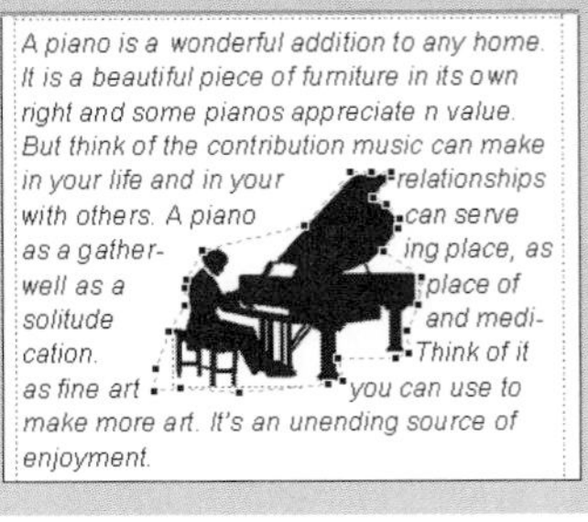

A piano is a wonderful addition to any home. It is a beautiful piece of furniture in its own right and some pianos appreciate n value. But think of the contribution music can make in your life and in your relationships with others. A piano can serve as a gather-ing place, as well as a place of solitude and medi-cation. Think of it as fine art you can use to make more art. It's an unending source of enjoyment.

FIGURE H-7: Image inserted in text box

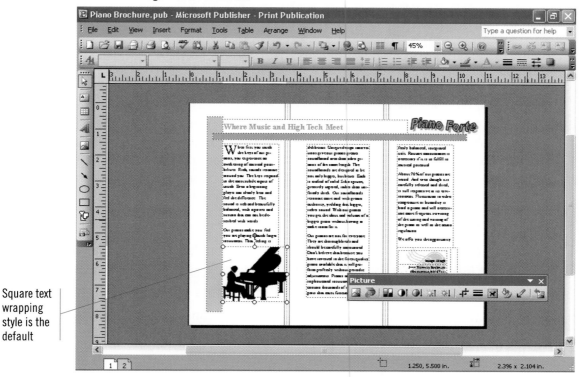

Square text
wrapping
style is the
default

FIGURE H-8: Text wrapped to image

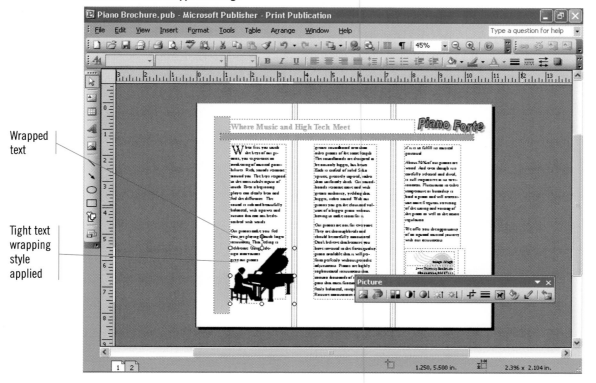

Wrapped
text

Tight text
wrapping
style
applied

Rotating a Text Box

You can rotate a text box to create interesting effects, or to reorient text for a specific purpose, such as folding a publication. By rotating text in selected text boxes, you can ensure that all text in the publication will be easy to read depending on its placement in the final, folded publication. You want to rotate a text box in the brochure to draw attention to important promotional text. You also want to rotate the recipients address and client's return address text boxes so they are "right side up" when the brochure is complete and folded for mailing. You want to use a rotated text box on the bottom of the first panel to add important text. First, you will create a text box, enter the promotional message, then rotate it into position on the page. Then, you'll create and rotate text boxes for the store's return address and the recipient's address. Both these new text boxes will appear in the middle panel of the brochure.

STEPS

1. **Click the** page 1 icon, **click the** Text Box button 🔲 **on the Objects toolbar, then drag to create a text box from** 7¾" H / 7¼" V **to** 10¼" H / 7¾" V

QUICK TIP

The promotional text should be brief but prominent; it is a visual analogy to a sound bite.

2. **Press** [F9], **if necessary, then type** In-Store Piano Lessons

3. **Press** [Ctrl][A], **click the** Font list arrow **on the Formatting toolbar, scroll if necessary and click** Arial Narrow, **click the** Font size list arrow **on the Formatting toolbar, click** 18, **click the** Bold button 🅱, **click the** Center button ▤, **then press** [Esc]
   Compare your screen to Figure H-9.

QUICK TIP

You can drag the text box into different positions and use the green rotation handle to fine-tune the positioning.

4. **Right-click the** text box, **click** Format Text Box, **click the** Size tab, **make sure that the height of the box is** 0.5" **and the width is** 2.5", **select the contents of the** Rotation text box, **type** –20, **then click** OK
   The text box is rotated -20˚.

5. **Click the** Fill Color list arrow 🎨▾ **on the Formatting toolbar, then click the** Accent 2 (RGB (255, 153, 153)) **color box**
   This text is more noticeable with the added fill color.

6. **Press** [F9], **click the** text box **at** 5" H / 6½" V, **click** Arrange **on the menu bar, point to** Rotate or Flip, **then click** Rotate Left 90˚
   The return address is now correctly placed and oriented for printing.

7. **Click** 🔲, **then drag** ✛ **from** 4½" H / 3" V **to** 7" H / 4½" V, **click** Arrange **on the menu bar, point to** Rotate or Flip, **then click** Rotate Left 90˚
   Compare your work to Figure H-10.

8. **Click the** Save button 🔲 **on the Standard toolbar**

FIGURE H-9: Completed text in text box

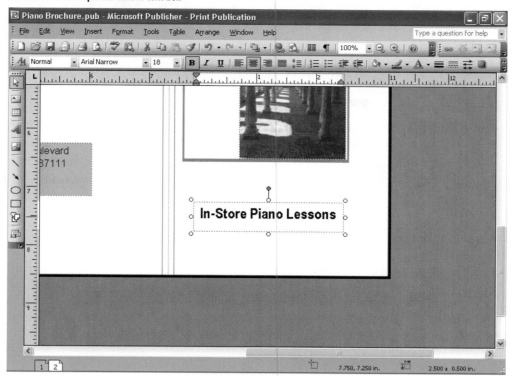

FIGURE H-10: Rotated text boxes

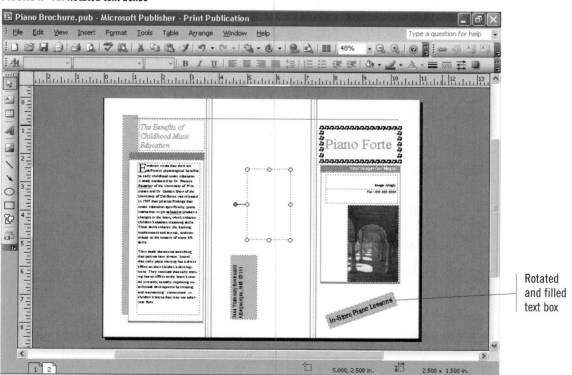

Rotated and filled text box

Understanding Mail Merge

A **mail merge** blends a publication that contains generic information with a data source that contains unique pieces of information. In Publisher, this feature is called **mail and catalog merge**. For example, a Publisher-generated gift certificate could contain generic text regarding the store's location and details about the gift, but unique text such as the first and last names of each recipient would come from a data source. Combining the two documents results in a set of customized versions of the publication. Figure H-11 shows an overview of a mail and catalog merge. Types of publications that can be customized include sales literature, postcards, greeting and invitation cards, catalogs, award certificates, gift certificates, and labels. You know that once the publication is complete, Piano Forte will want the brochure personalized with information it has collected about potential customers. Before you begin the mail merge process, you consider all the necessary steps.

DETAILS

- ### Select the recipients

  A **data source** is a file that contains information about the recipients. It is made up of fields organized into records. A **field** is a category of information—such as last name, first name, address, state, or zip code. A **record** is a set of information about an individual or an item—for example, a person's complete address. **Data source files** can come from several programs, but you will most likely use a database, a spreadsheet, a Microsoft Outlook contact list, or a table from a word processing program.

  If you don't have a data source file from another program, or prefer to create a new one, you can create one using Publisher. The Mail and Catalog Merge task pane guides you through the main steps: selecting or building a data source, selecting or creating the publication, previewing the merged publication, and completing the merge. The Mail and Catalog Merge task pane offers choices as to the type of information you can collect for the data source file, and even lets you add your own fields. Some commonly used mail merge information fields are address, city, zip code, country, e-mail address, and home phone.

- ### Create the publication

  A Publisher publication contains the generic information that appears in every merged publication. In the mail merge process, you insert a text box or a table frame that will contain the merge fields, where the unique information about the recipient is placed inside the publication. For example, you can insert the person's name in the Greeting line so that it will read "Dear John Smith." With the Mail and Catalog Merge task pane, it is easy to go back and edit the fields until you get exactly the publication you want.

- ### Consider Options

  Using the mail and catalog merge capabilities, you can filter and sort a subset of records. **Filtering** allows you to print, preview, or merge a portion of qualifying records. **Sorting** allows you to change the order in which the merged publications are printed or viewed.

- ### Preview the publications

  This feature allows you to look over the merged output before it is printed to catch any mistakes without wasting paper. This is particularly important since printing and mailing publications is so expensive. Paper, inks, envelopes, and even bulk postal rates are costly.

- ### Print the publication

  Publisher's Mail and Catalog Merge task pane uses dialog boxes to guide you through printing your publications.

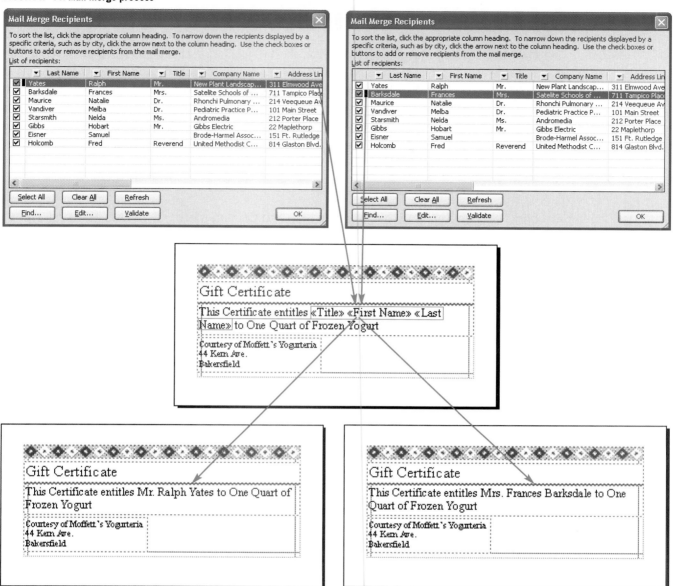

Design Matters

Catching costly errors

There are several types of spelling errors that demand your attention. The most obvious is the danger of misspelled words in a publication. Such errors make your company seem unprofessional. Another important spelling error is the misspelling of a person's name. Errors in people's names and titles can offend them. A simple misspelling or a misuse of Mrs. or Ms. may annoy potential clients to the point that they will not do business with your company. When in doubt, find a way to verify a potential misspelling: it pays off. Bulk mailings are often a one-way communication and you may never know that a recipient was offended.

Creating a Mail Merge

The **Mail and Catalog Merge task pane** is an effective tool for creating personalized publications. This feature guides you though the merging process and allows you to customize both your data source and your publication. It unites the power of the database and the functionality of the desktop publishing pro- gram.  Emma Rose, your contact at Piano Forte, has provided you with a data source containing a small group of customers. You want to test the merge on this smaller group before creating a merge docu- ment for their entire customer base. You want the merged address information to appear in the recipient text box you created in the middle panel of the second page.

STEPS

1. **Click** Tools **on the menu bar, point to** Mail and Catalog Merge, **then click** Mail and Catalog Merge Wizard

   The Mail and Catalog Merge task pane opens, displaying a brief introduction to merging, and the first in five steps in the merging process.

2. **Make sure the** Mail Merge option button **is selected, then click** Next: Select data source

3. **Click** Browse **in the Use an existing list section, open the file** PUB H-3.mdb **from the drive and folder where your Data Files are located, then click** OK **in the Mail Merge Recipients dialog box**

   The data source file is selected.

4. **Click** Next: Create your publication **at the bottom of the Mail and Catalog Merge task pane, if necessary click the text box at** 5½" H / 4" V **to select it, click** Address block **on the Mail and Catalog Merge task pane, adjust the settings in the Insert Address Block dialog box so they match the settings shown in Figure H-12, then click** OK

   The Insert Address Block dialog box provides a wide variety of ways to insert the recipient's name in the address block, and shows a preview of how it will look. On your screen, the address block field appears in the text box. It is difficult to read on the screen because it is rotated 90 degrees, but when the publications are printed and folded the recipient's address will be in just the right spot for mailing.

5. **Click** Next: Preview your publication **at the bottom of the Mail and Catalog Merge task pane**

   The address of the first recipient is inserted in the text box.

> **TROUBLE**
> If you added extra spaces to either the Title or Name fields, the spaces will appear in the text box, and your name and title will be shown with the extra spaces.

6. **Click** Edit recipient list, **click the first entry in the Mail Merge Recipients dialog box if necessary, then click** Edit

   Compare your screen to Figure H-13.

7. **Replace the first three fields in this record with your preferred title and your first and last names, click** Close, **then click** OK

   Your name and title appear in the text box on the brochure. Compare your screen to Figure H-14.

> **TROUBLE**
> If you find any mis- takes in the mail merge, use the link to the Previous task pane to go back and correct the mistakes. If necessary, print the pages again using the Test button.

8. **Click** Next: Complete the merge **at the bottom of the Mail and Catalog Merge task pane, click** Print, **make sure that the correct printer is selected, then click** Test **in the Print Merge dialog box**

   Examine your publication.

9. **Click** Cancel **to close the Print Merge dialog box, click the** Close button **on the Mail and Catalog Merge task pane, then click the** Save button 🖫 **on the standard toolbar**

FIGURE H-12: Insert Address Block dialog box

Formatting options for names

International mail requires that the country be specified; domestic mail does not

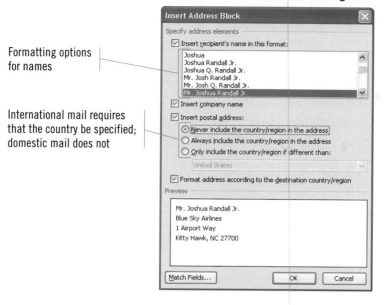

FIGURE H-13: Mail Merge Recipient's dialog box

Number of recipients on list

View is of first entry

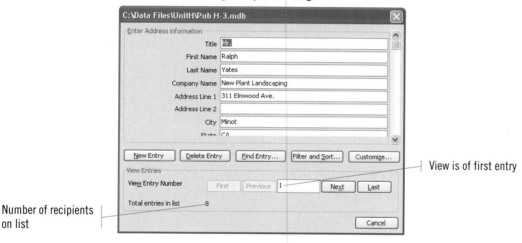

FIGURE H-14: Preview of the Mail Merge

Move back and forth between task panes

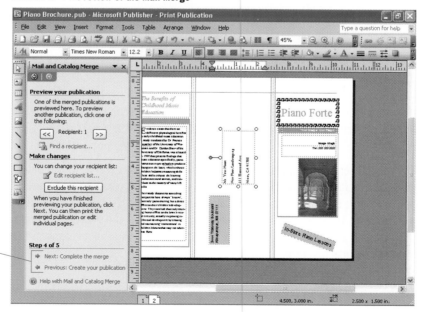

Publisher 2003

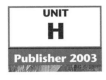

Preparing for Commercial Printing

Once your publication is completed, you can print it yourself, or send the files to a commercial printer for bulk printing with high-quality options and results. For professional output, it is important to consult with the printer during the design process to save time and expense. ▰▰▰▰ You know that once the project is complete and successfully tested, Piano Forte will want the brochure professionally printed. You examine the commercial printing options so you can start making arrangements.

DETAILS

- ### Consult the commercial printing professionals early

  Cost is important. You will need to know about quantity, quality, paper stock, binding, folding, trimming, and deadlines so that you can determine a budget and schedule. Ask your printer for recommendations on ways to reduce costs. For example, updating your graphics by doing your own scanning, or creating your own art files instead of relying on the printer's art services may reduce expenses.

- ### Determine the file format

  Once you select a printer, find out the required hand-off format. The **hand-off format** is the final format the printer receives. Publisher can create files in the PostScript or Publisher formats. You can also prepare your files in the CMYK format (composite postscript files in the cyan-magenta-yellow-black format), which many commercial printers prefer. There are advantages to using the Publisher format, but this option may also limit your commercial printing options. You also need to know if your printer prefers to accept transferred files on disks, by e-mail, by posting to an ftp site, or through some other means.

QUICK TIP
Once the file is saved as a PostScript, you cannot make any changes to it, so be sure to ask your commercial printer if it wants you to apply specific print settings.

- ### Explore the PostScript file format

  If your commercial printer doesn't accept Publisher files, or uses only Macintosh computers, you can use the **PostScript** file format. To do this, you can use Publisher's Help feature to install a PostScript printer driver on your computer, then follow the steps to use this driver. Figure H-15 shows the Save As PostScript File dialog box.

  Ask your commercial printing service if it wants you to apply any specific print settings, then save the publication in the PostScript format. Be aware that due to its large size, you may not be able to save a PostScript file directly to a floppy disk. Try saving to your hard drive, then copying to a floppy disk or other media, or transferring the file to the commercial printer via the Internet.

  Your printer may ask you for a CMYK PostScript file. CMYK, which stands for Cyan Magenta Yellow Black, is a color model used by many commercial printers. You can save a composite CMYK PostScript file by clicking Save As on the File menu, supplying a name for the file, clicking the Save as type list arrow, clicking PostScript, then clicking Save. Click Advanced Print Settings, click the Separations tab, click the Output list arrow, then click Composite CMYK. Select any additional options you want, then click Save.

- ### Learn about the Publisher format and the Pack and Go Wizard

  If your commercial printing service accepts Publisher format hand-off files, you can take advantage of several important features. The Publisher format is accessible with the Pack and Go Wizard, and verifies linked graphics, embeds TrueType fonts, and will pack all the files your printing service might need.

  The printing service can use Publisher format to do **pre-press work**. As part of this process, the printer can verify the availability of fonts and linked graphics, make color corrections or separations, and set the final printing options. Figure H-16 shows the Fonts dialog box, and Figure H-17 shows the Graphics Manager task pane. Using this task pane, you can easily determine the names, file types, and sizes of graphic objects in a publication. Each of these features gives your printing service important information about elements that make up your publication, and any potential problems.

FIGURE H-15: Save As PostScript File dialog box

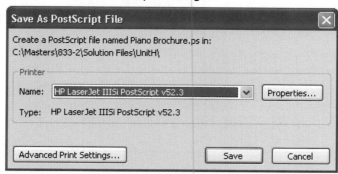

Save As PostScript File

Create a PostScript file named Piano Brochure.ps in:
C:\Masters\833-2\Solution Files\UnitH\

Printer

Name: HP LaserJet IIISi PostScript v52.3   ▼   Properties...

Type: HP LaserJet IIISi PostScript v52.3

Advanced Print Settings...   Save   Cancel

FIGURE H-16: Fonts dialog box

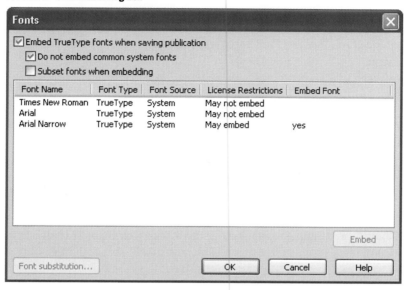

Fonts

☑ Embed TrueType fonts when saving publication
  ☑ Do not embed common system fonts
  ☐ Subset fonts when embedding

Font Name	Font Type	Font Source	License Restrictions	Embed Font
Times New Roman	TrueType	System	May not embed	
Arial	TrueType	System	May not embed	
Arial Narrow	TrueType	System	May embed	yes

Embed

Font substitution...   OK   Cancel   Help

FIGURE H-17: Graphics Manager task pane

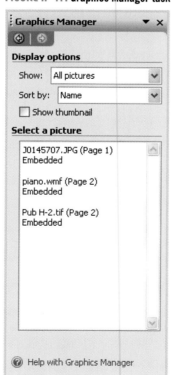

Graphics Manager   ▼ ✕

Display options

Show: All pictures   ▼

Sort by: Name   ▼
  ☐ Show thumbnail

Select a picture

J0145707.JPG (Page 1)
Embedded

piano.wmf (Page 2)
Embedded

Pub H-2.tif (Page 2)
Embedded

ⓘ Help with Graphics Manager

Publisher 2003

Using the Pack and Go Wizard

For this lesson, you will need a blank, formatted disk. You may need to put a publication on a disk to take to a commercial printing service, or to use at another computer. The **Pack and Go Wizard** lets you package all the fonts and graphic images needed to work with your publication elsewhere. You have arranged to have the Piano Forte brochure printed by a commercial printing service. They have requested that you provide the file on a disk, so you decide to use the Pack and Go Wizard to transfer the publication.

STEPS

1. **Click File on the menu bar, point to Pack and Go, then click Take to a Commercial Printing Service**

   The Pack and Go Wizard dialog box opens, as shown in Figure H-18. The first Pack and Go Wizard dialog box explains the advantages of using the wizard. The items included in the packaged publication file include embedded TrueType fonts and linked graphics. As part of the packing process, the wizard also prints the publication.

2. **Click Next**

   The second Pack and Go Wizard dialog box lets you determine where you want the packaged files.

3. **Make sure the A:\ option button is selected, place a blank formatted floppy disk in drive A, then click Next**

   The third Pack and Go Wizard dialog box lets you decide what attributes to include. You can embed TrueType fonts, include linked graphics, and create links for embedded graphics, or you can deselect any of these options, if necessary. By default, all three check boxes are selected.

4. **Click Next**

   The fourth Pack and Go Wizard dialog box is shown in Figure H-19. It lets you know the options you've selected, the file-naming scheme it will use, and how to unpack the files.

5. **Click Finish**

   As the Pack and Go Wizard works, you'll see that as the files are completed, several processes take place. The files are compressed and your publication (Piano Brochure.pub) is saved as packed01.puz. Once the publication has been successfully packed, the final Pack and Go Wizard dialog box opens, as shown in Figure H-20.

6. **Click OK**

   As part of the packaging process, the Wizard prints the publication.

7. **Click File on the menu bar, then click Exit**

Clues to Use

Taking files to another computer

You can also use the Pack and Go Wizard to take a publication to another computer, so that you can work on it elsewhere or give it to someone else to work on. The advantages are the same as when using this feature to provide the publication to a printer; the publication's files are compressed, and all the fonts and graphics travel with it, so you have everything you need to view and make changes. To use the Pack and Go Wizard to package files for another computer, click File on the menu bar, point to Pack and Go, then click Take to Another Computer. Click Next to advance through the dialog boxes, click Finish, then click OK.

FIGURE H-18: First Pack and Go Wizard dialog box

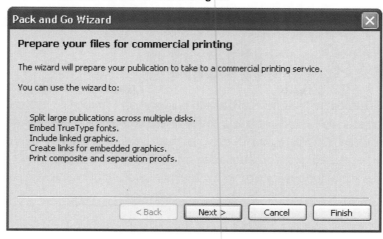

FIGURE H-19: Fourth Pack and Go Wizard dialog box

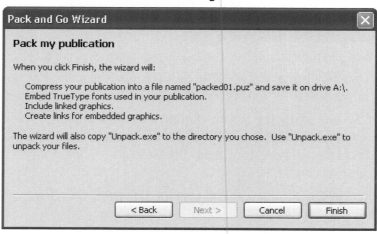

FIGURE H-20: Final Pack and Go Wizard dialog box

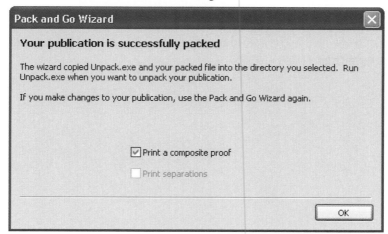

Capstone Project: Automotive Gift Certificate

You have learned the skills necessary to add BorderArt and WordArt to publications. You have wrapped text around objects and rotated text boxes. You have learned about and used the Mail and Catalog Merge feature and the Pack and Go Wizard, and the steps you should take for having your work printed commercially. You have been asked to create personalized gift certificates for select customers of an automotive service. You decide to enhance the certificate by adding thematic BorderArt before performing the mail merge.

STEPS

1. **Start Publisher, open the file** PUB H-4.pub **from the drive and folder where your Data Files are located, then save it as** Automotive Gift Certificate

2. **Enter an expiration date in the** text box **whose top-left corner is at** ½" H / 2½" V, **right-click the** text box **whose top-left corner is at** 4½" H / 1½" V, **click** Format Text Box, **click the** BorderArt button, **then click the** Firecrackers option

3. **Click the** Always apply at default size check box **to deselect it, click** OK, **change the Line weight to** 11, **click** OK, **click the** Line color list arrow ![icon] **on the Formatting toolbar, then click the** Accent 1 (Blue) color box

   The BorderArt pattern appears on the edge of the text box, as shown in Figure H-21.

4. **Click the text box at** 2½" H / 2" V, **click** Tools **on the menu bar, point to** Mail and Catalog Merge, **click** Mail Merge Wizard, **then click** Next: Select data source

5. **Click** Browse **under the Use an existing list section, open the file** PUB H-3.mdb **from the drive and folder where your Data Files are located, substitute your first and last names in the first record if necessary, then click** OK

   The data source file is selected.

6. **Click** Next: Create your publication **in the task pane, click** First Name **in the list box, then click** Last Name

   The First and Last Name fields appear in the text box, but there is no spacing between them.

TROUBLE

If your work needs editing, click Edit recipient list or Previous: Create your publication on the task pane to make corrections.

7. **Click between the double arrows separating the** First Name **and** Last Name **merge fields, press** [Spacebar], **then click** Next: Preview your publication

   Your first and last names appear in the text box.

8. **Click** Next: Complete the merge, **click** Print **in the Merge section of the task pane, make sure that the correct printer is selected, then click** Test

   Compare your publication to Figure H-22.

9. **Click** Cancel, **close the task pane, click the** Save button ![icon] **on the Standard toolbar, then exit Publisher**

FIGURE H-21: BorderArt applied to text box

FIGURE H-22: Test publication

Publisher 2003

Practice

▼ CONCEPTS REVIEW

Label each of the elements in the Publisher window shown in Figure H-23.

FIGURE H-23

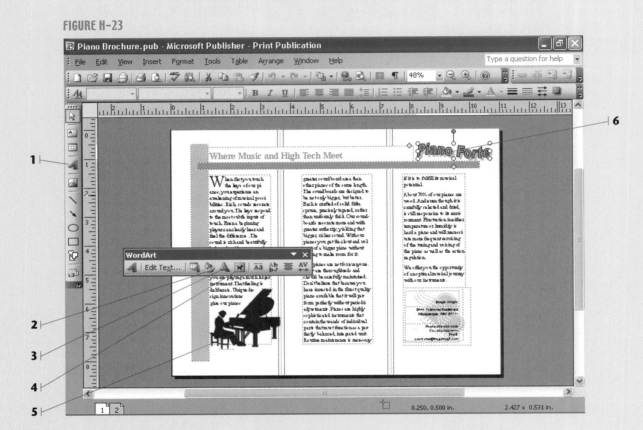

Match each of the buttons with the statement that describes its function.

7.
8.
9.
10.
11.
12.

a. Displays WordArt Gallery
b. Displays WordArt shapes
c. Formats WordArt
d. Edits wrap points
e. Changes line color
f. Inserts WordArt

Select the best answer from the list of choices.

13. Which feature blends two information sources together?
   a. File Blender
   b. Mail Marriage
   c. Mail and Catalog Merge
   d. WordArt

14. A file that contains information about the recipients of a mail merge is called a:
   a. Field.
   b. Record.
   c. Data source.
   d. Blend source.

15. **Which button is used to insert WordArt?**
    a.
    b.
    c.
    d.

16. **Which button is used to change a WordArt shape?**
    a.
    b.
    c.
    d.

17. **Which button is used to change how WordArt is aligned?**
    a.
    b.
    c.
    d.

18. **Each of the following is true about WordArt, except:**
    a. WordArt has a text wrapping menu.
    b. You cannot change character spacing in WordArt.
    c. You can resize WordArt.
    d. You can edit WordArt.

19. **You can make the following changes to BorderArt:**
    a. Customize BorderArt.
    b. Change the color of BorderArt.
    c. Change the point size of BorderArt.
    d. All of the above

20. **Which button is used to edit wrap points around a picture?**
    a.
    b.
    c.
    d.

▼ SKILLS REVIEW

Throughout these exercises, use the Zoom feature where necessary to work with the publication more easily.

1. **Add BorderArt.**
   a. Start Publisher.
   b. Open the file PUB H-5.pub from the drive and folder where your Data Files are located, then save it as **Gym Flyer**.
   c. Right-click the blue text box at 1" H / 2" V, click Format Text Box, then click BorderArt.
   d. Scroll through the list of Available Borders, then click Hearts.
   e. Click the Always apply at default size check box to deselect it, then click OK.
   f. Change the Line weight to 15, then click OK.
   g. Save your work.

2. **Design WordArt.**
   a. Click the Insert WordArt button on the Objects toolbar, then click the second box in the second row of the WordArt Gallery.
   b. Click OK, type **We Want You Back!** in the Text text box.
   c. Change the font size to 36 if necessary, make the text bold, then click OK.
   d. Reposition the WordArt so that its top-left corner is at 2" H / 1½" V.
   e. Apply the Double Wave 1 WordArt shape (the seventh shape in the third row).
   f. Add the Accent 2 (Gold) fill color to the WordArt.
   g. Save your work.

3. **Wrap text around an object.**
   a. Add the Heart AutoShape (first column, sixth row)
   b. Create an image of a heart whose top-left corner is at 1½" H / 5" V, and whose dimensions are 2½" H × 2½" V.
   c. Experiment by moving the wrap points to alter the shape of the wrapped text, then click the Undo button.
   d. Use the Fill Color list arrow and More Fill Colors to fill the heart with any shade of red you choose.
   e. Save the publication.

4. Rotate a text box.

  a. Draw a new text box anywhere that has the dimensions 1¾" H × ½" V.

  b. Type **We Miss You** in the text box, then change the font size to 20.

  c. Click the Bring to Front button on the Standard toolbar.

  d. Place the text box so that the top-left corner is at 1¾" H / 5¾" V (superimposed over the heart).

  e. Rotate the text box 25 degrees.

  f. Save your work.

5. Understand mail merge.

  a. Imagine that you are the owner of a flooring supply store. You are always looking for ways to communicate more effectively with your customers and your distributors. Given these goals, what kind of mail merge documents might you want to create?

  b. What types of information might be in the data source files for your company?

  c. What programs would you be likely to use to create these data source files?

6. Create a Mail and Catalog Merge.

  a. Start the Mail Merge Wizard.

  b. Select the file PUB H-3.mdb from the drive and folder where your Data Files are located as the data source, confirm that your first and last names and preferred title are in the first record, then click OK.

  c. Click Next: Create your publication, click the text box at 1½" H / 3" V to select it, press [F9], put the insertion point at the beginning of the text, then insert the Title and Last Name fields.

  d. Insert a space between the Title and Last Name merge fields.

  e. Go to the next task pane, then verify that your preferred title and last name are the first words in the text box.

  f. Go to the next task pane, click Print in the Merge section of the task pane, make sure that the correct printer is selected, then print a test. Click Cancel in the Print Merge dialog box.

  g. Save your work.

7. Prepare for commercial printing.

  a. Use the Web and your favorite search engine to research commercial printers and their requirements. Print at least one page that you find for a commercial printer.

  b. Make a list of requirements/suggestions from a commercial printer, or underline/highlight them on the Web page you printed.

8. Use the Pack and Go Wizard.

  a. Open the Pack and Go Wizard to take files to a commercial printing service.

  b. Use a blank, formatted floppy disk, if necessary.

  c. Answer **Next** to each of the Wizard dialog boxes, then click Finish in the last dialog box.

  d. Close the publication.

  e. Exit Publisher.

▼ INDEPENDENT CHALLENGE 1

As office manager for your company, you decide to make customized monthly calendars for the employees.

  a. Start Publisher and use the New Publication task pane to create a calendar using the Layers design in the Publications for Print category of the New from a design list.

  b. Use the Personal Information set of your choice to add appropriate information, and the color scheme of your choice.

  c. Save the publication as **Monthly Calendar** to the drive and folder where your Data Files are located.

  d. Add BorderArt of your choice, sized to 16 pt around the text box containing the month and year.

  e. Use the WordArt feature to create vertical text that reads **Go Team**. (*Hint*: The right side of the WordArt Gallery contains several vertical text templates.) Change the font size to 40 pt.

  f. Superimpose the WordArt over the filled text box to the left of the calendar.

  g. Modify the fill color of the WordArt to Accent 1.

  h. Type your name in the text box located at 2" H / 1½" V.

  i. Save and print the publication, then exit Publisher.

▼ INDEPENDENT CHALLENGE 2

The Believe It or Not Bookstore asks you to design a postcard announcing an upcoming book-signing event.

a. Start Publisher and use the New Publication task pane to create a schedule using the Schedule design in the Event Postcards section of the Publications for Print category of the New from a design list Gallery.

b. Use the Personal Information set of your choice to add appropriate information, and the color scheme of your choosing.

c. Save the publication as **Believe It or Not Postcard** to the drive and folder where your Data Files are located.

d. Add BorderArt around the Activities text box.

e. Modify the text at 2" H / 2" V with your own text.

f. Delete the object at 1" H / 1¾" V.

g. Delete the contents of the Activities text box.

h. Write appropriate text in the text box and add an image if you wish.

i. Add your name as the contact person.

j. Change any text as necessary to fit the theme of a book signing at the Believe It or Not Bookstore. Make up a suitable event title.

Advanced Challenge Exercises

- Edit the object in the center panel so it has multiple handles. (You can add wrap points if you choose.)
- Move the object to illustrate the effect of the multiple handles. Compare your publication to Figure H-24.

k. Save and print the publication, then exit Publisher.

FIGURE H-24

Publisher 2003

▼ INDEPENDENT CHALLENGE 3

Your Publisher skills convince you that you can open your own design shop, Design Center. First, you'll need business cards. You will use mail merge to personalize the cards for your employees and yourself.

a. Start Publisher, then choose a design in the Plain Paper Business Cards category of the Publications for Print category in the New from a design list.

b. Use the Personal Information set of your choice to add appropriate information, and add any color scheme you choose.

c. Save the publication as **Design Center Business Card** to the drive and folder where your Data Files are located.

d. Open the Mail and Catalog Merge Wizard, then select the file PUB H-3.mdb from the drive and folder where your Data Files are located as the data source.

e. Insert First and Last Name merge fields where you wish the names to appear on your business card.

f. Make sure the First and Last Name merge fields are separated by a space.

g. Preview the business card to make sure that your name appears. Make any necessary corrections.

h. Use the Print Merge dialog box to test print your business card.

i. Save the publication and exit Publisher.

 ▼ INDEPENDENT CHALLENGE 4

Image Magic is courting a potential client based in Toronto, Canada. The client wants Image Magic to design and lay out its monthly newsletter but wants to have the newsletter printed locally. They are concerned that it would be too difficult for you to transfer the files effectively to a commercial printing service in Canada. You tell the potential client that Publisher makes it easy to transport the publication. You decide to investigate this capability and create an informative flyer, so that you can solicit other long-distance clients who might have the same concerns.

a. Connect to the Internet and use your browser to go to www.microsoft.com. From there, search for information on commercial printing with Publisher. Another site that may contain information on this topic is www.business.com/directory/media_and_entertainment/publishing/printing/printers/commercial, or you can search on the topic using your favorite search engine.

b. Find out the key features and benefits of this Publisher feature, and print out any necessary information.

c. Start Publisher if necessary.

d. Use the Publication Gallery to create a flyer. Save the file as **Publisher Printing Options** to the drive and folder where your Data Files are located.

e. Use bulleted lists to briefly describe the benefits of the commercial printing features of Publisher.

f. Add BorderArt to call attention to a text box within the page.

Advanced Challenge Exercises

- Change the border art to a custom border using a piece of clip art.
- Add the same piece of clip art to the publication.
- Recolor the clip art. (*Hint*: Right-click the object, then click Format AutoShape.) Compare your publication to Figure H-25.

g. If necessary, make space for a new text box by deleting placeholder artwork.

h. Find at least one commercial printing service in Toronto that accepts Publisher files, and include its address on your flyer. (*Hint*: Look on Publisher's home page for directions on how to find a printing service.)

i. Make sure Your Name appears in the publication, save and print the publication, then exit Publisher.

FIGURE H-25

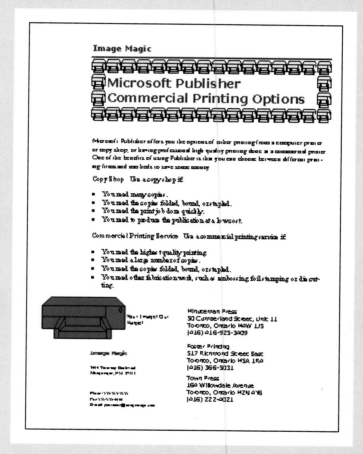

▼ VISUAL WORKSHOP

Use the New Publication task pane to create an Accessory Bar Price List Brochure as the initial design of a brochure for Craig's Toy Shop. Save this publication as **Toy Shop Brochure** to the drive and folder where your Data Files are located. Use Figure H-26 as a guide. The BorderArt around the text box at 9" H / 1½" V has a zigzag pattern. The style for the "Specializing In Model Airplanes" text comes from the WordArt Gallery—experiment to find the right style. Replace the store manager's name with your name. Save and print the first page.

FIGURE H-26

Back Panel Heading

This is a good place to briefly, but effectively, summarize your products or services. Sales copy is typically not included here.

Lorem ipsum dolor sit amet, consectetuer adipiscing elit, sed diem nonummy nibh euismod tincidunt ut lacreet dolor et accumsan

Craig's Toy Shop

Your Name,
Store Manager

Specializing In Model Airplanes!

Your Image! Our Magic!

Tel: 555 555 5555

Your Name,
Store Manager

Image Magic
214 Old Spanish Trail
Santa Fe, New Mexico 87501

Phone: 505-555-5555
Fax: 505-555-4444
Email: cxiksxcodxxxx@imagemagic.com

Caption describing picture or graphic.

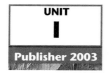

Working Efficiently

OBJECTIVES

Integrate with Office programs
Import a Word document
Use AutoCorrect
Record images
Embed and link objects
Use Design Checker
Understand speech recognition
Capstone Project: Dinner Invitation

Both choosing the right tool for the right job and choosing to do tasks in the best order help you to increase your effectiveness. Understanding how to integrate Publisher with other Office programs and peripheral devices means that you can join their strengths and work around their limitations. Learning how to use additional features, such as AutoCorrect and Speech Recognition, can speed up your work. AutoCorrect automatically fixes your typing errors as you type. Speech recognition software lets you create text and initiate commands vocally. ▰▰▰ Image Magic is holding a two-day computer-training course for its employees. The goals of the training sessions are to introduce the employees to efficient methods of working with Publisher and other Microsoft applications, as well as to use peripheral devices to enhance and speed up their work. You have been asked to organize and create course materials for this event.

Integrating with Office Programs

All Microsoft Office programs are designed to work together. Because the Office programs have a similar look and feel, your familiarity with one program can make it easier to use others. Another advantage of using Office programs is that you can easily transfer information or objects created in one program to another. One of the goals of the training course is to familiarize employees with business productivity software, and advise them on which programs are best suited to individual jobs. To make the training interactive, you decide to ask co-workers familiar with specific programs to speak about how they use them at Image Magic.

DETAILS

- ### Microsoft Word

  Almost everyone at Image Magic uses Word, a **word processing** program, to create letters, memos, reports, and stories. But not everyone is as familiar with Publisher as you are. You plan to educate employees about how they can import a Word document, such as the one shown in Figure I-1, into a publication, in order to take advantage of some features in Word, such as grammar checking and word count, which aren't available in Publisher.

- ### Microsoft Excel

  Many employees use Excel, an **electronic spreadsheet** program that automatically calculates and analyzes data and creates powerful charts. A **chart** is a graphical representation of data. Ricardo Fernandez, Image Magic's office manager, uses Excel to create budgets and financial statements, and to track customer billing and invoices. Figure I-2 shows an Excel worksheet with data and a chart. This chart is also shown in Figure I-3, after it was pasted into a publication in Publisher.

- ### Microsoft PowerPoint

  When they need to present information to a group of people, employees create professional visual presentations using PowerPoint. A **presentation** is a series of projected slides and/or handouts that a speaker refers to while delivering information. Together, Publisher and PowerPoint can make for an impressive and cohesive presentation using a slide show from PowerPoint and supporting documents from Publisher, which share similar fonts and colors. Maria Abbot, Image Magic's president, will use PowerPoint to create a slide show summarizing the company's growth and financial performance; she will give the presentation during the training session, and later at an annual meeting of investors, creditors, and clients.

- ### Microsoft Access

  Complex data can be organized, tracked, and updated using an Access database. A **database** is a collection of related information that is organized into tables, records, and fields. Information in a database can be sorted and retrieved in a variety of ways, and then used to make business decisions. Access databases can be used as a data source for Publisher mail merges. Nancy Garrott, Image Magic's marketing manager, uses Access to create and maintain a customer information database. She shares this information with the accounting department so it does not have to re-enter information about new customers and sales.

- ### Microsoft Outlook

  All employees use the Outlook **personal information manager** to keep track of business and personal contacts and to schedule appointments. Outlook contact lists can be used as data sources for mail merges in Publisher.

- ### Office tools

  All Office programs include **online collaboration**, the ability to share information over the Internet. Employees can schedule online meetings and have discussions over the World Wide Web. **Speech Recognition** lets them enter data and give commands verbally using a computer microphone. You can use the Research task pane to reference online information from reference sources such as the Encarta Dictionary, Thesaurus, eLibrary, Factiva Search, and MSN Search.

FIGURE I-1: Word document

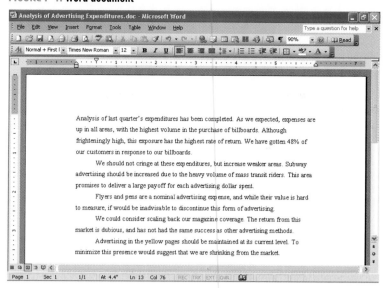

FIGURE I-2: Excel worksheet containing a chart

Pie chart

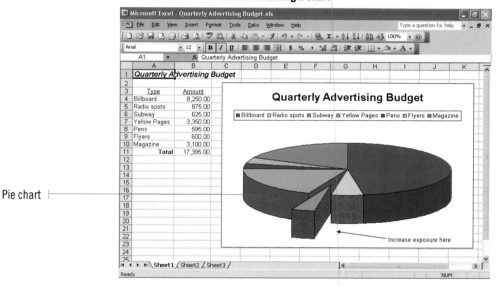

FIGURE I-3: Excel chart and Word story in publication

Word document imported into a Publisher newsletter

Excel chart supports the text

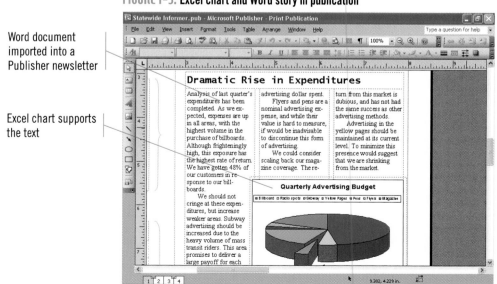

Importing a Word Document

You have already imported Word documents into text boxes. You have also edited a Publisher story in Word and returned it to Publisher. Publisher also lets you import Word documents directly into a publication, where you can automatically add design elements to ensure that all of your documents have similar designs and maintain the same look and feel. It also provides an easy way to enhance an unformatted Word document. ▰▰▰▰ You want to include a book review in the pre-course materials. This publication will be distributed one week before the training session and will be designed to raise questions about job effectiveness and to spark discussion.

STEPS

TROUBLE
If you get a warning box that you need a converter, contact your instructor or technical support person.

1. **Start Publisher, click** Publications for Print **in the New from a design list in the New Publication task pane if necessary, click** Import Word Documents, **then click the** Linear Accent Word Document **in the Publication Gallery**
   The Import Word Document dialog box opens.

2. **Navigate to the location where your Data Files are located, as shown in Figure I-4**

3. **Click the file** PUB I-1.doc **from the drive and folder where your Data Files are located, click OK in the Import Word Document dialog box, then save the publication as** Book Review
   The Word document is imported into a Publisher text box and the Word Import Options task pane opens.

TROUBLE
Your color scheme may differ from the one shown in the figure. This is not a problem.

4. **Click the** 2 Columns button **in the task pane, as shown in Figure I-5**
   The two-column format looks great and makes the document easier to read.

5. **Click the** Close button **on the task pane, then press** [F9]

6. **Click the** Document Title placeholder text, **then type** Sources of Power: How People Make Decisions
   The title of the book review is inserted, but it looks too small.

7. **Press** [Ctrl][A] **to select the text, click Format on the menu bar, point to** AutoFit Text, **then click** Best Fit
   The font size of the title is now larger.

8. **Right-click the** text box **whose top-left corner is at** 1" H / ½" V, **then click** Delete Object
   Page numbers are not necessary because this is a single-page publication. Compare your page to Figure 1-6.

9. **Press** [F9], **click the** Save button 🖫 **on the Standard toolbar, then close the publication**

FIGURE I-4: Import Word Document dialog box

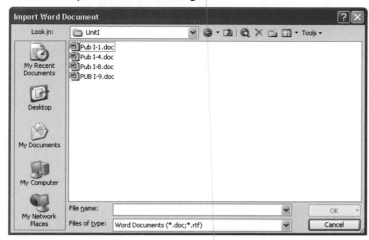

FIGURE I-5: Word Import Options task pane

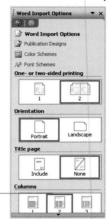

2-column format button

FIGURE I-6: Imported Word Document

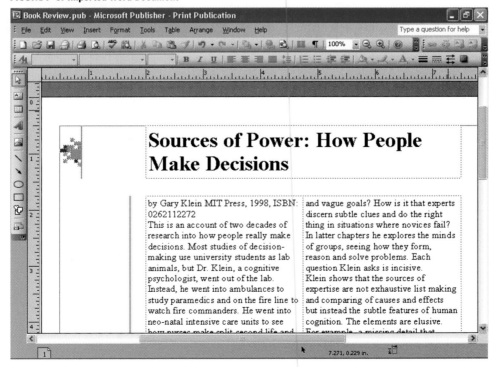

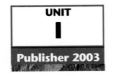

Using AutoCorrect

The **AutoCorrect** feature can detect and correct misspelled words, typos, and other common errors as you type. For example, if you type "yuo" followed by a space, AutoCorrect replaces the incorrect word with "you." In addition, AutoCorrect lets you quickly insert text, graphics, or symbols. For example, you can type "(tm)" to insert ™, or customize AutoCorrect to automatically replace abbreviations such as "potus" with President of the United States. ▰▰▰ You want to change the AutoCorrect settings to speed up your work and help avoid spelling errors as you generate training materials for the course. You review how AutoCorrect works and how it can be modified.

DETAILS

QUICK TIP
There are different versions of Microsoft Office depending on your dialect or language. Each has its own AutoCorrect feature and dictionary.

- ### Add to or change AutoCorrect entries

  AutoCorrect uses AutoCorrect entries, a list of commonly misspelled words and typos, to detect misusages and automatically correct them. It also contains some common symbols, such as ©, that can be substituted for specific keystrokes. You can easily add your own custom AutoCorrect entries or remove unwanted ones by clicking Tools on the menu bar, then clicking AutoCorrect. You can make additions or changes to AutoCorrect in the AutoCorrect: English dialog box. You can add an entry to AutoCorrect by typing the text you want replaced in the Replace text box, and the text that will replace it in the With text box. Once you create your entry, click Add, and the new AutoCorrect entry will be in effect. Figure I-7 shows a new entry added to AutoCorrect. You can delete an AutoCorrect entry by clicking the entry you want to delete, then clicking Delete. You can also use AutoCorrect to format as you type. By clicking the AutoFormat As You Type tab in the AutoCorrect dialog box, shown in Figure I-8, you can set this feature to automatically apply bullets and numbers to lists of text.

- ### Use AutoCorrect to correct capitalization errors

  AutoCorrect recognizes words that are commonly capitalized and corrects them when they are entered incorrectly. For example, the first word in a sentence, or the days of the week, are recognized and corrected if they are not capitalized. AutoCorrect also recognizes when the first two letters of a word have been capitalized incorrectly and makes the second letter lowercase. You can also add names or words that you want capitalized or in lowercase to the AutoCorrect entries.

- ### Use AutoCorrect to correct spelling errors

  AutoCorrect works differently than the Publisher Spell Checker. The Spell Checker does not automatically correct all of your spelling errors. After it identifies potential misspellings, it underlines the words with a red wavy line. As you edit your publication, you can decide whether the underlined words are truly misspelled. AutoCorrect, on the other hand, makes spelling corrections automatically. With AutoCorrect, you enter your common misspellings and the proper replacement spellings. It then identifies the misspellings and makes the replacements as you type.

- ### Prevent AutoCorrect from making specific corrections

  To modify AutoCorrect, you can turn options on and off, or edit the AutoCorrect entries. For the AutoCorrect capitalization and Spelling Checker options, you can also create an exceptions list that specifies which words should not be changed. For example, you can prevent AutoCorrect from capitalizing a word that you want to appear in lowercase for stylistic reasons.

FIGURE I-7: Entry added in AutoCorrect dialog box

List of capitalization errors
and AutoCorrect options

AutoCorrect entries
appear alphabetically

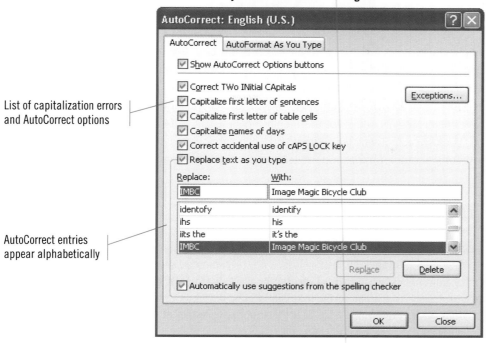

Deselect features to maintain
a design theme

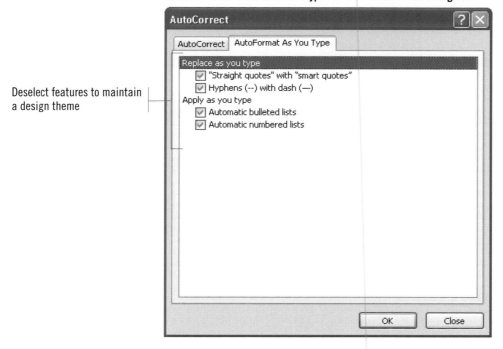

FIGURE I-8: AutoFormat As You Type tab in the AutoCorrect dialog box

Design Matters

Using tools wisely

AutoCorrect is a powerful tool. However, like all tools, it is important to recognize appropriate uses and limitations. There may be occasions when, for design or literary reasons, you want to turn off AutoCorrect features. Consider how the works of Mark Twain, James Joyce, e. e. Cummings, Lewis Carroll, and other English-speaking authors would have been altered by the tools found in software products. Knowing how and when to use a tool is vital. Knowing when and how to dispense with a tool is important, too.

Recording Images

Publisher is a powerful program because of its ability to handle both text and graphics. As your publications become targeted to a specific audience, your choice of graphic images will become targeted as well. Instead of relying on digital images created by others, you may wish to create your own. A **digital image** is a picture in an electronic file. The two most common methods of creating digital images are using a scanner and using a digital camera. █████ You want the training materials to foster a sense of inclusion and help all employees get to know each other. You decide to ask each employee to provide a favorite photo for you to scan, or to pose for a photograph that you will take with a digital camera.

DETAILS

- **Types of scanners**

  There are many kinds of scanners in use today, each with advantages and disadvantages. By far, the most popular scanners are the flatbed and sheetfed variety. Some common features to both types are that they come with their own software that must be loaded on the computer, and they must be connected to a computer. Most scanners come with **optical character recognition** (**OCR**) software for scanning and translating text documents. To scan an image into Publisher, you click Insert on the menu bar, point to Picture, then click From Scanner or Camera. The Insert Picture from Scanner or Camera dialog box opens, and the installed scanner appears, as shown in Figure I-9.

  - **Using a flatbed scanner**

    A **flatbed scanner** has a flat surface from which the image is scanned, and it is the best type for creating digital images from photos and printed materials. To scan an item, you place it face down on the scanner's glass surface, just as you would on a copy machine. Since you can remove the scanner's lid, you can scan large objects, such as books, because you can place the object face down on the glass. The biggest disadvantage of a flatbed scanner is that it takes up space on your desk because of its large flat glass surface.

  - **Using a sheetfed scanner**

    The biggest advantage of a **sheetfed scanner** is its size. Commonly the size of a portable printer, it takes up little space on a crowded desktop. Instead of placing a document on a flat piece of glass, you feed the document into the scanning system using rollers. This limits sheetfed scanners to scanning single sheets of paper, which makes scanning a page from a book or other bulky object impossible. Most sheetfed scanners are more adept at scanning text than photos.

- **Digital cameras**

  Unlike other cameras, a **digital camera** does not require film; it stores images on a memory device. Pictures are stored on the device until they are transferred to another storage medium or are deleted. The memory device can then be used again to take and store more images. The number of pictures a camera can save depends on the **resolution** (the density of **pixels**, or color dots) and the capacity of the memory device. Generally, the higher the resolution, the fewer pictures can be stored. Some digital cameras can store four times as many low-resolution pictures as high-resolution images.

  Once you take the pictures that you want, you must download them using a software program that comes with the digital camera. As with scanners, the software program must be installed on your computer to download the pictures. In addition, you need a way to transfer the images from the camera to the computer. Some cameras use a floppy disk to transfer the images, while some connect to a computer using a cable. Many digital camera software programs let you organize your images in digital photo albums; an example is shown in Figure I-10.

- **Copyright laws**

  Images that you take with either a digital camera or film camera are your property to use as you want. However, images from other sources, including magazines, books, and the Internet, are the intellectual property of others and may be copyrighted and have limitations placed on their use. Permission for you to use an image may be granted by the copyright holder; sometimes permission is received just by asking, and other times you may be required to pay a fee. It is your legal and ethical responsibility to only use images that belong to you or that you have permission to use.

FIGURE I-9: Insert Picture from Scanner or Camera dialog box

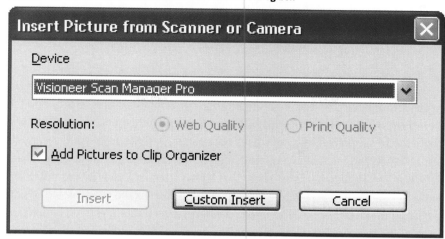

FIGURE I-10: Image Expert photo album

Design Matters

Studying color

Color is one of the most difficult areas of design to master, for a variety of reasons. Color perceptions and descriptions are subjective since the human eye can detect several million hues. Adding to that complexity is the limitation of language to deal meaningfully with so many shades of color. Also, between five to eight percent of males have some defect of color vision (females are much less affected because color-blindness is a male dominant trait). Considering the limitations of language and perception, a good way to study color is by using a color wheel. **Color wheels** teach color relationships by organizing colors in a circle so you can visualize how they relate to each other.

Embedding and Linking Objects

You can link or embed objects from other programs, such as pictures, charts, and tables, into a publication. An **embedded object** is a copy that is pasted into a publication. It maintains no ties to the original, so that if the original is modified, the copy does not change. A **linked object** is a copy that is connected to the original. When the original is modified, the copy is updated to reflect those changes. For example, you might want to include an Excel chart that shows quarterly sales in promotional literature for potential investors or informational literature for employees. If you link the chart instead of simply embedding it, then the chart in the publication will be updated whenever new data is entered into the Excel workbook. As part of the training literature, you want to include a chart of Image Magic's growth in a publication that documents the history of the company. Because you anticipate using the publication in the future with only minor changes, you want to explore different ways of importing the chart from Excel.

- **Embedded objects**

  An **embedded object** is created in another program and copied to a publication in Publisher. The **source file** contains the original information, and the **destination file** is the recipient of the information. There is no connection between the two programs, so if you modify the information in the source file, the information in the destination file does not change.

  The advantages of embedding are permanence and portability. You do not have to worry that a source file will be deleted, moved, or renamed, which would render the link between the files useless, or that its contents or formatting will change. Because the object is contained within your publication, it will stay the same unless you change it. An embedded object can always be edited using its original program by double-clicking it, but once the editing is done, the connection is again severed. To embed an object in any Office program, click the object, then click the Copy button 📋 on the Standard toolbar. You can embed the object by clicking the Paste button 📋 on the Standard toolbar, or by clicking the copied item on the Office Clipboard, as shown in Figure I-11.

  The disadvantages of embedding an object are that it increases the size of the publication, and if any changes are made to the source file, they are not updated in the destination file.

- **Linked objects**

  A **linked object** has a connection to the original object. When the object is updated in the source file, it is automatically updated in the publication (the destination file).

  Linking has two advantages over embedding. First, the publication file is smaller because it contains only links to the objects, not the objects themselves. Second, if changes are made to the source objects, they are automatically reflected in the publication when you view the objects. You can link an object in any Office program by clicking the object to select it, then clicking the Copy button 📋 on the Standard toolbar. Once the object is copied, click Edit on the menu bar, then click Paste Special. The Paste Special dialog box opens, showing the source of the copied data. Click the Paste Link option button, as shown in Figure I-12, then click OK.

  The disadvantages are that the contents may change and those changes will not be reflected in the surrounding text; the formatting may change and be disruptive to your design; and if you move, delete, or rename the source file, the link is broken.

FIGURE I-11: Objects copied the Office Clipboard

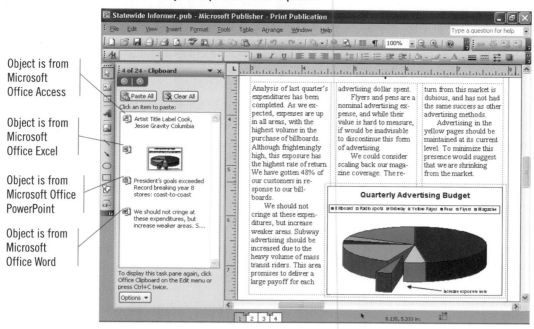

Object is from Microsoft Office Access

Object is from Microsoft Office Excel

Object is from Microsoft Office PowerPoint

Object is from Microsoft Office Word

FIGURE I-12: Paste Special dialog box

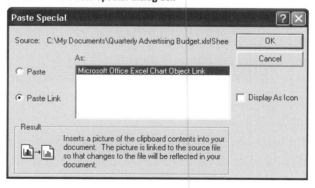

Clues to Use

Using Publisher E-mail

Publisher contains six e-mail wizards that can be used to create electronic publications. These publications are designed to contain hyperlinks. If you use Microsoft Office Outlook Express (version 5.0 or later), you can send a single publication page as the body of an e-mail message. You can use any of the 45 Master Design Sets to keep your e-mail messages consistent with your publication designs.

Using Design Checker

Because there are multiple elements of text and graphics in most publications, you can miss design problems in a casual review. **Design Checker** looks for errors in layout, alerts you, and suggests changes, but it does not fix the problems automatically. There may be times when your design choices may cause you to reject the Design Checker suggestions, but often it can help find areas of your publication that you can improve. ▰▰▰▰ You created a flyer containing intentional errors that can be used to dramatize the capabilities of the Design Checker feature. You want to use this publication so others can see how Design Checker works.

STEPS

1. **Open the file** PUB I-2.pub **from the drive and folder where your Data Files are located, then save it as** Training Flyer

   The flyer appears on the screen. It has two areas of color on the page.

2. **Click** Tools **on the menu bar, then click** Design Checker

   The Design Checker task pane opens. By default, it will check all pages, as well as the Master Page.

3. **Click** Design Checker Options **at the bottom of the Design Checker task pane, click the** Checks tab, **read all the selected features that Design Checker can examine, then make sure all your checkboxes contain a checkmark**

   See Figure I-13.

4. **Click** OK **in the Design Checker task Options dialog box**

   The errors found by the Design Checker do not have to be addressed or fixed in any particular order. Design Checker finds that part of the e-mail address went into the overflow area. Design Checker makes suggestions about possible remedies in the task pane. Several errors are listed in the task pane. The first error listed reads "Page has space below top margin." In order to go to a specific item listed in the task pane, you have to position the pointer over the item, then click the list arrow that appears to the right of the item.

5. **Click the list arrow to the right of item 2:** Picture is not scaled proportionally (Page 1) **on the Design Checker task pane, as shown in Figure I-14**

   Design Checker finds that the Image Magic logo does not have its original proportions, as shown in Figure I-14.

6. **Click** Fix: Rescale Picture

   The logo is resized to its original proportions.

7. **Click the list arrow next to** Story with text in overflow area (Page 1) **on the Design Checker task pane, click** Go to this Item, **point to the right border of the text until the pointer changes to ←→, drag the border to 3"H, then click anywhere in the** scratch area **to deselect the text box**

8. **Click the** list arrow **next to** Page has space below top margin (Page 1) **on the Design Checker task pane, click** Go to this item, **then press ↑ until the selected objects are at the top of the page**

   There are no more items in the Design Checker task pane.

9. **Make sure Your Name displays in the e-mail address in the lower-left text box, click the** Print button 🖨 **on the Standard toolbar, click the** Save button 🖫 **on the Standard toolbar, then exit Publisher**

FIGURE I-13: Design Checker Options dialog box

FIGURE I-14: Design Checker results

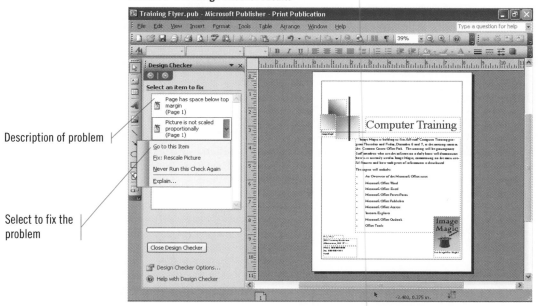

Description of problem

Select to fix the problem

Design Matters

Working with Design Checker

Design Checker is a good and valuable tool, but it is crucial to recognize its limitations. For example, Design Checker does not recognize WordArt as text; instead, it considers it an object, and does not recognize it when it is placed on an otherwise empty text box. It does not recognize color clashes, or insufficient white space in a publication. You can work around these limitations by visually inspecting a publication in addition to running Design Checker. In addition, there may be occasions when you wish to ignore the Design Checker suggestions in order to achieve a design goal. For example, you may want to change the proportions of an image to create an interesting visual effect, or simply to fill a space.

Publisher 2003

Understanding Speech Recognition

Speech recognition is an emerging technology that translates spoken language into computer commands or text. When you talk into a microphone connected to a computer, your words are converted into a text file by a software package.  You have heard a lot about speech recognition technology. You think a brief overview of the technology would interest employees at the training session and foster discussion about improving work practices at Image Magic. You consider some key issues related to speech recognition that you want to bring up at the training session.

DETAILS

- **Installation**

  Installation of the Speech Recognition component may require the installation of additional software from your Publisher CD, and requires answering some simple questions in several dialog boxes.

- **Training sessions**

  The first time you start the Speech Recognition feature the Training Wizard opens, as shown in Figure I-15. Training involves reading a series of paragraphs into your computer's microphone. Figure I-16 shows an explanatory dialog box that appears before the training session. The training sessions teach the software's speech module to recognize your voice, and teach you the correct speed and clarity that are understandable to the program, as shown in Figure I-17. Training sessions can be completed more than once, and repetition results in improved performance of the Speech Recognition module.

- **Using Speech Recognition**

  Once the Speech Recognition component is installed in Word, it is available for all Office applications (except Office Designer) and can be turned on by clicking Tools on the menu bar, then clicking Speech. With Speech Recognition turned on, the language bar appears in the application title bar.

Clues to Use

Choosing a microphone

Many newer computers come with a microphone already installed, allowing you to easily use the speech recognition feature. If your computer did not come with this accessory, use the Web to research manufacturers and styles, and to learn which models work best with your system. Connect to the Internet, then use your browser and your favorite search engine to search on "PC microphones" or "PC sound systems."

FIGURE I-15: Welcome to Office Speech Recognition dialog box

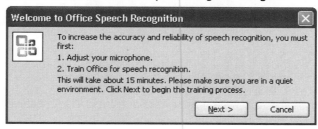

FIGURE I-16: Voice Training dialog box

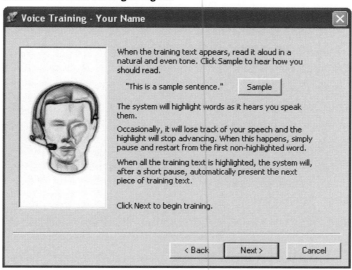

FIGURE I-17: Voice Training dialog box

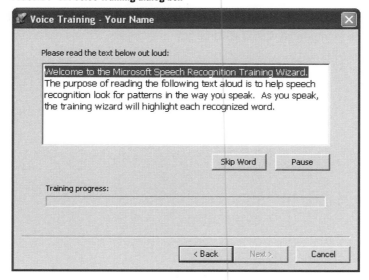

Publisher 2003

Capstone Project: Dinner Invitation

You have learned the skills necessary to transform Word documents into publications. You have learned about and used Design Checker. You have also learned about using alternative input devices: scanners, digital cameras, and speech recognition, as well as linking and embedding objects. ████ The president is inviting the staff of Image Magic to a formal dinner. The invitations will be engraved so you want them to be perfect when you hand the file over to the printer. You decide to use the Design Checker.

STEPS

1. **Start Publisher, open the file** PUB I-3.pub **from the drive and folder where your Data Files are located, then save it as** Dinner Invitation

   The invitation appears on the screen with two elements of color alongside the text at the top and bottom.

2. **Click** Tools **on the menu bar, then click** Design Checker

   The Design Checker task pane opens, as shown in Figure I-18. By default, it will check all pages, as well as the Master Page.

3. **Click the** Object has no line or fill (Page 1) **list arrow, then click** Fix: Delete Object

   The first item in the task pane has been checked off and is no longer displayed.

4. **Click the** Page has space below top margin (Page 1) **list arrow, then click again to close it**

   Design Checker finds that there is more than 1 inch of blank space at the top of page 1. This white space is intentional since it allows you to personalize the invitations with a quick note of thanks to each employee, recognizing their hard work.

5. **Click the** Picture is not scaled proportionally (Page 1) **list arrow, then click** Fix: Rescale Picture

   This item in the Design Checker task pane has been corrected and is no longer displayed.

6. **Click the** Page has space below top margin (Page 2) **list arrow,** click Go to this Item, **then drag the selected objects to the top of the page**

   The remaining items in the Design Checker task pane are not troublesome to you.

7. **Scroll so page 3 is visible, then delete the extra spaces between the words "some" and "business"**

   Compare your work to Figure I-19.

8. **Click the** Save button 🖫 **on the Standard toolbar, then exit Publisher**

   Examine your printed page. If you find any mistakes, go back and correct the mistakes. If necessary, print the pages again.

FIGURE I-18: Design Checker task pane

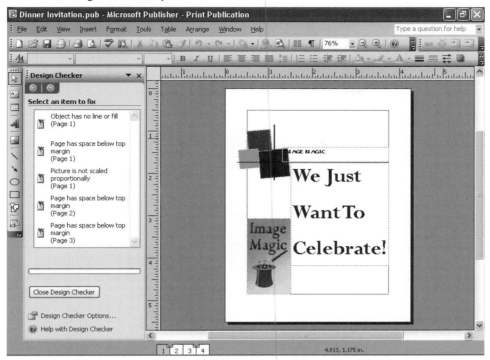

FIGURE I-19: Completed Dinner Invitation

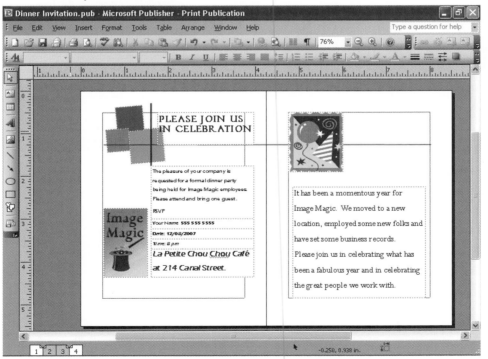

Practice

▼ CONCEPTS REVIEW

Label each of the programs that created the Office Clipboard contents shown in Figure I-20.

FIGURE I-20

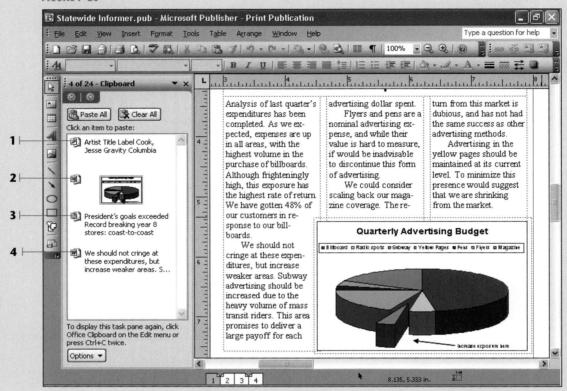

Match each of the features with the statement that describes its function or attribute.

5. **Embedded object**

6. **Design Checker**

7. **Digital cameras**

8. **AutoCorrect entries**

9. **Linked object**

10. **Flatbed scanner**

a. Finds problems such as an object in non-printing areas of the page

b. Maintains a connection to the source file

c. Creates images free of copyright restrictions

d. List of common misspellings

e. Transforms images or text into electronic files

f. Must be double-clicked for editing

Select the best answer from the list of choices.

11. **A linked object:**
    a. Can never be updated.
    b. Is updated when the source file is changed.
    c. Is updated by double-clicking on the object.
    d. Has to be removed from the publication for updating.

12. **Which Microsoft product can you use to organize data into tables, records, and fields?**
    a. Access
    b. Excel
    c. Outlook
    d. PowerPoint

13. **Which Microsoft product can you use to exchange e-mail across the Internet?**
    a. Access
    b. Outlook
    c. Excel
    d. PowerPoint

14 **AutoCorrect is used to do everything listed below, except:**
    a. Correct misspelled words.
    b. Find and correct typos.
    c. Correct errors in capitalization.
    d. Correct layout and design errors.

15. **Each of the following is true, except:**
    a. Word documents can be imported directly into Publisher.
    b. Word can be used to edit stories written in Publisher.
    c. Stories written in Word are created in text boxes by default.
    d. One reason to import Word documents into Publisher publications is to maintain design consistency by adding design elements.

16. **You can use Design Checker to:**
    a. Correct misspelled words.
    b. Find and correct typos.
    c. Correct errors in capitalization.
    d. Correct layout and design errors.

17. **To detect and correct misspellings, AutoCorrect uses:**
    a. A list of AutoCorrect entries.
    b. The main dictionary.
    c. The custom dictionary.
    d. A thesaurus.

18. **You can use a copyrighted image in a publication if:**
    a. You ask permission of the copyright holder.
    b. You copy it from the World Wide Web.
    c. You credit the copyright owner in a footnote.
    d. You receive written permission from the copyright holder.

19. **An embedded object:**
    a. Can never be updated.
    b. Is updated automatically.
    c. Is updated by double-clicking on the object.
    d. Has to be removed from the publication for updating.

20. **Design Checker can check for:**
    a. Text in the overflow area.
    b. Blank pages.
    c. Subject verb agreement.
    d. Clashing colors.

21. **You can use Microsoft Excel to:**
    a. Create presentations.
    b. Create charts.
    c. Write e-mails.
    d. All of the above

▼ SKILLS REVIEW

1. **Integrate with Office programs.**
    a. You work for a chain of restaurants and are responsible for creating menus, advertisements, business plans, and monthly special flyers. List at least three ways in which you could integrate Office programs to create these materials on a regular basis.
    b. You work for a non-profit organization dedicated to pet adoptions. What tasks could you perform using Office programs?
    c. You work for a small, family-owned plumbing company. How could you use Office products to make this business more efficient?

2. **Import a Word document.**
    a. Start Publisher, then create a new publication using the Bars Word Document in the Publisher Gallery.
    b. In the Import Word Document dialog box, select the file PUB I-4.doc in the drive and folder where your Data Files are located, click OK, then save the publication as **Astronomy Story**.
    c. Make the publication two columns, close the task pane, then press [F9].
    d. Replace the Document Title placeholder text with **Doing Astronomy Correctly**.
    e. Change the title font size to 18 point.
    f. Click the Save button on the Standard toolbar, then close the file, but do not exit Publisher.

3. **Use AutoCorrect.**
    a. Examine the list of default AutoCorrect entries. Are any entries that you know you will need missing?
    b. Will any of the default entries cause problems in your everyday use?

4. **Record images.**
    a. Find two images, then scan them.
    b. Open a new, blank publication, then save it as **Scanning Practice** in the drive and folder where your Data Files are located. Insert the two images, place your name somewhere on the page as well as the title 'Scanning Practice', then print the page.

5. **Embed and link objects.**
    a. Think of a real-world situation in which linking an object, such as financial data, would be advantageous. One example might be a book distributor working with several warehouses across the country. How could linking help to keep inventory reports in this sort of business up to date?

6. **Use Design Checker.**
    a. Open the file PUB I-5.pub from the drive and folder where your Data Files are located, then save it as **New IM Newsletter**.
    b. Start Design Checker.
    c. Ignore the item **Object encroaches nonprinting region (Page 1)** if it appears in the list.
    d. Ignore the item that says **Picture is not scaled proportionally (Page 1)**.
    e. Fix items 2 and 3 that say **Object is not visible (Page 1)**.
    f. Fix the remaining problems by either deleting empty text boxes, scaling objects proportionally or bringing objects forward.
    g. Print page 1 of the publication.
    h. Save the publication and close Publisher.

▼ SKILLS REVIEW (CONTINUED)

7. Understand speech recognition.

a. If you have a microphone and speakers attached to your computer and you completed the Speech Recognition wizard in the lesson, make a list of two simple tasks in which you could use the speech recognition feature. (*Hint:* You could create a text box, then use the speech recognition feature to fill it. Or, you could select a text box, then use the speech recognition feature to open the Format Text Box dialog box.)

b. Write down what tasks you accomplished, then try each task and rate the feature's effectiveness.

▼ INDEPENDENT CHALLENGE 1

As the office manager for your local Chamber of Commerce, you decide to spend time working with employees to improve their skills. One of the employees needs help with a postcard announcing an upcoming event. You will use Design Checker to find and fix problems.

FIGURE I-21

a. Start Publisher, then open the file PUB I-6.pub from the drive and folder where your Data Files are located.

b. Save the publication as **Potluck Supper Postcard**.

c. Use Design Checker to find and correct any problems.

d. Adjust the text point size so that all of the text is visible and no words are hyphenated.

Advanced Challenge Exercises

■ Scan artwork appropriate to this publication.

■ Place the artwork in the publication.

■ Make any necessary adjustments such as cropping, or changing the way the text wraps around the image, then compare your work to Figure I-21.

e. Include **your name** in the e-mail address.

f. Save and print the publication, then exit Publisher.

▼ INDEPENDENT CHALLENGE 2

Some friends from an art school are giving a party with the theme "Bad Taste is in Your Face". You agreed to make a flyer in the worst taste you can imagine to announce the party.

a. Start Publisher, then open the file PUB I-7.doc from the drive and folder where your Data Files are located.

b. Save the publication as **Party Flyer**.

c. Use Design Checker to find and correct any problems it identifies in the flyer.

d. Correct any text spacing problems not found by Design Checker.

e. Correct any typos or misspellings.

f. Substitute your name for the e-mail address.

g. Save and print the publication, then exit Publisher.

Publisher 2003

▼ INDEPENDENT CHALLENGE 3

You have been researching the topic of color psychology in preparation for a talk you are giving to graphic designers later this month. You wrote up a summary of your notes in a Microsoft Word document, and have decided that you want to provide a hard copy of the summary to people attending the talk. You decide to import the document into Publisher so that you can create a sharp-looking publication to hand out to attendees.

a. Start Publisher, click Publications for Print in the New from a design list, then click Import Word Documents.

b. Click the Blocks Word Document design.

c. In the Import Word Document dialog box, open the file PUB I-8.doc from the drive and folder where your Data Files are located, click OK, then save the publication as **Color Psychology Story**.

d. Click the One-sided printing button on the task pane, then click Yes in the warning box.

e. Close the task pane, then press [F9].

f. Delete the page number text box.

g. Click the Document Title placeholder text, type **The Psychology of Color, by**, then type **your name**.

h. Select the text, click the Font Size list arrow on the Formatting toolbar, then click 20.

Advanced Challenge Exercises

- Change the number of columns to 2.
- Create shapes for some of the colors mentioned in the publication, then arrange and group them.
- Compare your publication to Figure I-22.

i. Save and print the publication, then exit Publisher.

FIGURE I-22

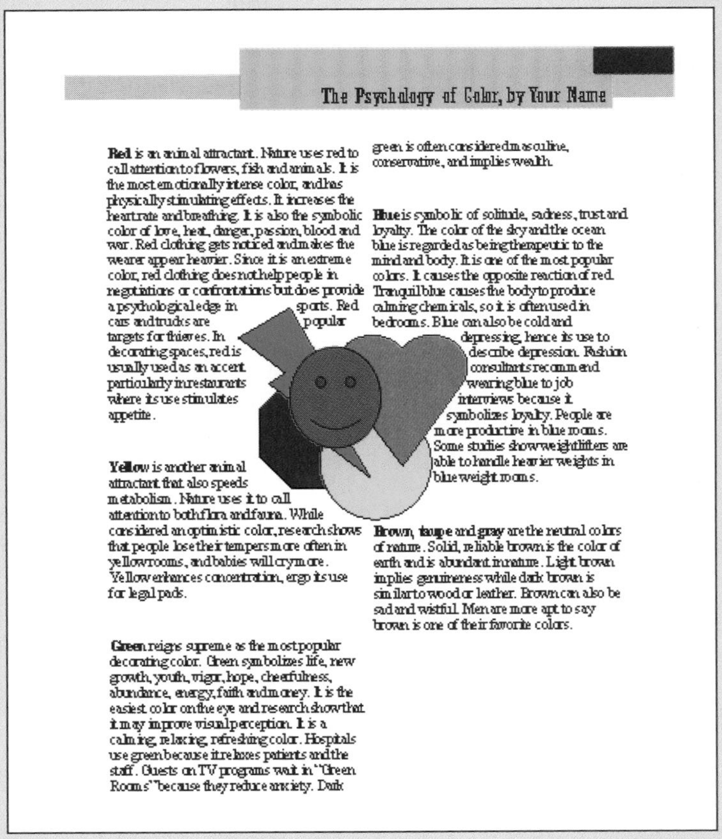

The Psychology of Color, by Your Name

Red is an animal attractant. Nature uses red to call attention to flowers, fish and animals. It is the most emotionally intense color, and has physically stimulating effects. It increases the heart rate and breathing. It is also the symbolic color of love, heat, danger, passion, blood and war. Red clothing gets noticed and makes the wearer appear heavier. Since it is an extreme color, red clothing does not help people in negotiations or confrontations but does provide a psychological edge in sports. Red cars and trucks are targets for thieves. In decorating spaces, red is usually used as an accent particularly in restaurants where its use stimulates appetite.

Yellow is another animal attractant that also speeds metabolism. Nature uses it to call attention to both flora and fauna. While considered an optimistic color, research shows that people lose their tempers more often in yellow rooms, and babies will cry more. Yellow enhances concentration, ergo its use for legal pads.

Green reigns supreme as the most popular decorating color. Green symbolizes life, new growth, youth, vigor, hope, cheerfulness, abundance, energy, faith and money. It is the easiest color on the eye and research shows that it may improve visual perception. It is a calming, relaxing, refreshing color. Hospitals use green because it relaxes patients and the staff. Guests on TV programs wait in "Green Rooms" because they reduce anxiety. Dark green is often considered masculine, conservative, and implies wealth.

Blue is symbolic of solitude, sadness, trust and loyalty. The color of the sky and the ocean blue is regarded as being therapeutic to the mind and body. It is one of the most popular colors. It causes the opposite reaction of red. Tranquil blue causes the body to produce calming chemicals, so it is often used in bedrooms. Blue can also be cold and depressing, hence its use to describe depression. Fashion consultants recommend wearing blue to job interviews because it symbolizes loyalty. People are more productive in blue rooms. Some studies show weightlifters are able to handle heavier weights in blue weight rooms.

Brown, taupe and gray are the neutral colors of nature. Solid, reliable brown is the color of earth and is abundant in nature. Light brown implies genuineness while dark brown is similar to wood or leather. Brown can also be sad and wistful. Men are more apt to say brown is one of their favorite colors.

▼ INDEPENDENT CHALLENGE 4

You consider yourself artistic with good instincts about design, but wish you knew more about colors and how to choose them. Use your browser and search engine to explore articles about color wheels on the World Wide Web. Create a brief description of color wheels in Word, then import it into Publisher.

a. Connect to the Internet, then use your browser and favorite search engine to explore the term "color wheel."

b. Find out the key features and benefits of color wheels and print out any information that will help you write a brief Word document about the subject.

c. Use the information you gathered online to write a short Word document about color wheels, then save it as **Color Wheel Story** to the drive and folder where your Data Files are located.

d. Use the New Publication task pane and Publication Gallery to pick any Word document template of your choosing in Publisher.

e. Import your Word document into Publisher.

f. If possible, find an image of a color wheel and insert it into the publication.

g. Save the publication as **About the Color Wheel** to the drive and folder where your Data Files are located.

h. Change the title to **About the Color Wheel, by**, then type **your name**.

i. Select the one-sided printing option.

j. Save and print the publication, then exit Publisher.

FIGURE I-23

About The Color Wheel, by Your Name

The **Color Wheel** shows how colors are related. It is laid out so that any two primary colors (red, yellow, blue) are separated by the secondary colors (orange, violet, purple and green) which are made by combining two primary colors.

Primary Colors are basic and cannot be mixed from other elements. They are analogous to prime numbers in mathematics. You can mix two primaries to get a **Secondary Color**. Each Secondary Color on the Color Wheel is bounded by two primaries. Those are the components that you mix to get that Secondary Color.

Color complements are color opposites. These colors contrast each other in the most extreme way possible. They help to make each color seem more active.

All light travels as waves. Color complements have drastically different wavelengths and, consequently, cause some perception problems for a viewer if they are placed close to each other in a design or in art. The cones and rods of the eye cannot separate the information, so we sometimes detect a quivering or optical distortion when two complements are used near each other.

▼ VISUAL WORKSHOP

Use the New Publication task pane and Publication Gallery to create the Import Studio Word Document publication. This is the initial design of a story you are importing from Word. Import the file PUB I-9.doc into the publication, save the publication as **Presenting Designs**. Use Figure I-24 as a guide for enhancing the publication and including or removing additional elements such as your name. Move any of the objects on the page to make the publication easier to read, and use the Best Fit AutoFit feature. The clip art shown in the sample can be found by searching for meeting (it is j0233018.wmf). Save and print the first page.

FIGURE I-24

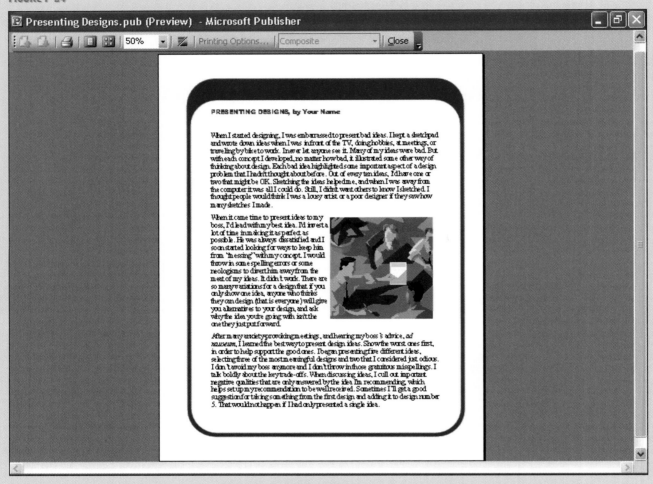

UNIT
J
Publisher 2003

Creating Web Documents

OBJECTIVES

Plan a Web site	
Design a Web site	
Create a Web site	
Add hyperlinks	
Modify a background	
Test a Web site	
Publish a Web site	
Convert a publication to a Web page	
Capstone Project: Personal Web Site	

Publisher has Web capabilities and graphics tools that make it easy to create multi-page Web sites. You can create professional-looking sites with attractive backgrounds, useful navigation bars, and interesting links. You can test a finished site with a browser, and publish it to the Internet so that others can access it. Before you create a Web site, you must identify your goals and resources. Image Magic has decided to create a company Web site and has asked you to begin planning and designing the site. The primary purpose of the Web site is to introduce potential customers to Image Magic and provide contact information.

Planning a Web Site

The steps in planning a Web site are similar to planning a paper publication, but with some important differences. You must begin by considering how much time, money, and expertise are available for your Web site. Because of the dynamic nature of a Web site, it may require more resources than a typical paper publication. For example, paper publications are a form of one-way communication, where the reader does not interact with the document. Web sites, on the other hand, must be interactive, so that readers can navigate the site, use hyperlinks, and provide information or ask questions. Another difference is that Web sites must be maintained and their content updated to attract multiple visits. ▰▰▰ You think about the key questions necessary to plan a Web site.

DETAILS

- ### What are the constraints?

  Time, money, expertise, and competing needs are the limiting factors in most enterprises. Being aware of budgetary, scheduling, and technical limits may influence your selection of a target audience and consequently, your design. A few of the things you should consider before designing a Web site are shown in Figure J-1. Image Magic has only a limited budget for the initial Web site, and wants it published as soon as possible. You will be the primary designer of the site, though the company may hire someone later to maintain and expand the site so that it can be used for customer service activities such as order tracking.

- ### Who is the target audience?

  The Internet makes it difficult to identify who is actually visiting your site because anyone can access it, but you can take steps to reach your target audience. The more narrowly you can define the characteristics of your ideal audience, the more you can tailor the content, design, and access to your Web site so that the site appeals to them. This may influence your choice of design elements, the amount of text you include on each page, and the degree of interactivity in the site. Image Magic has a profile of its current average client and designs its Web site according to that profile's tastes.

- ### What is the desired effect of the Web site?

  Are you trying to sell something, persuade, teach, motivate, inform, or solicit a contribution of time or money? Deciding what effect you want is the first step to obtaining it. The answers to those questions will help you decide whether the site should give technical support, or be a clearinghouse of information, an electronic catalog, or another type of site. Visitors to the Image Magic site will want to know the benefits of becoming a customer, and may want to see links to existing clients.

- ### What response do you want?

  Do you intend the site to simply provide information, or do you want feedback? If you want people to interact with your site, what structure should the feedback take? Do you want to solicit and register people for attendance at an event? Do you want e-mail inquiries for additional information, such as a catalog? Do you want multiple visits to your Web site? If you plan to collect money, do you want to collect credit card information? How will you deal with tariffs and taxes and other barriers to international trade? Your answers to these questions will help you to reexamine and reevaluate the constraints and the desired effect of your Web site. Image Magic plans to install a customer survey as part of its future Web site. This will make the site more interactive, and encourage feedback from clients.

- ### What will you do with the responses?

  If you offer people a product in exchange for money, or offer some free service such as additional information by mail, or an e-mail response, you must be able to deliver on your offer. If you don't have enough merchandise or other materials prepared for a timely response, you risk alienating customers and potential customers who show interest in your products or services. If you don't have adequate resources to deal with the potential responses your Web site will generate, then you should adjust your goals accordingly. It is the goal of Image Magic to respond to all e-mail inquiries within 24 hours.

Web Site Planning Constraints

- Budget limitations
- Limiting technologies
- Staffing needs (current and future requirements)
- Development staff (programmers, designers, etc.)
- Maintenance staff (e-mail responses)
- Security issues (prevention of hacking)
- Privacy issues (guarding clients' personal information)
- Web site transactions (credit cards, order processing)
- Customer service issues (pre-sales questions, customer support, warranties, returns, etc.)
- Foreign language services

Clues to Use

Planning and customer service

One of the most problematic areas of planning is customer service. Even with earnest research efforts to try to anticipate the need for your product or service, the marketplace determines the actual demand for a product or a service. Underestimating this demand can lead to outstripped supply. Overestimating demand can lead to idle capacity, underutilized workers, and eventually, perhaps, layoffs and/or bankruptcy. When developing a Web site, carefully consider the developmental and maintenance costs. Unless there is value in a return visit, either to purchase additional product, or read updated content, the number of visits to a site will drop off. Changing content requires an investment of time and energy on the part of developers and management. You must plan for direct contact with visitors to your site too. While e-mail responses can be standardized and automated to respond to customer needs, someone has to make sure that the responses are timely and accurately answer the customers' questions. If you do not satisfy your customers' needs, someone else will.

Designing a Web Site

Before creating a Web site, it's a good idea to decide on the design of the site, including how you want elements to appear on the pages. Although you'll probably make many modifications to your initial design over time, a master design with a list of required elements can help you work more effectively. The elements may include a logo, colors, font selections, and other items that support you or your business's identity. As you plan the content of the Image Magic Web site, you want to present the company in the best possible light. To accomplish this, you want to incorporate success stories and accolades from credible outside sources.

DETAILS

- ### Create an outline or a sketch

  The first step in preparing a Web site is to prepare an outline. The outline should include a list of the elements to place on each page. Information you might want to have on a page includes: a title, introductory paragraph, contact information, links to other sites and other pages, and graphic images. For the Image Magic Web site, you have decided to create four pages. You want the primary page, or **home page**, to briefly describe Image Magic, including what they can do for customers and how they can be contacted. You also want a page for the company's success stories, or **testimonials**, in the form of a list of satisfied clients and some of their comments. And you want to include a page promoting an upcoming design clinic.

- ### Decide on a navigation structure

  Before you work on the Web site, you should consider the number of pages for the site and how they will be linked together. Each page should be linked to the home page, and it should be easy for a reader to jump from page to page. Figure J-2 illustrates a typical Web site navigation structure.

- ### Add links to other sites

  In addition to linking associated pages within your site, you can also provide helpful links to other Web locations of interest to your readers. If you have a page that lists Image Magic's clients, you might include links to the clients' Web sites. By including your clients on your corporate Web site, they become ambassadors for your company. These links also serve to promote your corporate clients. While there is no legal requirement to ask permission to link to another site, it is a good idea to seek the cooperation of clients, and keep them updated on how you represent their interests.

- ### Add graphics, backgrounds, and design elements

  QUICK TIP

  GIF stands for Graphics Interchange Format.

  A few well-placed graphic images can enhance your Web site by breaking up blocks of text and making your pages more attractive. You can use any Clip Art images on your pages, and Publisher provides **animated GIFs**—images with movement—for Web page use on the Clip Art on Office Online Web site. Using one of the over 200 backgrounds available can make your pages eye-catching. The Design Gallery contains a variety of elements designed specifically for Web pages. Additional buttons appear on the Objects toolbar to add Web-related elements, and the Web Site Options task pane lets you quickly add response forms and navigation bars to your Web pages.

- ### Critically examine the page

  Because Publisher shows you exactly how your page looks by letting you view it in a browser, you can monitor your progress as you work. Figure J-3 shows the sample Image Magic home page, and Figure J-4 shows the design clinic page. Pages 2, 3, and 4 are linked to the home page, and the vertical navigation bar is present on each page, making it easy for a reader to jump to any page on the site. It's a good idea to occasionally step back and imagine that you're seeing your work for the first time. Ask yourself if you find the pages easy to read and navigate. See if the pages look attractive.

- ### Preview the Web site and test the links

  If your pages include links to other Web sites, make sure that the links are correct. Periodically check the links to make sure that they work as intended. There is software available that can test links automatically, but you must still manually test them to make sure that the content on the sites to which you are linking is still relevant and appropriate.

FIGURE J-2: Typical Web site navigation structure

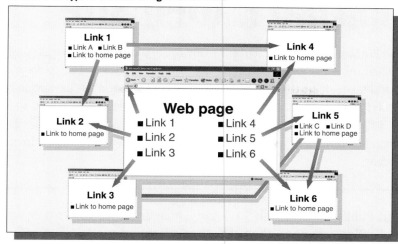

FIGURE J-3: Image Magic home page

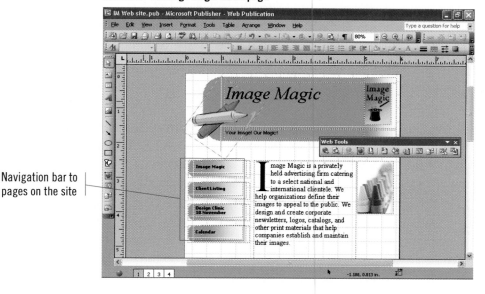

Navigation bar to pages on the site

FIGURE J-4: Design clinic page

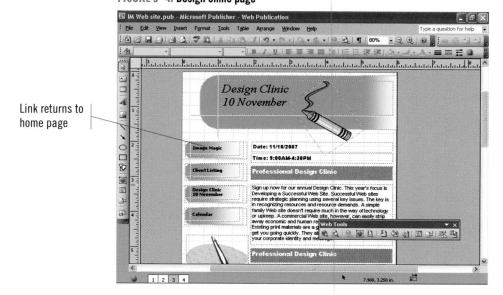

Link returns to home page

Creating a Web Site

The New Publication task pane contains many options for creating Web sites. Like other publications, Web sites created using the New Publication task pane have coordinated colors and placeholders for graphic images and text. Additionally, the Web Site Options task pane offers navigation bar choices, form elements, background sounds, and background textures. You can easily create Web sites using the Easy Web Site Builder, 3-Page Web Site, Project Sales, and Professional Services. ████ You decide to use the New Publication task pane, the Publication Gallery, and the Easy Web Site Builder to get a quick start on your new design ideas.

STEPS

1. **Start Publisher, click** Web Sites and E-mail **in the New from a design list in the New Publication task pane, then click the** Crisscross Easy Web Site **in the Publication Gallery**
   The Easy Web Site Builder dialog box opens.

2. **Select the checkboxes shown in Figure J-5, then click** OK
   If you only wanted the Web site to have a single page, you would leave all the checkboxes deselected.

3. **Click** Edit **on the menu bar, click** Personal Information, **click** Secondary Business, **click the** Include color scheme in this set check box **if necessary, click the** Select a color scheme list arrow, **click** Iris, **then click** Update

4. **Save the publication as** IM Web Site **to the drive and folder where your Data Files are located**

   > **QUICK TIP**
   > The unit of measurement in Web page rulers is in **pixels**. Tick marks are in increments of 8 pixels.

5. **Click anywhere in the publication, press** [F9], **right-click the** picture frame at 672 H / 384 V, **point to** Change Picture, **click** From File, **click the file** PUB J-1.tif **from the drive and folder where your Data Files are located, click** Insert, **then press** [Esc]
   The Image Magic logo replaces the picture placeholder on the page.

   > **TROUBLE**
   > If this image is not available, choose a similar image.

6. **Click the** Picture Frame button 🖼 **on the Objects toolbar, click** Empty Picture Frame, **then drag** ✛ **below the navigation bar from** 16 H / 384 V **to** 176 H / 544 V **click** 🖼, **click** Clip Art, **type** paints **in the Search for text box in the Clip Art task pane, then click** Go
   The Photographs checkbox in the Results should be list should contain a checkmark.

7. **Point to the image shown in Figure J-6, click the** list arrow, **then click** Insert **on the menu**
   The empty picture frame is filled with the image of the paint cans.

8. **Right-click the** text frame at 384 H / 288 V, **point to** Change Text, **click** Text File, **click the file** PUB J-2.doc **from the drive and folder where your Data Files are located, then click** OK
   The document file replaces the placeholder text.

   > **TROUBLE**
   > A warning box appears when you add a drop cap if the insertion point is not in the paragraph.

9. **Click anywhere** within **the paragraph, click** Format **on the menu bar, click** Drop Cap, **click the first choice in the second row, click** OK, **then click the Save button** 🖫 **on the Standard toolbar**
   Compare your page to Figure J-7.

FIGURE J-5: Easy Web Site Builder dialog box

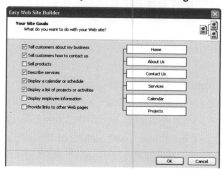

FIGURE J-6: Clip Art task pane

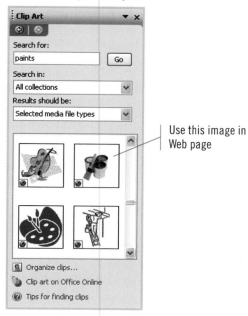

Use this image in Web page

FIGURE J-7: Home page with image and text replaced

Drop cap

Text file inserted in Web page

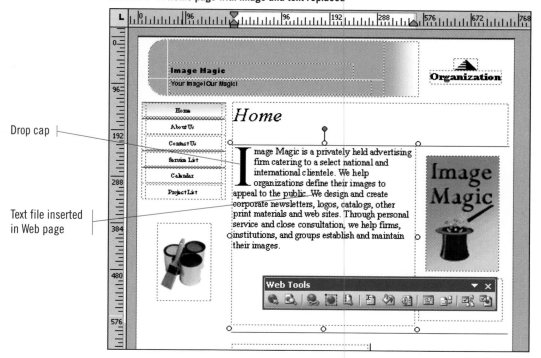

Adding Hyperlinks

You use a hyperlink each time you click an area on a page and jump to another Web site. **Hyperlinks**, or **links**, are electronic connections to locations within a Web site or elsewhere on the Internet. Links are included on Web pages to make the reader's experience more pleasurable and efficient. You can create links to your own or other pages, Web sites, e-mail addresses, and documents on a specific computer. Publisher automatically links pages added to a Web site with a navigation bar. A **navigation bar** is a row or column of buttons on a Web page containing links to each of the site's sub pages. It's easy to add pages to a Web site. Publisher comes with 26 templates, including the Photo Gallery, Project List, and Services, that are made for specific page type additions. You want to add an additional page to the Web site, and include a link to a client's Web page.

STEPS

1. **Close the task pane, click** Insert **on the menu bar, then click** Page

    The Insert Web Page dialog box opens, as shown in Figure J-9. You can choose from a variety of page styles.

2. **Click** Related links, **make sure that the** Add hyperlink to navigation bars check box **is selected, then click** OK

    The newly inserted page 2 is now the current page, and the default heading is "Related Links". There is now a new entry at the bottom of the navigation bar whose heading is identical to the current page title.

3. **Click the text** Web site or page name 1, **press [F9], then type** Course Technology

    The company name, Course Technology, appears.

4. **Select the text** Course Technology, **then click the** Insert Hyperlink button 🔗 **on the Web Tools toolbar**

    The Insert Hyperlink dialog box opens.

5. **Click the** Existing File or Web Page button **if necessary, type** http://www.course.com **in the Address text box as shown in Figure J-10, then click** OK

    The selected Course Technology text changed color and is underlined, indicating that it is a hyperlink.

6. **Click the text beneath the Course Technology link, type** A publisher of high-quality technology textbooks and other electronic training materials., **then press [Esc] twice**

7. **Click the** Save button 💾 **on the Standard toolbar**

    Compare your page to Figure J-11.

Clues to Use

Modifying a navigation bar

You can modify the text and order of pages within a navigation bar by clicking anywhere within the bar, then clicking the Click to edit options for this Navigation Bar button 🖉. When the Navigation Bar task pane opens, click Add, remove, and reorder links. The Navigation Bar Properties dialog box opens, as shown in Figure J-8.

FIGURE J–8: Navigation Bar Properties dialog box

FIGURE J-9: Insert Web Page dialog box

FIGURE J-10: Insert Hyperlink dialog box

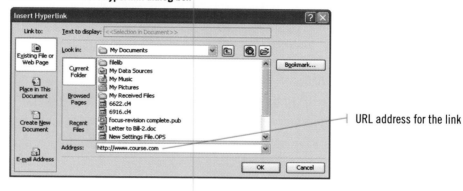

URL address for the link

FIGURE J-11: New page with hyperlink added

Underlined text indicates a hyperlink

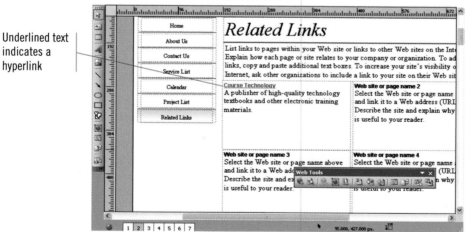

Publisher 2003

Clues to Use

Adding a hyperlink to an e-mail address

By adding a hyperlink to an e-mail address, you can make it easy for your readers to keep in touch. Because the Internet is a fairly impersonal medium, this kind of contact with readers can be invaluable. It can lead you to new ideas, and new sources of content, and expand your network. Complaints can be particularly valuable because they help you identify problems that might otherwise escape notice. To establish a hyperlink to an e-mail address, first select the text that you want to be the link, open the Insert Hyperlink dialog box by clicking the Insert Hyperlink button on the Web Tools toolbar, click E-mail Address, then enter a valid address in the E-mail address text box. You can confirm that the hyperlink is attached to the selected text by placing your pointer over the hyperlink. When you do this, a ScreenTip displays.

Modifying a Background

The background of the pages on a Web site can be modified to have different colors and textures, or no texture at all. The addition of carefully chosen background colors and textures enhances a Web site's design by adding visual interest and an illusion of depth. You can easily modify the background colors and textures individually on each page, or on all the pages, using Master Page view. You want to modify the background texture so that it has a pattern, but still allows the text to be easily readable.

STEPS

1. **Click** View **on the menu bar, then click** Master Page
    With the Master Page view selected, the design elements are no longer visible.

2. **Click** Format **on the menu bar, click** Background, **click** More backgrounds **in the Background task pane, then click the** Texture tab **in the Fill Effects dialog box**

3. **Click the third box in the first row**
    A sample appears in the lower-right corner of the dialog box, and the name of the texture, "Parchment," appears below the samples, as shown in Figure J-13.

4. **Click** OK
    The Master Page has a light beige, textured background that will add visual interest and an illusion of depth when the design elements are visible.

5. **Press** [Ctrl][M], **then click the** page 1 icon **on the status bar**
    With the design elements visible, the texture creates a pleasing appearance with the rest of the page.

6. **Click the** Save button 🖫 **on the Standard toolbar, then compare your screen to Figure J-14**

Design Matters

Creating a custom color scheme

You can create your own custom color schemes, just like those included in the Publisher Color Scheme list. Custom color schemes include main, accent, and hyperlink colors, as well as background textures. You create a custom color scheme by making selections in the Color Schemes task pane. Click Custom color scheme at the bottom of the Color Schemes task pane. Click the Custom tab in the Color Schemes dialog box, shown in Figure J-12, if necessary. You can now change the color scheme selections. Click the list arrows for any of the Scheme colors in the New column, then click a color from the palette. When all your selections are made, you can name the scheme by clicking the Save Scheme button, typing a name for the scheme, then clicking OK twice.

FIGURE J-12: Custom tab in the Color Schemes dialog box

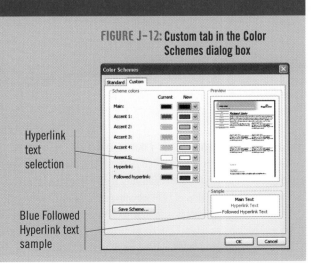

Hyperlink text selection

Blue Followed Hyperlink text sample

FIGURE J-13: Texture tab in Fill Effects dialog box

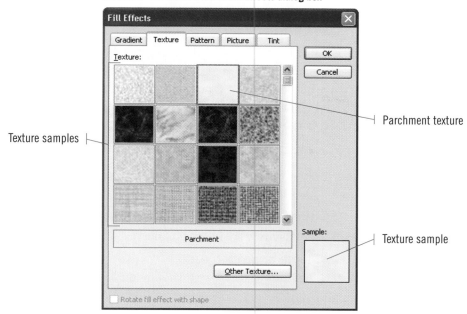

Texture samples

Parchment texture

Texture sample

FIGURE J-14: Web page background texture modified

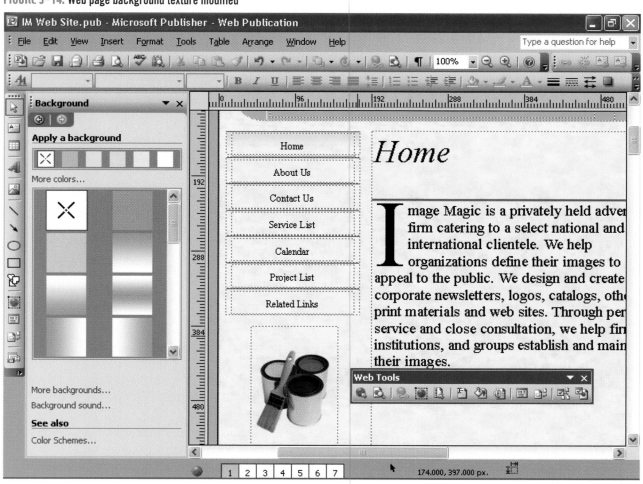

UNIT
J

Publisher 2003

Testing a Web Site

On a Web site, the potential for embarrassment caused by typos, misspellings, and awkward or poor design is worldwide. It is important to test and critique your Web site before publishing it to the Internet. Careful examination of the publication, first using Design Checker, and then the Web Page Preview feature, can help you identify and correct errors before they become public. ▰▰▰▰ You want to preview the publication in Internet Explorer.

STEPS

1. **If the Web Tools toolbar is not open, click** View **on the menu bar, point to** Toolbars, **then click** Web Tools

> **TROUBLE**
>
> Your page may look different depending upon which browser is installed.

2. **Click the** Web Page Preview button 🔍 **on the Web Tools toolbar**

   The Web page opens in your browser. The first page of the Web site appears, as shown in Figure J-15.

3. **Click** Related Links **on the navigation bar**

   Page 2 of the IM Web site appears on the browser screen, as shown in Figure J-16.

4. **Connect to the Internet**

   If you are unsure how to connect to the Internet, contact your instructor or technical support person. If you are unable to connect to the Internet, skip Steps 4 and 5.

> **TROUBLE**
>
> You will not be able to test the hyperlink if you cannot connect to the Internet.

5. **Click the** Course Technology link

   The Course Technology Web site now appears on the browser screen.

6. **Click the** Close button **on the browser window**

7. **Click the** Save button 🖫 **on the Standard toolbar in the Publisher window, then close the publication**

Clues to Use

Renaming a Web page

The name of each page displays when you position the pointer over the page icon at the bottom of the screen. This name is generated automatically when you create the page, so it may not be to your liking. You can change the name of the page by right-clicking the page icon, then clicking Rename. Type the new name in the Page title text box in the Web Page Options dialog box, then click OK.

FIGURE J-15: Web Page preview of Page 1

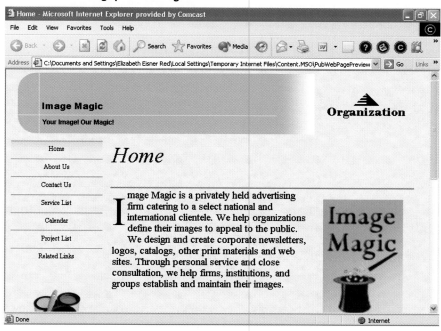

FIGURE J-16: Web Page preview of Related Links page

Hyperlink to Course Technology Web site

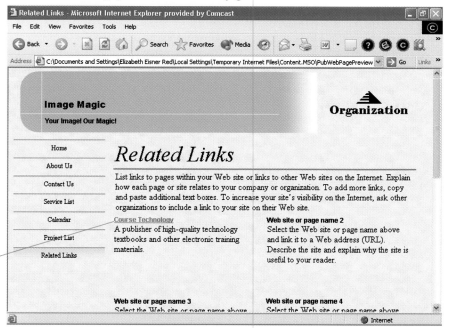

Publishing a Web Site

Once your Web site is finished, you will want to publish it to the Internet so that others can see it. Publisher offers several ways to do this. The following instructions are for Windows XP. Before you can publish a Web site to the Internet, you must create a Network Place for the site. A **Network Place** is a shortcut to a location on a Web server where your pages will reside. Before beginning the publishing process, you must get a **Uniform Resource Locator (URL)** from your **Internet Service Provider (ISP)**. Once the Image Magic Web site is complete, it will need to be published to the Internet. You research the steps required to do this so that you will be familiar with the procedure.

DETAILS

Read below to understand how to publish a Web site, but *do not* follow the instructions at this time.

- **Creating a Network Place**

  The first step in creating a Network Place is to contact your ISP and get an address for your files. Once this is complete, click File on the menu bar, then click Publish to the Web. Click OK to close the warning box if necessary, then click My Network Places in the Publish to the Web dialog box, as shown in Figure J-17. Use the Add Network Place Wizard, shown in Figures J-18 and J-19, to establish a connection to the URL. To start this wizard, double-click Add Network Place in the My Network Places folder in My Computer or Windows Explorer.

- **Saving the publication as a Web page**

  To save the publication as a Web page, you must use the Publish to the Web Page dialog box, which is available by clicking Publish to the Web on the File menu or clicking the Publish to the Web button on the Web Tools toolbar. Open My Network Places, double-click the site you want, double-click the folder in which you want your files published, then click Save.

- **Publishing to the Web incrementally**

  Once your site is ready to be uploaded to the Web, you can publish it. Later, as you make changes to your files, you can publish incrementally to the Web. This means that you won't have to republish each file, just the ones that have been updated. You can change the incremental option by clicking Tools on the menu bar, then clicking Options. Click the Web tab in the Options dialog box, select the Enable incremental publish to the Web check box, then click OK.

Design Matters

Adding design elements

There is a wide variety of design elements for Web pages, which can be found on the Microsoft Office Clip Art and Media Web site, including some that create movement and sound. Animated GIFs and sound clips will not be visible or heard within Publisher. They are only displayed or played with a browser. You can attract attention by creating moving images or using an animated GIF. The **Graphics Interchange Format (GIF)** is commonly used on the Web because of its small file size, which makes it quick to download. Additionally, you can add sounds to your Web pages so that people with sound-capable computers will be able to hear them when the page opens. You can install most commonly used sound formats by clicking Background sound at the bottom of the Web Site Options task pane, then typing the name of the sound file in the File name text box of the Web Page Options dialog box.

FIGURE J-17: Publish to the Web Page dialog box

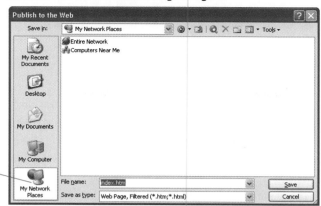

My Network Places button

FIGURE J-18: Add Network Place Wizard dialog box

FIGURE J-19: Insert URL in the Add Network Place Wizard dialog box

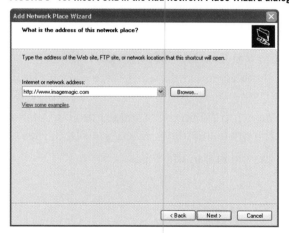

Publisher 2003

Clues to Use

Increasing Web site traffic

The key to a successful Internet site is its accessibility to all Web users. After all, if no one sees your site, the caliber of its design is irrelevant. At minimum, you want to contact interested parties by e-mail to let them know of your site. You also want to register your Web site with several **search engines**, special Web sites that search for and report on information found on the Internet. Because many search engines compile their indices using keywords, the descriptive reference words found on a page, it is important to include those words. Additionally, there are several listing services on the Internet that will make submissions to the search engines, and provide information on maximizing the amount of traffic to your site.

Converting a Publication to a Web Page

By using existing documents in a Web site, you can increase your site's usefulness to a reader, and make additional use of your written work. Using Publisher, it is easy to convert a publication such as a newsletter or brochure to a Web page. Publisher even stores design elements that must be removed to fit the Web site design. Design elements removed during the conversion process are added to the Extra Content tab in the Design Gallery so they can be retrieved if needed elsewhere. Once a publication is converted to a Web site, you can modify the design and create your own hyperlinks. In the future, you plan to convert several Image Magic publications to Web pages, including a new information brochure on the company. You decide to start creating the brochure, and then use this work-in-progress to test the conversion process.

STEPS

1. **Click** File **on the menu bar, click** New, **then click** Brochures **in the Publications for Print category in the New from a design list in the New Publication task pane**

2. **Click the** Borders Informational Brochure
   The brochure is created and appears on the screen.

QUICK TIP

You can switch to the Color Scheme task pane to find out which color scheme is currently in use.

3. **Apply the** Secondary Business Personal Information set **using the** Lilac color scheme, **then save the publication as** Brochure Conversion **to the drive and folder where your Data Files are located**

4. **Click the** text frame **at 9" H / 5" V, type** Image Magic Brochure, **then press [Esc] twice**

5. **Click** Convert to Web **publication at the bottom of the Brochure Options task pane, as shown in Figure J-20**
   The Convert to Web Publication dialog box appears.

6. **Click** Next **to save a print version of the publication, then click** Finish **to add a navigation bar**

7. **Click the** Zoom text box, **type** 50, **then press [Enter]**
   The publication has been converted to a Web site, as shown in Figure J-21. Although the print version of this publication has been saved, the Web version has not yet been saved.

8. **Click the** Save button 🖫 **on the Standard toolbar, then save the publication as** Converted Brochure **to the drive and folder where your Data Files are located**

9. **Click** File **on the menu bar, then click** Exit

Clues to Use

Using Web mode

Once a print publication is converted to a Web publication, you are using the Web mode. The Web mode includes the Web Tools toolbar, which contains commonly used tools. The Web mode specifically tailors Web publications for optimal effectiveness when viewed in a browser. You can view your publication in your installed browser by clicking the Web Page Preview button 🔍 on the Web Tools toolbar.

By clicking on the menu bar, then clicking Edit with Microsoft Office Word, you can edit the browser document using all the tools available in Microsoft Word (assuming this program is installed on your computer). In Publisher, the Web Tools toolbar allows you to make changes and additions to hyperlinks and navigation bars.

FIGURE J-20: Brochure before conversion to a Web site

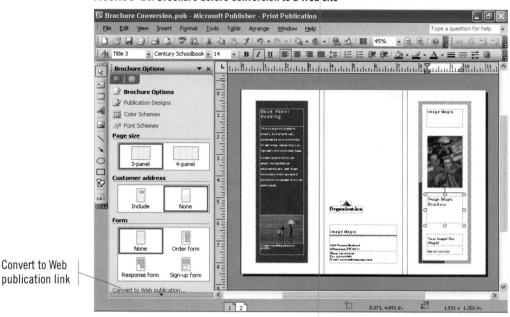

Convert to Web publication link

FIGURE J-21: Web site after conversion from a brochure

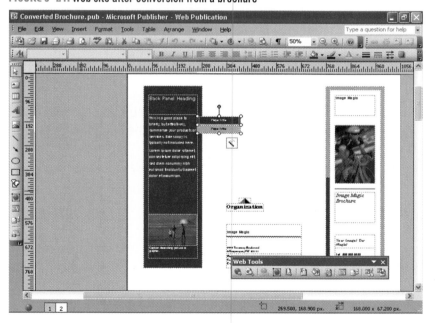

Clues to Use

Converting a Web site to a print publication

You can also convert a Publisher-designed Web site into a brochure or newsletter. Once the Web site you want to convert is open, and the Web Site Options task pane is open, click the Convert to Print Layout button at the bottom of the task pane, then click the type of print publication you want.

Capstone Project: Personal Web Site

You have learned about planning, designing, creating, testing, converting, and publishing Web sites. Additionally, you have added hyperlinks and modified a Web site's background. ▨▨▨ You want to make it easier for people to get to know you so you have created a personal Web site that contains your resume and a calendar. You want to add an e-mail button to make it easier for visitors to the page to contact you.

STEPS

1. **Start Publisher, then open the file** PUB J-3.pub **from the drive and folder where your Data Files are located**

   The Web site opens on the screen.

2. **Save the publication as** Your Name's Web Site **to the drive and folder where your Data Files are located, then press** [F9]

   The Design Gallery contains many design elements specifically created for use on Web sites.

3. **Click the** Design Gallery Object button 🖼 **on the Objects toolbar, then click** Buttons **in the Categories list**

   You can easily find a variety of design elements specifically made for insertion on Web pages, as shown in Figure J-22.

4. **Click** Email Framed Oval **from the Web Buttons list, then click** Insert Object

   The button is inserted onto the Web page.

5. **Using** ⸜⃕ **drag the** object **so that the upper-left corner is at** ½" H / 4½" V, **then click the text** E-mail

6. **Click the** Insert Hyperlink button 🖴 **on the Web Tools toolbar, click the** E-mail Address button, **type** yourname@imagemagic.com **in the E-mail address text box, click** OK, **then click anywhere on the** scratch area **to deselect the e-mail button**

   The e-mail hyperlink is created. Compare your page to Figure J-23.

7. **Click the** Save button 🖫 **on the Standard toolbar, print the first page of the Web site, then close Publisher**

FIGURE J-22: Buttons category in the Design Gallery

FIGURE J-23: Text box added to Web site

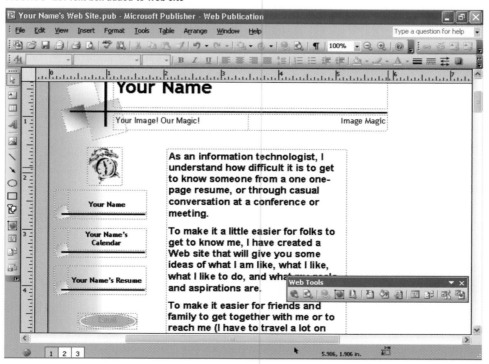

Publisher 2003

Practice

▼ CONCEPTS REVIEW

Label each of the elements in the Publisher window shown in Figure J-24.

FIGURE J-24

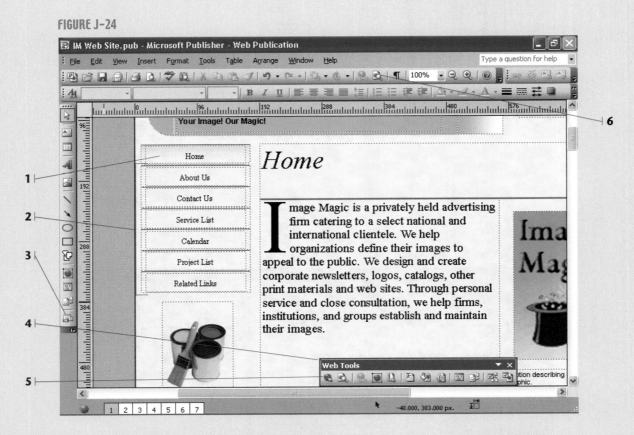

Match each of the buttons or terms with the statement that describes its function.

7.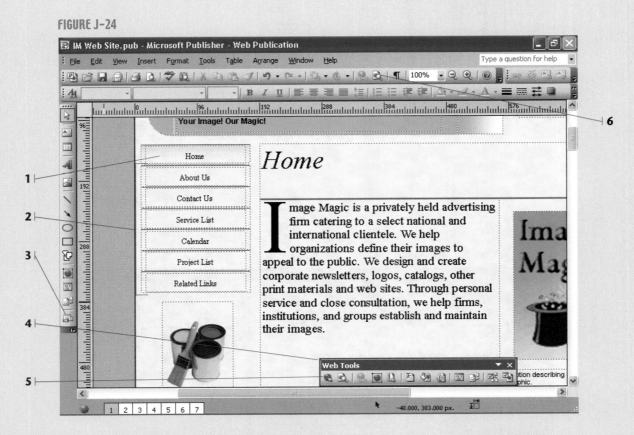

8. **Animated GIF**

9. **Navigation bar**

10.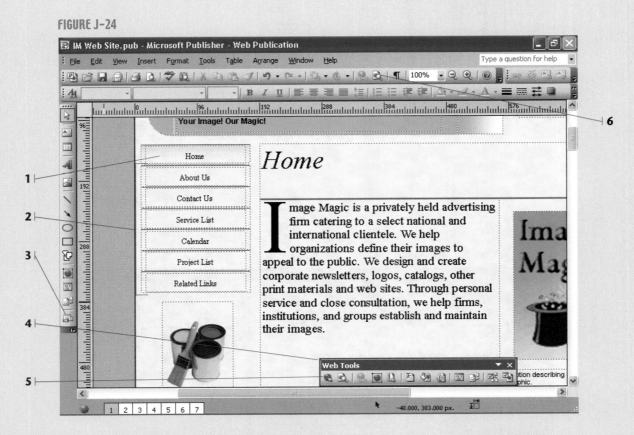

11. **Network Place**

12.

a. Views page in browser

b. Creates a hyperlink

c. Image with movement

d. Contains Web design elements

e. Buttons on a Web page containing links to sub pages

f. Shortcut to a location on a Web server where pages will reside

Select the best answer from the list of choices.

13. You can modify a Web page's background texture using the:
    a. File menu.
    b. Edit menu.
    c. Format menu.
    d. All the above

14. Add sound clips to a Web page using the:
    a. Objects toolbar.
    b. Web site options task pane.
    c. Format menu.
    d. Programs menu.

15. Which button would you use to add a hyperlink to a page?
    a.
    b.
    c.
    d.

16. Which statement about hyperlinks is true?
    a. You can add a hyperlink to any object.
    b. The only object to which you can add a hyperlink is an animated GIF.
    c. You cannot add a hyperlink to a text frame.
    d. A hyperlink cannot be used with e-mail.

17. Each of the following is true about a navigation bar, except:
    a. Publisher creates one automatically as part of a Web site.
    b. It can contain an animated GIF.
    c. It can be horizontal or vertical in design.
    d. It is automatically updated when a page is added.

18. Which of the following can be hyperlinks on a Web page?
    a. Other Web sites
    b. E-mail addresses
    c. Web pages on your own Web site
    d. All of the above

19. Which statement is true about animated GIFs?
    a. They only display movement in a browser.
    b. They display movement in Publisher and a browser.
    c. They cannot be added to the Clip Gallery.
    d. They are available for a fee from Microsoft Design Gallery.

20. GIF stands for:
    a. Great Image Format.
    b. Graphics Interchange Format.
    c. Good Image Format.
    d. None of the above

21. Which button can you use to add a Design Gallery element to a page?
    a.
    b.
    c.
    d.

▼ SKILLS REVIEW

Throughout these exercises, use the Zoom feature when necessary to adjust your view of the page.

1. **Planning a Web Site.**
   a. You own Ladders By Mail, a small business that sells a wide variety of ladders to individuals and other businesses. You specialize in high-quality ladders for indoor and outdoor use, and in timely shipment or delivery. You are planning a Web site for Ladders By Mail. What are your constraints?
   b. Who is your target audience?
   c. Do you want your Web site to be interactive? If so, what type of interaction do you think will be effective in attracting potential customers?

2. **Designing a Web Site.**
   a. Make a list of the type of information you want to display and the number of pages that will be required.
   b. Make preliminary sketches of the pages that will be required.

3. **Create a Web Site.**
   a. Start Publisher.
   b. Use the New Publication task pane and the Web Sites and E-mail category in the New from a design list to create a Web site for Ladders By Mail. Select the Bubbles Easy Web Site and do not select any check boxes in the Easy Web Site Builder dialog box. Use the Secondary Personal Information Set and the the Citrus color scheme.
   c. Save the file as **Ladders By Mail Web Site** to the drive and folder where your Data Files are located.
   d. Replace the Home Page Title text at 288 H / 64 V with **Ladders By Mail**.
   e. Replace the text in the frame at 96 H / 16 V with **Your Name, Owner**.
   f. Replace the logo text (at 672 H / 48 V) with the company name, then save your work.

4. **Add hyperlinks.**
   a. Insert a Related links page after the home page. (*Hint*: Make sure that the hyperlink is added to the Web navigation bar.)
   b. Change the title on page 2 at 288 H / 160 V and on the navigation bar to **Happy Customers**.
   c. Click the Web site or page name 1 text, then type **Microsoft Corporation**.
   d. Select the Microsoft Corporation text, then click the Insert Hyperlink button on the Web Tools toolbar.
   e. Make sure that the Existing File or Web Page button is selected, enter the Internet address **http://www.microsoft.com**, then click OK.
   f. Save your work.

5. **Modify a background.**
   a. Open the Master Page, display the Background task pane, click More backgrounds, then click the Texture tab in the Fill Effects dialog box.
   b. Click the Blue tissue paper texture, the first sample in the third row.
   c. Click OK.
   d. Return to Normal view.
   e. Save your work.

6. **Test a Web site.**
   a. Display the Design Checker task pane make a note of any errors other than alternative text and space below margins, then close the Design Checker.
   b. Click the Web Page Preview button on the Web Tools toolbar.
   c. Click Happy Customers on the navigation bar on page 1.
   d. Click Microsoft Corporation. (*Hint*: If you are not connected to the Internet, you will not be able to view the Microsoft Web site. Skip Steps d and e.)
   e. Close the browser.
   f. Print the current page.
   g. Save and close the Web site publication.

7. Publishing a Web Site.

   a. Using your own ISP as an example, investigate the procedure you would use to publish the Web site for Ladders By Mail.

   b. Find out if your ISP has any hosting fees or space limitations.

8. Convert a publication to a Web page.

   a. Use the New Publication task pane and the Publication Gallery to create a brochure for Ladders By Mail. Select the Bubbles Informational Brochure, use the Secondary Personal Information Set (using appropriate names, etc.), then apply the Citrus color scheme and change the logo text to reflect the company name.

   b. Save the file as **Ladders By Mail Brochure** to the drive and folder where your Data Files are located.

   c. Click Convert to Web publication in the Brochure Options task pane, making sure that you save the print publication before the conversion, and add a navigation bar.

   d. Make sure Your Name displays in the email address at the bottom of the center panel on page 1.

   e. Save the file as **Ladder Brochure Conversion** to the drive and folder where your Data Files are located.

   f. Move the navigation bar to the top of the center panel on page 1, then save your work and print page 1 of the Web site.

   g. Close the publication.

   h. Exit Publisher.

▼ INDEPENDENT CHALLENGE 1

You are the proud owner of a very successful rare comic book store in Binghamton, NY. You decide to expand your store, Comix Alive, by designing a Web site. This way, you will be able to retain all the university student customers who leave town after graduation.

   a. Start Publisher, use the New Publication task pane and the New from a design list to create a new Web site based on the Blocks Easy Web Site design.

   b. Your Web site should contain only the Home page.

   c. Use the Personal Information Set of your choice, an appropriate slogan for the store, and the Fjord color scheme.

   d. Save the publication as **Comix Alive Web Site** to the drive and folder where your Data Files are located.

   e. Change the title of the home page to **Your Name's Comix Alive**.

   f. Insert a Related links page after the home page.

   g. Select the Web site or page name 1 text listed on page 2.

   h. Create a hyperlink to any comic book site. Use your favorite search engine to find a site.

   i. Save the publication, print the first page of the publication, then exit Publisher.

▼ INDEPENDENT CHALLENGE 2

Your family asks you to create a newsletter that can be distributed to everybody, and you know that a request for a Web site isn't far behind. Thinking ahead, you want to prepare a simple mock-up of a family newsletter, convert it to a Web site, then suggest it to the family at your next gathering.

    a. Start Publisher, then use any newsletter design in the Publication Gallery to create a new publication, accepting all the defaults.

    b. Use the Personal Information Set of your choice to enter appropriate information, customize all information, such as newsletter and logo text, then change the color scheme to one of your choice.

    c. Save the publication as **Family Newsletter** to the drive and folder where your Data Files are located.

    d. Make modifications you feel are necessary to give family members a feel for the newsletter, but make sure that the newsletter masthead contains your last name. (For example, the masthead might be "Your Name's Family News.")

    e. Place your name in one of the headlines on page 1.

    f. Save your work and print the first page of the newsletter.

    g. Convert the publication to a Web site.

    h. Save the converted publication as **Family Web Site** to the drive and folder where your Data Files are located.

Advanced Challenge Exercises

    ■ Use the Design Gallery Object button to add a Web button on the home page.

    ■ Create a hyperlink to the Web button that allows a user to send e-mail to you.

    ■ Rename pages 2 and 3 as **Page 2** and **Page 3**.

    i. Save the Web site, print the home page, then exit Publisher.

▼ INDEPENDENT CHALLENGE 3

You are creating a Web site for Jackie's Joke Shop, a novelty store. The company's management team is not technologically sophisticated but they believe they need a Web site to be competitive in their local market. You need to plan and then create the Web site.

    a. Write down a list of key questions that management should consider before pursuing their planning process.

    b. Sketch out two Web site plans. One plan involves creating a Web site describing the shop, and showing their location, phone number and an e-mail link at minimal cost. The other option is more involved. In addition to informing potential customers about Jackie's, it would, at moderate cost, let them sell a limited number of items over the Internet.

    c. Make a recommendation of which plan they should choose. Support your recommendation in terms that will be understandable given your client's limited knowledge of technology.

    d. Based on your recommendation, use Publisher to create a Web site using the design and style of your choice.

    e. Save the publication as **Joke Shop Web Site** in the drive and folder where your Data Files are located.

    f. Include your name, address and phone number in the Web site.

    g. Save the Web site, print the home page, then exit Publisher.

INDEPENDENT CHALLENGE 4

You have seen how dynamic Web sites look when they contain animated GIFs, or other sources of animation. But you have probably also seen Web sites that go overboard in gimmickry and silly design stunts that distract from their message. In this exercise you are asked to use your own judgment about what is bad design.

a. Connect to the Internet and use your favorite search engine to search on **bad Web site design** or **worst of the Web**, then locate two examples of poorly designed Web sites.

b. Start Publisher. Use the New Publication task pane and the Publication Gallery to create a Flyer. Use the Personal Information Set of your choice to enter appropriate information, customize any information such as a company name or logo text, then apply the color scheme of your choice. Save the publication as **Bad Web Site Design Flyer**.

c. Describe the Web sites you chose in the flyer and list the sites by their URL.

d. Modify the flyer to include your name.

e. Describe what could be done to improve those Web sites.

Advanced Challenge Exercise

■ Using the URLs you entered in Step c, create hyperlinks to the sites.

f. Print the flyer, as shown in Figure F-25, exit the browser, then exit Publisher.

FIGURE J-25

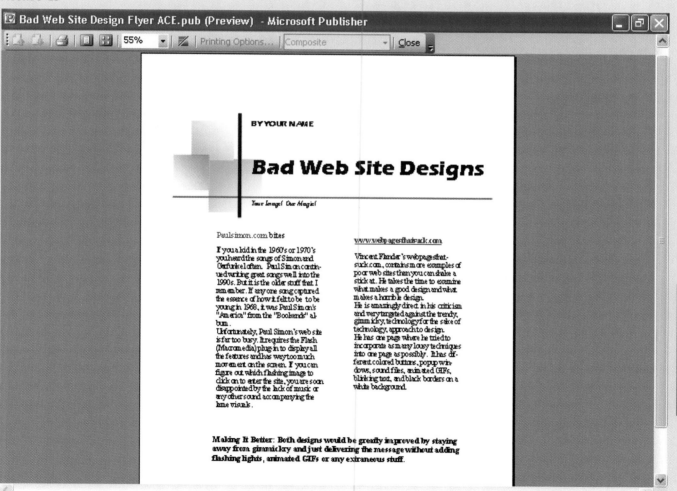

Publisher 2003

▼ VISUAL WORKSHOP

Use the New Publication task pane and the Publication Gallery to create the Southwest Easy Web Site. Save the Web site to the drive and folder where your Data Files are located as **Ultimate Traveler Web Site**. Use the Secondary Personal Information Set and the Garnet color scheme Add two additional story pages (Colorado Adventures and New Mexico Adventures), and change the background to Canvas. Insert the images PUB J-4.tif and PUB J-5.tif (found in the drive and folder where your Data Files are located) into the home page. Replace any text, and resize and rearrange any elements, using Figure J-26 as a guide. Include your name in a text box on page one, then print page one.

FIGURE J-26

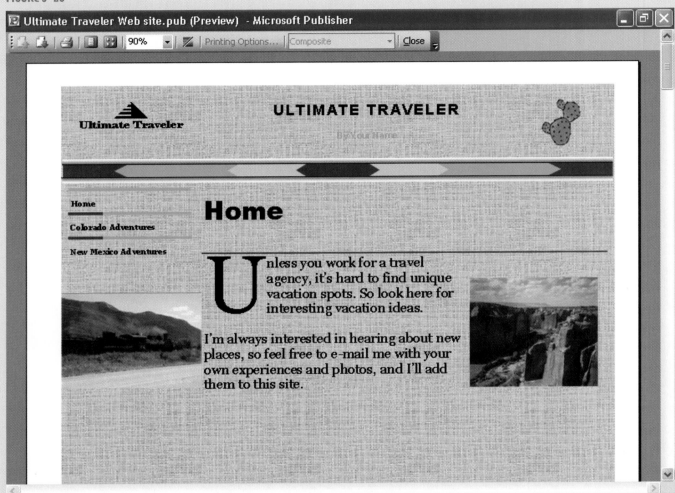